California Wine Winners

2003

Results of the 2002 Wine Judgings

Edited by
J.T. DEVINE

Printed in the United States of America.

ISBN 1-881796-09-4
ISSN 0883-4423

To order additional copies of this book or copies of any of the previous eighteen editions, please send $13.25 to the address below specifying which year's competition results you want to receive.

VARIETAL FAIR
P.O. Box 432
Graton, CA 95444
707 • 823 • 8795

TABLE OF CONTENTS

INTRODUCTION

This is a report of all the medals awarded to California wines in the 2002 round of wine judgings. Take a look at the inside front cover to see what competitions we include and how to read the first section. The book covers the 22 most popular varietals and blends, as listed in the Table of Contents.

ORGANIZATION

The first section alphabetically lists award winners under specific varietals. Each varietal section is subdivided into groups containing those who have won nine awards, eight awards, seven awards, etc. Within these subdivisions, wines are listed alphabetically and identified by vintage, appellation and price. Across from each wine a symbol denotes what award was won in each judging. These symbols are: (double gold or special award) G (gold), S (silver), or B (bronze).

A few wines are grouped together under larger families of related wines. In these "Other..." sections, the varietal or proprietary name is listed before the appellation.

The second part of the book is an alphabetical listing of all winning wineries, including both physical and web site addresses where available. Inside the back cover is a key to these listings. Under each winery, winning wines are listed. Each wine is followed with a number in parentheses which indicates how many awards that wine won. Exact medals can then be easily found in the front section. Single-medal winners are listed only in the back, with the award and competition identified.

The last four pages have a key to wines $13.00 or less which have won gold medals.

COMPETITIONS

The competitions start in February and end in late June. The judgings have specific entry requirements (see statistics chart on pages 6 and 7) including the amount of wine to be available for purchase by the public. Some wines entered in early judgings sell out and cannot entered in the later ones. Keep your copies of this book to compare awards in previous/subsequent years.

The statistics chart also shows the number of entered wines that win medals in each competition. Since this book only covers wines from California and does not include every varietal judged (Fruit wines, Port, etc.) we note the number of awards from each judging reflected in this book.

ADDITIONAL NOTE

In an effort to keep the size of this publication small, we have deleted from the back of the book wineries that do not receive at least four total points plus have less than three wine entries. This means wineries that have one or two single Bronze medal winners or a single Silver medal winner are not listed. This list totalled 191 wineries producing 240 wines. Apologies to anyone who is offended by the omissions. If, for whatever reason, you would like this additional data, please contact the publisher.

POINT COUNTS & REGION COMPARISONS

The first page of each varietal section ranks the top dozen or so winners by weighting the value of each award. Double Golds, Sweepstakes, and other special merit awards = 7 points. (We do not include every competition's "best of class" or "best of region", when they are basically "semi-finalists" for a higher award). Gold = 5 points, Silver = 3 points, and Bronze = 1. The values are arbitrary; it is just another way of looking at the awards.

Also included is a graph that shows how many points of those weighted medals were taken by certain regions of the state. The regions refer to those areas where the grapes were grown, not necessarily where the wineries are located. These regions are:

North Coast..................... Lake, Mendocino, Marin and Solano Counties.
Sonoma.......................... Sonoma County (11 Appellations).
Napa.............................. Napa County (5 Appellations).
Bay Area........................ Alameda, Contra Costa, San Mateo, Santa Clara and Santa Cruz Co.
No. Central Coast......... Monterey and San Benito Counties.
So. Central Coast.......... San Luis Obispo and Santa Barbara Co.
South Coast.................... L.A., Orange, Riverside, San Diego and Ventura Counties.
Sierra Foothills................ Amador, Calaveras, El Dorado, Mariposa, Nevada, Placer, Tuolomne, Yuba Counties.
Other.............................. All other California Counties
California........................ Non-specified blends from above.

COMPETITIONS	ENTRIES # Wines # Wineries	MEDALS Total # in book	AWARDS IN BOOK Σ G S B
LOS ANGELES COUNTY FAIR P. O. Box 2250 Pomona, CA 91769 (909) 623-3111	+3,400 +450	- 1050	54 136 395 465
ORANGE COUNTY FAIR P. O. Box 11059 Costa Mesa, CA 92627 (714) 708-1636	2940 +425	1158 1003	17 182 377 427
RIVERSIDE INTERNATIONAL 18745 Bert Road Riverside, CA 92508-8908 (909) 780-7584	2511 469	1541 971	38 110 290 533
SAN FRANCISCO INTERNATIONAL 3145 Geary Blvd., #437 San Francisco, CA 94118-3000 (415) 345-9000	3810 918	1921 981	40 62 293 586
WEST COAST WINE COMPETITION 536 B Street, 1st Floor Santa Rosa, CA 95401 (707) 566-3810	+1450 +225	934 818	21 91 440 266
CALIFORNIA STATE FAIR P. O. Box 15649 Sacramento, CA 95852 (916) 263-3159	+2300 +425	- 923	60 137 390 3336
NEW WORLD INTERNATIONAL P. O. Box 5306 Diamond Bar, CA 91765 (775) 484-9765, ext. 31	2276 473	262 880	65 126 345 344
PACIFIC RIM INTERNATIONAL 689 South "E" Street San Bernardino, CA 92408-1978 (909) 888-6788	+2200 +400	1098 688	19 78 227 364
SAN DIEGO COMPETITION P. O. Box 880881 San Diego, CA 92168 (619) 421-9463	2050 +420	788 580	23 74 213 270

2002 Entry Deadline Judging Dates	ENTRY Fee Bottles to Send Min. Produced Min. Inventory at judging	WINNERS Require-ments after Judging	JUDGING SCOPE Geographic Area Covered Judging Categories Entry Restrictions
LOS ANGELES April 15 May 15-17	$50.00 Six - 120 Gal.	Golds only to sell 3 cs. to fair	Any wine from the World Some judged in vintage groups. Limit of two entries per class.
ORANGE CO. May 14 Jun 1-2	No charge Six None "Some"	All winners invited to pour at the fair	California wines available in Orange Co. Judged in price categories. Not all entries voluntary.Current releases only.
RIVERSIDE April 13 May 4-5	$30.00 Four 500 Gal 50 Cases	All entries invited to pour at the fair	Any wine from anywhere in the world. Some judged in vintage groups.
SAN FRAN. May 31 June 22-25	$60.00 Five None 50 Cases	Wineries to reserve one case to sell to the fair	Any wine in the world. No limit on number of entries. Wines judged in vintage groupings.
WEST COAST March 29 May 17-19	$55.00 Four - -	None	Wines produced in CA, WA, OR, ID, NV British Columbia or Mexico
STATE FAIR May 31 June 21-23	$32.00 Six 480 Gal. 240 Gal.	Reserve to sell up to 10 cases for the fair	Any California wine. Wines judged in 10 geogrpahical groups. Limit of 3 entries per class per region.
NEW WORLD Jan 25 Feb. 17-18	$35.00 Six None "Some"	All entries invited to pour at awards	Any wine from the New World. All wines judged in price groups. Must be available to buy in at least one state.
PACIFIC RIM Mar 22 April 18-19	$40.00 Four None No minimum	Golds are required to pour at events	Wines from any Pacific Rim country. Judged in residual sugar & price categories.
SAN DIEGO April 5 April 26-27	$40.00 Four 300 Gal. 125 Cases	All winners to donate 1 case for charity sale	Any U. S. vinifera wine. Some judged in vintage groups. No limit on number of entries, except same wine in 2 classes.

Cabernet Sauvignon

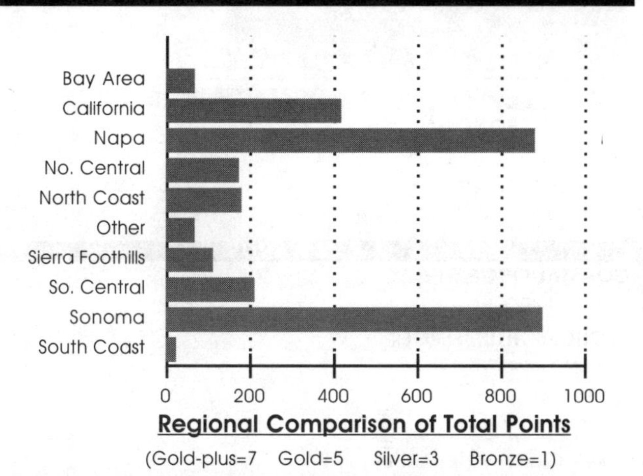

Regional Comparison of Total Points

(Gold-plus=7 Gold=5 Silver=3 Bronze=1)

Highest Individual Wine Totals

29 **KENDALL-JACKSON WINERY**
'98, Great Estates, Napa Vly., $49.00

26 **MICHEL-SCHLUMBERGER**
'99, Dry Creek Vly., $29.00

25 **RODNEY STRONG**
'97, Northern Sonoma Rsv., $40.00

24 **GEYSER PEAK**
'99, Alexander Vly., Kuimelis Vnyd. Block Collection, $26.00

24 **GEYSER PEAK**
'99, Sonoma Co. Rsv., $40.00

24 **RIOS-LOVELL WINERY**
'00, Livermore Vly., Estate, $18.00

24 **V. SATTUI WINERY**
'99, Napa Vly., Suzannes Vyd., $25.00

24 **RODNEY STRONG**
'99, Sonoma Co., $18.00

24 **TURNING LEAF**
'99, Central Coast Rsv., Oak Aged, $10.00

23 **FORCHINI VINEYARDS**
'99, Dry Creek Vly. Rsv. , $26.00

23 **RAYMOND**
'99, Napa Vly. Rsv., $40.00

Cabernet Sauvignon

Wine	L.A.	Orange	Riverside	San Fran	West Coast	State Fair	New World	Pacific Rim	San Diego
9 AWARDS									
GALLO OF SONOMA '99, Sonoma Co. Rsv., Barrel Aged $13	G	B	B	B	S	S	S	S	B
RODNEY STRONG '97, Northern Sonoma Rsv. $40	G	G	S	S	S	S	B	B	B
8 AWARDS									
COASTAL RIDGE WINERY '99, California $7	G	B	B	S	S	B	S	S	
MICHEL-SCHLUMBERGER '99, Dry Creek Vly. $29	S	S	S	B		Σ	S	B	G
NAPA RIDGE '97, Napa Vly. Rsv. $20	S		B	B	S	B	B	S	B
PERRY CREEK VINEYARDS '99, El Dorado Estate $14		G	S	B	S	B	S	S	B
V. SATTUI WINERY '99, Napa Vly., Suzannes Vyd. $25	S	G	S	S	S	G		B	B
RODNEY STRONG '99, Sonoma Co. $18	S	G	B	B	S	S	G	S	
7 AWARDS									
FETZER '98, Napa Vly., Rsv. $40		B	G		S	S	S	G	B
FORCHINI VINEYARDS '99, Dry Creek Vly. Rsv. $26	B	S	S		G	Σ	B		S
GALLO OF SONOMA '97, Alexander Vly., Barelli Creek Vnyd. $28	G	B	B	Σ			B	B	S
GREENWOOD RIDGE VINEYARDS '99, Mendocino Ridge Estate $30	S	S	B	B			S	S	S
GROVE STREET '99, Alexander Vly. $39	G	S	B	B	G	S	B		
HARMONY CELLARS '99, Paso Robles $16	B	B	S	B	G	G	S		
VICTOR HUGO '99, Paso Robles $18	S		B	B	S	S	B	B	
KENDALL-JACKSON WINERY '99, Grand Rsv., California $30	B	S	B	S	B		B	S	
KENDALL-JACKSON WINERY '98, Great Estates, Napa Vly. $49	S	S	G			B	G	G	Σ

Cabernet Sauvignon

L.A.	Orange	Riverside	San Fran	West Coast	State Fair	New World	Pacific Rim	San Diego	Wine
7 AWARDS									
B	Σ	B	B	S		G		G	**RAYMOND** '99, Napa Vly. Rsv. $40
B	B	B	S	S			S	G	**WINDSOR VINEYARDS** '98, Alexander Vly., Simoneau Ranch $19.75
6 AWARDS									
B		S	B	B		S	B		**BAREFOOT CELLARS** '99, Knights Vly. Rsv. $15
B	B	Σ		B	G		B		**BARTHOLOMEW PARK** '99, Sonoma Vly., Kasper Vnyd. $40
S	B	G		S	Σ		B		**BERINGER** '99, Founders Estate, California $12
	B	B	S	B		S	B		**BRUTOCAO** '99, Mendocino Co., Brutocao Vnyd. $20
B	B		B	B	S		S		**BUEHLER VINEYARDS** '99, Napa Vly. $22
B	B	B	B	S				S	**EBERLE** '99, Paso Robles Estate $28
S		S	B	G	G		B		**ECHELON** '00, California $15
S		B		G	S	S		B	**FOREST GLEN WINERY** '99, Oak Barrel Selection, California $10
	G	G	B	B	G		G		**FREI BROTHERS WINERY** '99, Alexander Vly. Rsv. $24
	G	G	S	S		G	S		**GEYSER PEAK** '99, Alexander Vly., Kuimelis Vnyd. Block Collection $26
		S	B	Σ		G	G	S	**GEYSER PEAK** '99, Sonoma Co. Rsv. $40
	B	S			S	B	S	S	**GUENOC** '98, Napa Vly., Beckstoffer, Rsv. $41
		G	B	S	S	S	B		**KENDALL-JACKSON WINERY** '97, Great Estates, Napa Vly. $49
G	S	Σ	B	G			B		**MIRASSOU** '99, Central Coast, Coastal Selection $11
G	S	G	G	S	S				**RIOS-LOVELL WINERY** '00, Livermore Vly., Estate $18

Cabernet Sauvignon

Winery	L.A.	Orange	Riverside	San Fran	West Coast	State Fair	New World	Pacific Rim	San Diego
6 AWARDS									
V. SATTUI WINERY '99, Napa Vly., Morisoli Vnyd. $32	S	G	B	S	S				B
ST. SUPÉRY '99, Napa Vly., Dollarhide Ranch $70	G		S	B	S		G		G
STELTZNER VINEYARDS '99, Napa Vly., Stags Leap District $32	Σ	G	B			S		B	B
STERLING VINEYARDS '99, Napa Vly., Diamond Mtn. Ranch $40	B	S		B		Σ		B	S
STONEGATE '99, Napa Vly. $40	B	B	G	B			B	B	
M. TRINCHERO WINERY '99, Napa Vly. Lewelling Vnyd. $60	S	B	S	G	S				S
TURNING LEAF '99, Central Coast Rsv., Oak Aged $10	S		B		G	Σ	Σ		B
WATTLE CREEK '98, Alexander Vly. $45	G		G		S	B		B	S
WINDSOR VINEYARDS '98, Paso Robles $12.50	B	B	B		S		S		S
5 AWARDS									
AMBERHILL '99, California $12	S	S		B	S		S		
BARTHOLOMEW PARK '99, Sonoma Vly., Desnudos Vnyd. $40	B	G		B	B				B
BELL WINE CELLARS '98, Napa Vly., Baritelle Vnyd. $55			G		S		S	S	B
CANYON ROAD WINERY '00, California $10	B		B		B			S	S
CARMENET VINEYARD '99, Dynamite, North Coast $17.25		B	G		B		G	S	
CASTORO CELLARS '99, Paso Robles $14		B		S	S		B	B	
CECCHETTI SEBASTIANI CELLAR '99, Central Coast $13	B		B	B	S			B	
COOPER-GARROD '97, Santa Cruz Mtns. George's Vnyd. $35	G		B			G		B	B
DOMAINE ST. GEORGE WINERY '00, Dry Creek Vly., Wells Vnyd. $15	B		B	B	Σ	S			

Cabernet Sauvignon

5 AWARDS

L.A.	Orange	Riverside	San Fran	West Coast	State Fair	New World	Pacific Rim	San Diego	Wine
	B	B	B	G	B				**EOS** '00, Paso Robles, Estate $18
B	B	B		S	S				**FIELD STONE WINERY** '98, Alexander Vly. Rsv. $40
S		B	G	B				S	**GALLO OF SONOMA** '97, Dry Creek Vly., Frei Vnyd. $28
S		B		B		B		B	**GAN EDEN** '97, Mendocino Co. Limited Rsv. $40
	B	S	B			S	B		**GEYSER PEAK** '99, Sonoma Co. $17
S		G		S			S	B	**GUENOC** '98, North Coast $17
S		B		G	S			S	**GUENOC** '00, California $14
B	S			B			B	B	**GUNDLACH-BUNDSCHU WINERY** '99, Sonoma Vly., Rhinefarm Vnyd. $30
	S	B		G			S	S	**KENDALL-JACKSON WINERY** '98, Great Estates, Alexander Vly. $49
		S		S		S	S	B	**KENDALL-JACKSON WINERY** '98, Vintner's Rsv., California $16
Σ	S	B		S		G			**LAKE SONOMA WINERY** '98, Alexander Vly. $21
B	S	B				S	B		**LOCKWOOD VINEYARD** '99, Monterey Co. Estate $17
		B		B	S	B	B		**J. LOHR ESTATE** '98, Paso Robles Hilltp Vnyd. $32
	S			G		B	S	B	**MARCELINA VINEYARDS** '98, Napa Vly. $30
B		G		B	S		B		**LOUIS M. MARTINI** '99, Sonoma Vly., Monte Rosso Vnyd. $50
B	S	B		B				S	**MERIDIAN VINEYARDS** '97, Monterey Co., Coastal Rsv. $28
S		B				S	G	S	**MICHEL-SCHLUMBERGER** '97, Dry Creek Vly. Rsv. $65
B	B		B	S		S			**MIDNIGHT CELLARS** '99, Nebula, Paso Robles $25

Cabernet Sauvignon

	L.A.	Orange	Riverside	San Fran	West Coast	State Fair	New World	Pacific Rim	San Diego
5 AWARDS									
MONTPELLIER VINEYARDS '99, California $7		S	S		B		S	B	
NAPA RIDGE '99, Lodi $9		G	G		S	B	G		
NEVADA CITY WINERY '99, Sierra Foothills $16	B	B	B			S		S	
PEIRANO ESTATE VINEYARDS '99, Lodi Estate $10	B		S		S		B	G	
RAYMOND '98, Napa Vly., Generations $80	Σ	S	B		S				S
RUTHERFORD RANCH '99, Napa Vly. $14	S	G			S			B	S
RUTHERFORD VINTNERS '99, Stanislaus Co., Barrel Select $9		S	B		B		S	S	
V. SATTUI WINERY '99, Napa Vly. $21		Σ	B	B	S	G			
V. SATTUI WINERY '99, Napa Vly., Preston Vnyd. $32	B	G		S	S				S
SEBASTIANI VINEYARDS & WINERY '98, Sonoma Co. Four Generations $21		S	S		B			S	B
SILVER RIDGE VINEYARDS '99, California Barrel Select $10	B		B		S		S	B	
VILLA MT. EDEN '99, Napa Vly., Grand Rsv. $22	S		G	G	B	G			
WINDSOR VINEYARDS '99, Mendocino Co., Rsv. $16.75	B	G			S		S	B	
WINDSOR VINEYARDS '99, Paso Robles $12.50	B	B	B		B			B	
WINDSOR VINEYARDS '98, Sonoma Co., Signature Series $27.25		S	S		S		Σ		S
YORKVILLE CELLARS '99, Yorkville Highlands, Rennie Vnyd. $19			B	G	S	S			B
4 AWARDS									
ANTERRA '98, Napa Vly. Rsv. $37	B	S			B		S		
ARMIDA WINERY '99, Dry Creek Vly., Scharf Vnyd. $30	S	S			S				S

Cabernet Sauvignon

4 AWARDS

Wine	L.A.	Orange	Riverside	San Fran	West Coast	State Fair	New World	Pacific Rim	San Diego
BAREFOOT CELLARS 'NV, California $6	B		B				S		B
BEAULIEU '98, George de Latour, Napa Vly. Rsv. $100					S	B	G	S	
BELVEDERE '98, Sonoma Co., Healdsburg Ranches $22		Σ		S		G	G		
BERINGER '98, Knights Vly. $26	B		B		B			B	
BIANCHI VINEYARDS '99, Barrel Select, California $9	S	B		B				B	
BIG HORN CELLARS '98, Napa Vly., Coombsville Vnyd. $40	B			S		S	S		
BUEHLER VINEYARDS '98, Napa Vly. Estate $40	B		S		B			B	
CECCHETTI SEBASTIANI CELLAR '97, Napa Vly. $50			B	B	B			B	
CONCANNON VINEYARD '97, Livermore Vly. Rsv. $25					S		B	B	S
DARK STAR CELLARS '99, Paso Robles $20	B	S			S				G
DELICATO '00, California $8	S		S				B		B
DOMAINE ST. GEORGE WINERY '99, California Barrel Rsv. $10		S	B		S	B			
DRY CREEK VINEYARD '99, Sonoma Co. $21		S	B	B				B	
FETZER '99, Valley Oaks, California $10			B			S	S	B	
FETZER '98, Barrel Select, North Coast $20	B				S	B	G		
FIELD STONE WINERY '99, Alexander Vly. $24		B	B			G			B
FLORA SPRINGS '99, Napa Vly., Wild Boar Vnyd. $60	Σ			B		Σ		B	
GALLO OF SONOMA '97, Dry Creek Vly. Stefani Vnyd. $28	G	S	B	S					

Cabernet Sauvignon	L.A.	Orange	Riverside	San Fran	West Coast	State Fair	New World	Pacific Rim	San Diego
4 AWARDS									
GALLO OF SONOMA '97, Northern Sonoma Estate $70				Σ			Σ	S	G
GEYSER PEAK '98, Napa Vly., Vallerga Vnyd. Block Collection $35		B	B		B		B		
GRGICH HILLS '98, Napa Vly. $50			S		B		B	S	
GROVE STREET '99, Napa Vly. $39	G			G		Σ	B		
EMILIO GUGLIELMO WINERY '99, Central Coast, Vnyd. Selection $10	S	B		S		S			
IMAGERY SERIES '99, Sonoma Vly., Sunny Slope Vyd. $50				B	S	G		B	
IMAGERY SERIES '98, Sonoma Vly., Sunny Slope Vyd. $50	B			B				S	S
INDIAN SPRINGS VINEYARDS '99, Nevada Co. $20		S		G	S				S
MERIDIAN VINEYARDS '99, California $11		S		S	S	S			
CHARLES B. MITCHELL VINEYARDS '00, El Dorado Rsv. $25		B	G			B			B
MONTERRA WINERY '00, Monterey Co. $13	Σ	G	B						Σ
J. PEDRONCELLI '99, Alexander Vly., Morris Fay Vnyd. $16				B	B		S	B	
PEPPERWOOD GROVE '00, California $9			Σ		B	S			B
RAYMOND '99, Napa Vly. Estate $23	S			S	S		B		
JEFF RUNQUIST WINES '00, Paso Robles, Colina Poca Vnyd. $25	Σ		S				S		S
SEQUOIA GROVE VINEYARDS '99, Napa Vly. $29		S			B		Σ	B	
SEVEN PEAKS '99, Central Coast $14	S			B	S				B
SILVER ROSE CELLARS '99, Napa Vly. $34		B	B	S		S			

Cabernet Sauvignon

L.A.	Orange	Riverside	San Fran	West Coast	State Fair	New World	Pacific Rim	San Diego	Wine
									4 AWARDS
	S				S		B	S	**SMITH & HOOK** '99, Santa Lucia Highlands $18
B	S				S	B			**ST. SUPÉRY** '99, Napa Vly. $24
G	B		G					B	**STERLING VINEYARDS** '99, Napa Vly. $24
	S			S		B		S	**RODNEY STRONG** '98, Alexander's Crown Vnyd. $28
B	B		B	S					**TRELLIS VINEYARDS** '99, Sonoma Co. $16
S	S				Σ			G	**M. TRINCHERO WINERY** '98, Napa Vly., Chicken Ranch Vnyd. $30
				B	G	G	S		**M. TRINCHERO WINERY** '98, Napa Vly., Mario's Rsv. $45
S		B		B			B		**TRINITY OAKS** '99, California $10
		B		B		B		B	**VAN ASPEREN** '98, Napa Vly. $22
		B	B	S		S			**WATTLE CREEK** '99, Alexander Vly. $45
S	B	B			B				**WILSON CREEK WINERY & VINEYARD** '00, Temecula, Rsv. $35
									3 AWARDS
S	S		B						**ATLAS PEAK VINEYARD** '96, Napa Vly., Consenso Vnyd. $30
				S		S	S		**BEAULIEU** '99, Napa Vly. $17
B				B			S		**BEAULIEU** '99, Rutherford $25
	G	B		B					**BEL ARBOR** '00, California $7
S			B		B				**BOEGER** '99, El Dorado Estate $15
S	S		S						**BONTERRA** '99, North Coast $17
S		B			S				**RAYMOND BURR VINEYARDS** '98, Dry Creek Vly. $38

Cabernet Sauvignon

Winery	L.A.	Orange	Riverside	San Fran	West Coast	State Fair	New World	Pacific Rim	San Diego
3 AWARDS									
CAMELLIA CELLARS '98, Dry Creek Vly., Lencioni Vnyd. $45	S	B		B					
CAMELOT WINERY '99, California $9	B				S			S	
CHATEAU MARGENE '99, San Luis Obispo $30		B	B	S					
CLOS DU BOIS '99, Alexander Vly. Rsv. $21		B		B		S			
CLOS DU BOIS '99, Sonoma Co. $17		S		S		S			
CONCANNON VINEYARD '98, Central Coast Selected Vnyd. $11.50	B		B					S	
CONN CREEK '98, Napa Vly., Limited Release $26	S		B		B				
COOPER-GARROD '98, Santa Cruz Mtns. Estate $28			B			B	B		
CROZE '99, Napa Vly. $38				S	S	S			
DIAMONDBACK VINEYARDS '99, Mendocino Co. Estate $28		B		B		B			
DRY CREEK VINEYARD '98, Dry Creek Vly. Rsv. $35		S					S	S	
FOLEY ESTATES '99, Santa Ynez Vly., La Cuesta Vnyd. $35	S	S		S					
FOLIE A'DEUX '99, Napa Vly. $26		B		S			S		
FOLIE A'DEUX '98, La Grande Folie, Napa Vly. $65	B	S	G						
FOXHOLLOW VINEYARDS '99, California, Barrel Select $9			B				S	G	
HUNT CELLARS '99, Paso Robles, Destiny Vnyd. $24	S			B		S			
IRONSTONE VINEYARDS '99, California $10		S		B	S				
JEKEL VINEYARDS '99, Central Coast $16		B				G		B	

Cabernet Sauvignon

3 AWARDS

L.A.	Orange	Riverside	San Fran	West Coast	State Fair	New World	Pacific Rim	San Diego	Wine
		S				G	S		**ROBERT KEENAN** '98, Napa Vly. $36
		Σ				S	G		**KENDALL-JACKSON WINERY** '98, Grand Rsv., California $40
S	S		S						**KATHRYN KENNEDY** '99, Estate, Santa Cruz Mtns. $125
B	S			S					**KENWOOD VINEYARDS** '99, Sonoma Co. $20
	S	S		S					**KENWOOD VINEYARDS** '99, Sonoma Vly. Jack London Vnyd. $35
B				B		S			**LIONS PEAK** '98, Paso Robles $24
G		S				B			**METTLER FAMILY VINEYARDS** '99, Lodi $24
G		B			S				**MICHAEL-DAVID PHILLIPS** '00, Lodi $24
	S		B					Σ	**MONTICELLO CORLEY FAMILY** '99, Napa Vly., Jefferson Cuvee $34
		B				S	B		**MURPHY-GOODE** '99, Alexander Vly. $22
	S	S	S						**NAPA RIDGE** '99, Napa Vly. $12
S		B		S					**REDWOOD CREEK WINERY** '98, California $8
G			B		G				**ROSENBLUM CELLARS** '99, Mount Veeder, Yates Vnyd. $59
S		G				B			**ROUND HILL VINEYARDS** '99, California $9
			S				B	S	**SALMON CREEK CELLARS** '99, California $7
	G	S		S					**SEBASTIANI VINEYARDS & WINERY** '98, Sonoma Vly. $30
	S			S			S		**SEQUOIA GROVE VINEYARDS** '99, Rutherford Rsv. $55
B				S	B				**SMITH-MADRONE** '99, Napa Vly. $37

Cabernet Sauvignon

Wine	L.A.	Orange	Riverside	San Fran	West Coast	State Fair	New World	Pacific Rim	San Diego
3 AWARDS									
ROBERT STEMMLER '98, Sonoma Co. $28	S		B				S		
STONEHEDGE '00, Napa Vly. $25				B		B	S		
RODNEY STRONG '98, Alexander Vly., Alden Vnyds. $30		B			B				S
VAN ASPEREN '98, Napa Vly. Signature Rsv. $36	G				S				S
WINDSOR VINEYARDS '98, North Coast, Private Rsv. $20.75					S		G		S
2 AWARDS									
ALBERTONI VINEYARDS '99, California $13	B			B					
ALEXANDER VALLEY VINEYARDS '99, Alexander Vly. Estate $20			B				S		
ARBIOS CELLARS '99, Alexander Vly. $30	S		S						
ARROW CREEK WINERY '99, California $10		B					B		
BENZIGER '99, Sonoma $19				B		S			
BIG HORN CELLARS '98, Napa Vly. Soda Canyon Vnyd. $19.50			S				G		
BRADFORD MOUNTAIN WINERY '98, Dry Creek Vly., Headwater Vnyd. $40		S				G			
BUENA VISTA '98, Carneros Estate $22		S				B			
BUTTERFIELD STATION '00, California $8		G				G			
CEDAR MOUNTAIN WINERY '98, Livermore, Blanches Vnyd. Rsv. $22			B					S	
CHANDELLE OF SONOMA '00, Sonoma Co. $15			G		S				
CHAPPELLET '99, Signature, Napa Vly. $44								B	G
CHIMNEY ROCK '99, Napa Vly., Stags Leap $45		S					S		

L.A.	Orange	Riverside	San Fran	West Coast	State Fair	New World	Pacific Rim	San Diego	Cabernet Sauvignon
									2 AWARDS
	B						S		**CLONINGER CELLARS** '99, Carmel Vly., Quinn Vyd. $19
	B				S				**CLOS DU BOIS** '98, Alexander Vly., Briarcrest $43
		B					S		**CORBETT CANYON VINEYARDS** '00, California Rsv. $7
G		G							**COSENTINO WINERY** '99, Napa Vly. Rsv. $80
	G					G			**CYPRESS VINEYARD** '99, California $10
		B					B		**DUNNEWOOD** '99, North Coast $15
		S					B		**FETZER** '99, Central Coast 5 Rivers Ranch $13
				B		B			**FOPPIANO VINEYARDS** '99, Russian River Vly., Estate $17.50
			B					B	**FOPPIANO VINEYARDS** '00, Russian River Vly., Estate $18
		B						B	**FRATELLI PERATA** '98, Paso Robles $18
		S	G						**FRATELLI PERATA** '97, Paso Robles Riserva $40
						S	B		**FREI BROTHERS WINERY** '98, Alexander Vly. Rsv. $24
G			B						**GALLO OF SONOMA** '94, Dry Creek Vly., Frei Vnyd. $18
S			Σ						**GALLO OF SONOMA** '94, Northern Sonoma Estate $60
G			S						**GALLO OF SONOMA** '92, Northern Sonoma Estate $50
B			G						**GALLO OF SONOMA** '91, Northern Sonoma Estate $50
						S		S	**GEYSER PEAK** '98, Alexander Vly., Kuimelis Vnyd. Block Collection $26
		S					B		**HAGAFEN CELLARS** '99, Napa Vly. $36

Cabernet Sauvignon

	L.A.	Orange	Riverside	San Fran	West Coast	State Fair	New World	Pacific Rim	San Diego
2 AWARDS									
HANNA '99, Alexander Vly. $25							S	Σ	
HAWLEY WINES '99, Dry Creek Vly.	S					S			
HELLER ESTATE '97, Carmel Vly./Monterey Rsv. $100				S		S			
HRM 'NV, Central Coast $8				G		G			
HUSCH VINEYARDS '99, Mendocino Co., La Ribera Vnyd. $19	B			B					
ICARA CREEK WINERY '97, Alexander Vly., Hillside Vnyd. $60	G			S					
IMAGERY SERIES '99, Alexander Vly., Ash Creek Vyd.	S							B	
IMAGERY SERIES '98, Alexander Vly., Ash Creek Vyd. $50					B			B	
JEKEL VINEYARDS '99, Monterey Co. $16				B	S				
KENDALL-JACKSON WINERY '97, Alexander Vly. Single Vnyd. Series Buckeye $43			S	Σ					
KENDALL-JACKSON WINERY '97, Stature Napa Vly. $125		S		S					
J. LOHR ESTATE '99, Seven Oaks, Paso Robles $15		B			S				
LOUIS M. MARTINI '99, California $12	S		S						
MC MANIS FAMILY VINEYARDS '01, California $9				Σ		Σ			
MC NAB RIDGE '99, Mendocino Co. Rsv. $18		B				G			
MILL CREEK VINEYARDS '98, Sonoma Co. $19.50			B				B		
MONTHAVEN '99, California $10		B					B		
MOSS CREEK '97, Napa Vly., Raney Rock $65							S		B

Cabernet Sauvignon

2 AWARDS

L.A.	Orange	Riverside	San Fran	West Coast	State Fair	New World	Pacific Rim	San Diego	Wine
	B	S							**NATHANSON CREEK CELLARS** 'NV, California $6
			S		S				**PARADISE RIDGE** '99, Sonoma $27
	B			G					**PARDUCCI WINE CELLARS** '99, Mendocino Co., Vintner Select $11
			B				B		**J. PEDRONCELLI** '99, Dry Creek Vly., Three Vnyds. $15
B							S		**J. PEDRONCELLI** '00, Sonoma Co., Vintage Select
			B		B				**R. H. PHILLIPS** '00, Dunnigan Hills, Estate $9
						S	G		**MICHAEL POZZAN WINERY** '99, Napa Vly., Matthew's Cuvee $15
	S							S	**QUAIL RIDGE** '99, Rsv., Napa Vly. $60
				B		S			**RENAISSANCE** '97, Sierra Foothills $24
B					B				**RENAISSANCE** '95, Premier Cuvee
	S		S						**SADDLEBACK CELLARS** '99, Napa Vly. $48
B								B	**V. SATTUI WINERY** '00, Sattui Family, California $15
		B						G	**SAUSAL WINERY** '99, Alexander Vly. $24
B	G								**SAWYER CELLARS** '99, Napa Vly., Rutherford, Estate $46
			B	S					**SILVER STONE** '99, California $9
S	G								**STEVENOT** '99, Calaveras Co. $16
S					G				**STONE CELLARS** '00, California
	G			G					**STONE CREEK** '99, North Coast, Chairman's Rsv. $17

Cabernet Sauvignon

2 AWARDS

Wine	L.A.	Orange	Riverside	San Fran	West Coast	State Fair	New World	Pacific Rim	San Diego
STONEHEDGE '00, California $10						B	S		
SYLVESTER '99, Paso Robles, Kiara Rsv. $15				S				B	
TARA BELLA WINERY '99, Napa Vly. $55		B		Σ					
TARA BELLA WINERY '99, Sonoma Co. $42		S		B					
THORNTON '00, South Coast $14					B	B			
M. TRINCHERO WINERY '98, Family Selection $17					B		G		
TURNING LEAF '00, California	B							B	
WINDSOR VINEYARDS '99, North Coast, Vintner's Rsv. $20.75				G		S			
WINDSOR VINEYARDS '97, Alexander Vly., Private Rsv. $23.50							S	B	

880
PEAK
WINERY

Chardonnay

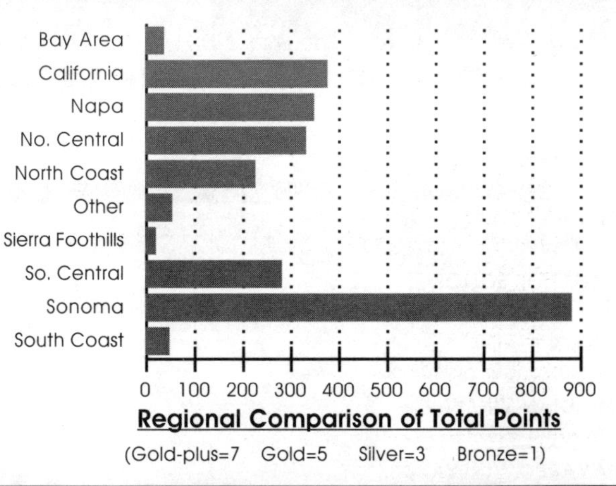

Regional Comparison of Total Points

(Gold-plus=7 Gold=5 Silver=3 Bronze=1)

Highest Individual Wine Totals

29 **GEYSER PEAK**
'00, Carneros-Sonoma Vly., Ricci Vnyd. Block Collection, $21.00

28 **GEYSER PEAK**
'00, Alexander Vly. Rsv., $23.00

28 **NAVARRO VINEYARDS**
'00, Mendocino Co., $14.00

26 **RUTHERFORD VINTNERS**
'00, Stanislaus Co., Barrel Select, $9.00

24 **MERIDIAN VINEYARDS**
'99, Santa Barbara Co., Limited, $22.00

23 **LA CREMA**
'99, Russian River Vly., $30.00

23 **LAURIER**
'00, Los Carneros, Sonoma, $16.00

22 **GLORIA FERRER**
'00, Carneros, Sonoma, $20.00

20 **BAYSTONE**
'00, Russian River Vly., Saralee's Vnyd., $20.00

20 **LA CREMA**
'00, Sonoma Coast, $18.00

20 **MIRASSOU**
'00, Monterey Co., Zabala Vnyd., $24.00

Chardonnay

Chardonnay	L.A.	Orange	Riverside	San Fran	West Coast	State Fair	New World	Pacific Rim	San Diego
9 AWARDS									
GEYSER PEAK '00, Carneros-Sonoma Vly., Ricci Vnyd. Block Collection $21	B	S	Σ	B	S	G	S	G	B
8 AWARDS									
GLORIA FERRER '00, Carneros, Sonoma $20	S	G	B	B	S	S		G	B
GALLO OF SONOMA '99, Dry Creek Vly., Stefani Vnyd. $22	G	S		B	S	B	B	B	B
GEYSER PEAK '00, Alexander Vly. Rsv. $23	S	S	Σ	B	S		S	B	Σ
MERIDIAN VINEYARDS '99, Santa Barbara Co., Limited $22	S	S	S	B	S	S	G	S	
NAVARRO VINEYARDS '00, Mendocino Co. $14	S	S	S	S	S	S	G	G	
RAYMOND '00, Monterey Co. Estates $15	S	B	B	B	B	B	G		B
7 AWARDS									
BAREFOOT CELLARS 'NV, California $6	S		B		S	Σ	S	B	B
BONTERRA '00, Mendocino Co. $15		S	B	B	S	S	B	S	
FETZER '01, Sundial, California $9	B	B			S	S	S	S	S
GALLO OF SONOMA '00, Sonoma Co. Rsv., Barrel Ferm. $11		G	B	B	S		S	S	S
GRGICH HILLS '99, Napa Vly. $33	S	B	S	S	S		S	B	
KENDALL-JACKSON WINERY '99, Great Estates, Sonoma Coast $28	B		B	S	B	B	S		B
KENDALL-JACKSON WINERY '00, Santa Maria Vly., Camelot Bench, Estate Series $17			B	B	S	S	G	S	B
KENDALL-JACKSON WINERY '00, Vintner's Rsv., California $12	S	B	S	B	S		B		B
LA CREMA '99, Russian River Vly. $30	G		B	B	S		G	G	S

Chardonnay

7 AWARDS

L.A.	Orange	Riverside	San Fran	West Coast	State Fair	New World	Pacific Rim	San Diego	Wine
G	B	B	Σ	B	S		G		**LAURIER** '00, Los Carneros, Sonoma $16
B	S	G	B	S		B	G		**NAVARRO VINEYARDS** '00, Anderson Vly. Premiere Rsv. $18
S	B	B		S	S	B		S	**RAYMOND** '00, Napa Vly. Rsv. $20
		B	B	S	G	B	S	B	**STONE CELLARS** '00, California $8

6 AWARDS

L.A.	Orange	Riverside	San Fran	West Coast	State Fair	New World	Pacific Rim	San Diego	Wine
S	S	G	B				G	S	**BAYSTONE** '00, Russian River Vly., Saralee's Vnyd. $20
	B		B	Σ	S	S	B		**CANYON ROAD WINERY** '00, California $9
S	B	S	B			G	B		**FETZER** '00, Mendocino Co. Barrel Select $14
S	S	B	B	B		B			**FIRESTONE VINEYARD** '00, Santa Barbara Co. $16
	S	B	B		S	B		G	**GROVE STREET** '99, Sonoma Co. $15
B		B			B	B	S	S	**HUSCH VINEYARDS** '99, Anderson Vly., Rsv. $25
	S	B		G		S	S	B	**KENDALL-JACKSON WINERY** '99, Great Estates, Sonoma Vly. $37
B	B	B		S	G		G		**KENDALL-JACKSON WINERY** '00, Great Estates, Arroyo Seco $37
G		B	S		S	B		B	**LAKE SONOMA WINERY** '00, Russian River Vly. $15
		S	B		S	B	S	S	**J. LOHR ESTATE** '99, Arroyo Seco Arroyo Vista Vnyd. $25
S		B	B			B	S	S	**J. LOHR ESTATE** '00, Arroy Seco Riverstone Estates $15
B	S		S	B		B	B		**LOUIS M. MARTINI** '00, Russian River Vly., Del Rio Vnyd. $22
S				B	B	B	S	S	**MC ILROY WINES** '00, Russian River Vly., Aquarius Ranch $22
S		S	B	S	G	G			**MIRASSOU** '00, Monterey Co., Zabala Vnyd. $24

Chardonnay

Chardonnay	L.A.	Orange	Riverside	San Fran	West Coast	State Fair	New World	Pacific Rim	San Diego
6 AWARDS									
RUTHERFORD VINTNERS '00, Stanislaus Co., Barrel Select $9		G	S		S	S	G	Σ	
SALMON CREEK CELLARS '00, California $7	S	S	B	B	B			G	
SUTTER HOME '00, California $6	S		S	B	B	S	B		
WATTLE CREEK '99, Alexander Vly. $25	S	S	S				B	G	S
WINDSOR VINEYARDS '00, Alexander Vly. Murphy Ranch $15.75	S		B		S	B	G	B	
WINDSOR VINEYARDS '00, Russian River Vly., Signature Series $18.75	S		S	B	B	S		B	
5 AWARDS									
BARGETTO '00, Santa Cruz Mtns, Regan Vnyd. $20			B		B	B	B	B	
BOGLE '00, California $9	S		B		B		G	B	
CHATEAU SOUVERAIN '99, Russian River, Winemakers Rsv. $25		B		S			B	S	B
CHATEAU ST. JEAN '00, Sonoma Co. $15	S		Σ		B		B		G
FREI BROTHERS WINERY '00, Russian River Vly. $17				B		B	S	G	G
GALLO OF SONOMA '99, Russian River Vly. Laguna Vnyd. $24			B	B			B	G	S
GEYSER PEAK '00, Sonoma Co. $12	S			S			S	B	B
GUNDLACH-BUNDSCHU WINERY '00, Sonoma Vly., Rhinefarm Vnyd. $20	S	B	B	B	B				
IMAGERY SERIES '99, Carneros, Ricci Vnyd. $25	B				B	B		B	G
JEKEL VINEYARDS '00, Monterey Gravelstone $13	S		B	B		S	S		
KENDALL-JACKSON WINERY '99, Great Estates, Monterey Co. $28			S		S		S	S	B

Chardonnay

5 AWARDS

L.A.	Orange	Riverside	San Fran	West Coast	State Fair	New World	Pacific Rim	San Diego	Chardonnay
	G	S	B	S			S		**KENDALL-JACKSON WINERY** '00, Great Estates, Santa Barbara $28
	S	S	Σ	S				S	**MERIDIAN VINEYARDS** '00, Santa Barbara Co. $10
S			B	B	S	G			**MIRASSOU** '00, Monterey Co., Coastal Selection $10
S	B	B				B		B	**MONTERRA WINERY** '00, Monterey Co. $13
	B	B	B	S			B		**PEIRANO ESTATE VINEYARDS** '99, Lodi Estate $10
B	S		B	G	Σ				**ROBERT PEPI WINERY** '01, Napa Vly. $14
B			B	B	Σ			S	**RUTHERFORD RANCH** '00, Napa Vly. $14
G	B			Σ	B			B	**SMITH-MADRONE** '99, Napa Vly. Estate $25
Σ		B	B	S				G	**ST. SUPÉRY** '99, Napa Vly. $19
	B		S		B	S		G	**STERLING VINEYARDS** '00, North Coast $17
B			B	S		S	S		**RODNEY STRONG** '98, Chalk Hill Vnyd. Rsv. $30
		B	B	S	B	G			**RODNEY STRONG** '00, Sonoma Co., Chalk Hill Estate $18
		B		G		B	B	B	**M. TRINCHERO WINERY** '99, Napa Vly., Mario's Rsv. $30
S		B	S				S	B	**M. TRINCHERO WINERY** '00, Family Selection, California $14
	G		B	S		S	B		**TURNING LEAF** '00, Coastal Rsv., North Coast $10
G		B		S			G	B	**WATTLE CREEK** '00, Alexander Vly. $25
S		S	B		B			Σ	**WHITE OAK VINEYARDS** '00, Russian River Vly. $17
S			B	B	B	B			**WINDSOR VINEYARDS** '00, North Coast $12

Chardonnay

	L.A.	Orange	Riverside	San Fran	West Coast	State Fair	New World	Pacific Rim	San Diego
4 AWARDS									
ANAPAMU '00, Monterey Co. $16			S	B	B			G	
BAILEYANA VINEYARD '00, Edna Vly., Firepeak Vnyd. $30	B	S				B		S	
BAILEYANA VINEYARD '00, San Luis Obispo-Monterey $18			B				B	S	B
BEAULIEU '00, Carneros $18		B		B	S		B		
BIG HORN CELLARS '99, Carneros, Camelback Vnyd. $16	S	S		B					S
BUEHLER VINEYARDS '00, Russian River Vly. Rsv. $30		S			S	B		B	
CECCHETTI SEBASTIANI CELLAR '00, Central Coast $13				S	G	S	B		
CHATEAU ST. JEAN '99, Alexander Vly., Robert Young Vnyd. $25		G		B			B	B	
CLONINGER CELLARS '00, Santa Lucia Highlands Estate $17	Σ	S				B		B	
CORBETT CANYON VINEYARDS '00, California Rsv. $7			B	S		S	B		
DE LORIMIER WINERY '99, Alexander Vly., Clonal Select $24	G			B				S	S
EAGLE CASTLE WINERY '00, Paso Robles $16		G	S					B	B
ECHELON '00, Central Coast $12.50	B				S		B	B	
EDMEADES '00, Anderson Vly. $18			B	S	S	S			
EDNA VALLEY VINEYARD '00, Edna Vly., Paragon Vyd. $16.50			B	B	G			S	
FETZER '00, 5 Rivers Ranch, Central Coast $13	B		S		S	B			
FORESTVILLE VINEYARD '00, Russian River Vly. Rsv. $12	S	B	B		B				
GALLO OF SONOMA '98, Northern Sonoma Estate $45		S					S	G	B

Chardonnay

4 AWARDS

L.A.	Orange	Riverside	San Fran	West Coast	State Fair	New World	Pacific Rim	San Diego	Wine
					S	S	B	S	**GEYSER PEAK** '00, Russian River Vly. $16
			B	B	S		B		**GUENOC** '99, Guenoc Vly. $15
		B			G	B	B		**GUENOC** '99, Guenoc Vly., Geneviere Magoon Rsv. $27
S		S		S			B		**INGLENOOK ESTATE CELLARS** 'NV, California $8
S		G	S					S	**JEKEL VINEYARDS** '99, F O S, Monterey Co. Rsv. $22
G			G	G			G		**LA CREMA** '00, Sonoma Coast $18
		B	G		S	B			**MARCELINA VINEYARDS** '00, Carneros $22
S			B	B			B		**MEADOR ESTATE** '99, Block 9, Arroyo Seco $30
G		S		S		B			**MERIDIAN VINEYARDS** '99, Rsv., Edna Vly. $14
B		G	B	B					**ORFILA VINEYARDS** '99, California Coastal Rsv. $18
B		B				S	G		**ROBERT STEMMLER** '99, Sonoma Co. $20
S		G				G	G		**STONEHEDGE** '00, Monterey Co. Rsv. $15
		B			B		B	B	**STUHLMULLER VINEYARD & WINERY** '99, Alexander Vly. $23
		S		S		G		S	**TRINITY OAKS** '99, California $10
		B	B		G			S	**VALLEY OF THE MOON** '00, Sonoma Co. $16
S					S	G	G		**WENTE VINEYARDS** '00, Riva Ranch, Arroyo Seco $16
B	B	B		S					**WINDSOR VINEYARDS** '00, Russian River Vly. Preston Ranch $15.75
S	B			S		S			**WINDSOR VINEYARDS** '00, Sonoma Co., Barrel Fermented $17.75

Chardonnay

Chardonnay	L.A.	Orange	Riverside	San Fran	West Coast	State Fair	New World	Pacific Rim	San Diego
3 AWARDS									
ABUNDANCE WINERY '00, Santa Maria, Bien Nacido Vnyd. $21	S				B				B
ALEXANDER VALLEY VINEYARDS '00, Alexander Vly. Estate $15.25			S		S			B	
BAREFOOT CELLARS '00, Sonoma Co. Rsv. $10	B		B						B
BEAULIEU '00, Carneros Rsv. $28	Σ			B				S	
BELVEDERE '00, Russian River Vly. $20		B		S			S		
BERINGER '99, Napa Vly., Private Rsv. $35				S			B	S	
BERINGER '00, Founders Estate, California $12			B			S			B
BIG HORN CELLARS '99, Napa-Carneros Grand Rsv. $24	S			B					B
BUEHLER VINEYARDS '00, Russian River Vly. $15	Σ		B						B
BUENA VISTA '99, Carneros Estate $18	B	S				G			
CALLAWAY COASTAL '99, Rsv., California $14	S	S				B			
CASTORO CELLARS '00, Central Coast $12			G		S				B
CINNABAR '99, Santa Cruz Mtns. Estate $25	B	G		B					
COASTAL RIDGE WINERY '99, California $7	S				G		B		
DOMAINE ALFRED '00, Califa Chamisal Vnyd., Edna Vly. $32	G					G			G
DOMAINE ST. GEORGE WINERY '00, California Barrel Rsv. $10	B	S		B					
DRY CREEK VINEYARD '00, Sonoma Co. $16							B	B	S
FOLEY ESTATES '00, Santa Barbara Co. Barrel Select $38	G	G				S			

Chardonnay

3 AWARDS

L.A.	Orange	Riverside	San Fran	West Coast	State Fair	New World	Pacific Rim	San Diego	Chardonnay
				B	B			S	**FOREST GLEN WINERY** '00, Oak Barrel Fermented, California $10
		B		S	B				**GALLO OF SONOMA** '00, Russian River Vly. Laguna Vnyd. $22
B		G					S		**GUENOC** '00, Guenoc Vly. $14.50
		B		B			B		**HANDLEY** '99, Anderson Vly. Estate $16
		B	B				S		**HANDLEY** '00, Anderson Vly. Estate $16
			S	S			G		**HANDLEY** '00, Dry Creek Vly., Handley Vnyd. $18
B			B		B				**WILLIAM HILL WINERY** '00, Napa Vly. Rsv. $23
	B		B				S		**HOP KILN WINERY** '01, North Coast $12
	S				B		S		**HUSCH VINEYARDS** '00, Mendocino Co. $14
G	B		B						**J WINE COMPANY** '99, Russian River Vly. Estate $32
	G	B					B		**JANKRIS VINEYARD** '00, Central Coast $14
		S				B	G		**KENDALL-JACKSON WINERY** '98, Great Estates, Sonoma Coast $28
				S		S	S		**KENDALL-JACKSON WINERY** '00, Grand Rsv., California $20
		B		B	S				**KENWOOD VINEYARDS** '00, Russian River Vly. Rsv. $20
S	S		B						**LINCOURT** '00, Santa Barbara Co. $18
B			S					G	**MARTIN & WEYRICH WINERY** '00, Edna Vly., Edna Ranch $18
B		B			G				**MC MANIS FAMILY VINEYARDS** '01, River Junction $9
		B					B	B	**MIDNIGHT CELLARS** '00, Equinox, Paso Robles $16

Chardonnay

3 AWARDS	L.A.	Orange	Riverside	San Fran	West Coast	State Fair	New World	Pacific Rim	San Diego
MILL CREEK VINEYARDS '99, Dry Creek Vly. $15		S	S			S			
MONTICELLO CORLEY FAMILY '00, Napa Vly., Estate $24		B				B			G
NAPA RIDGE '00, Napa Vly. $12			G			Σ		S	
PARDUCCI WINE CELLARS '00, Mendocino Co., Vintner Select $10	Σ	G			S				
J. PEDRONCELLI '00, Dry Creek Vly., F. Johnson Vnyd. $14	B			B			S		
PERRY CREEK VINEYARDS '00, El Dorado Estate $12	S			S	B				
R. H. PHILLIPS '99, Toasted Head, Dunnigan Hills Giguiere Ranch $25			B					B	B
PHOENIX VINEYARDS '00, Napa Vly. Rsv. $18			B	S		B			
REDWOOD CREEK WINERY '00, California $8			B	S	B				
ROSENBLUM CELLARS '00, Edna Vly., Paragron Vnyd. $19					S	B	B		
ROSENBLUM CELLARS '00, Russian River Vly., Loan Oak, Rsv. $25					S		S	B	
ROUND HILL VINEYARDS '00, California $9	B					B	S		
SAN SIMEON CELLARS '00, Monterey $15		B		S		S			
SAPPHIRE HILL VINEYARDS '00, Russian River Vly. Rsv. $30		B		S	S				
SEBASTIANI VINEYARDS & WINERY '99, Sonoma Co. $16		B			B				B
SEVEN PEAKS '00, Central Coast $10	S		G					B	
ST. SUPÉRY '99, Napa Vly., Dollarhide Ranch $30					S			B	B
ST. SUPÉRY '00, Napa Vly. $19	Σ			B		B			

L.A.	Orange	Riverside	San Fran	West Coast	State Fair	New World	Pacific Rim	San Diego	Chardonnay
3 AWARDS									
S			B			Σ			**ST. SUPÉRY** '00, Napa Vly., Dollarhide Ranch $35
			B	S			G		**STERLING VINEYARDS** '00, Carneros, Winery Lake $25
B							S	G	**STONEGATE** '00, Napa Vly. Estate $22
			B	S		G			**RODNEY STRONG** '00, Sonoma Co. $14
		B		B		S			**TALUS** '00, California $9
		G					S	B	**THORNTON** '00, South Coast Dos Vinedos Cuvee $10
B			B	B					**TREFETHEN** '00, Napa Vly. Estate $22
Σ		B			G				**VAN ROEKEL VINEYARDS** '01, Temecula $9
B		S						B	**VAN ROEKEL VINEYARDS** '00, Temecula Estate $10
		S	B		S				**VENTANA VINEYARDS** '00, Monterey Arroyo Seco Goldstripe $14
				S		B	S		**WINDSOR VINEYARDS** '00, Russian River Vly., Vintner's Rsv. $21.75
2 AWARDS									
	S				B				**ABUNDANCE WINERY** '00, Clarksburg, Clos d'Abundance $21
B						S			**AMBERHILL** '00, California $10
B				S					**ARMIDA WINERY** '99, Russian River Vly. $19
B					G				**ARMIDA WINERY** '99, Russian River Vly. Rsv.
	S				G				**ARMIDA WINERY** '00, Alexander Vly., Stuhlmuller Vnyd. $25
					G			B	**ARROW CREEK WINERY** '00, California $10
	S					B			**BAILEYANA VINEYARD** '99, Edna Vly., Firepeak Vnyd. $30

Chardonnay

2 AWARDS	L.A.	Orange	Riverside	San Fran	West Coast	State Fair	New World	Pacific Rim	San Diego
BARON HERZOG WINE CELLARS '00, California $13				S			S		
BEL ARBOR '00, California $6					S		S		
BENZIGER '00, Carneros $16	S	S							
RAYMOND BURR VINEYARDS '00, Dry Creek Vly. $28		B		B					
BUTTERFIELD STATION '01, California $8		G					B		
CAMELOT WINERY '00, California $9				S			S		
MAURICE CAR'RIE WINERY '00, Temecula $9	S		B						
CHANDELLE OF SONOMA '00, Sonoma Co. $13.50			S		B				
CHATEAU SOUVERAIN '00, Sonoma Co. $14					S		B		
CLOS DU BOIS '00, Alexander Vly. Rsv. $16				B		G			
COASTAL RIDGE WINERY '00, California $7				B		G			
CONCANNON VINEYARD '99, Central Coast, Rsv. $20					S			B	
CUVAISON '00, Napa Carneros $24		B			S				
CUVAISON '00, Napa Vly. $22							B	B	
DE LOACH VINEYARDS '00, California $11				B			B		
DE LOACH VINEYARDS '00, Russian River Vly. $18				S				B	
DE LORIMIER WINERY '99, Alexander Vly., Estate $16				B				B	
DIABLO CREEK '01, California $8							G		B

Chardonnay

L.A.	Orange	Riverside	San Fran	West Coast	State Fair	New World	Pacific Rim	San Diego	
2 AWARDS									
			B		G				**DIABLO GRANDE** '01, Fruit of the Vine Diablo Grande $18
	S				S				**DOMAINE SONOMA WINERY** '99, Sonoma Co., Chalk Hill $14
S				S					**DOMAINE ST. GEORGE WINERY** '99, California Barrel Rsv. $10
			B		B				**DOMAINE ST. GEORGE WINERY** '99, Chalk Hill, Blasi Vnyd. $14
					B		B		**DRY CREEK VINEYARD** '99, Dry Creek Vly. Rsv.
					S	G			**EDGEWOOD** '00, Napa Vly. $22
	S				S				**GARY FARRELL** '00, Russian River Vly., Westside Farms $34
						S	S		**FETZER** '00, Monterey Co., Rsv.
	S		B						**FOLEY ESTATES** '00, Santa Maria Vly., Bien Nacido Vnyd. $35
					B	B			**FOPPIANO VINEYARDS** '00, California Riverside Collection $7.50
B	B								**FOXHOLLOW VINEYARDS** '99, California, Barrel Select $9
		B				S			**J. FRITZ WINERY** '99, Russian River Vly. $22
			S	B					**GALLO OF SONOMA** '99, Northern Sonoma Estate $50
			G			S			**GUENOC** '00, Guenoc Vly., Geneviere Magoon Rsv. $27
S			S						**EMILIO GUGLIELMO WINERY** '00, Carneros Private Rsv. $16
		B				S			**HACIENDA WINERY** '99, California Clair de Lune $7
				B			S		**HANNA** '00, Russian River Vly. $19

Chardonnay

2 AWARDS

Wine	L.A.	Orange	Riverside	San Fran	West Coast	State Fair	New World	Pacific Rim	San Diego
HARMONY CELLARS '00, San Luis Obispo Co. $15	G								S
HEITZ WINE CELLAR '00, Napa Vly., Cellar Selection $30	S			B					
WILLIAM HILL WINERY '00, Napa Vly. $16	G			B					
HOP KILN WINERY '00, Russian River Vly., Griffin Vnyd. $18			B	B					
HRM '00, Central Coast $8				B		S			
INDIAN SPRINGS VINEYARDS '00, Nevada Co. $14.50			B				B		
KIRKLAND RANCH WINERY '00, KRV Napa Vly. $22				B		B			
KOEHLER WINERY '00, Santa Barbara Co., Estate $15	G			B					
KOEHLER WINERY '00, Santa Barbara, Winemaker Select $20		G		S					
KUNDE ESTATE WINERY '99, Sonoma Vly. Rsv. $35	S			B					
LA CREMA '00, Russian River Vly. $30				B		S			
LAFOND '00, Santa Ynez Vly., Santa Rita Hills $18		B		B					
LAMBERT BRIDGE WINERY '00, Sonoma Co. $20		B	B						
LOCKWOOD VINEYARD '98, Monterey Co. Rsv. $35	S								S
LOCKWOOD VINEYARD '00, Monterey Co., San Lucas $15			B					S	
J. LOHR ESTATE '01, Painter Bridge California $7				Σ		Σ			
J. LOHR ESTATE '00, Cypress California $10				S		B			
LUCAS & LEWELLEN '00, Santa Barbara Co., Old Adobe Vnyd. $24			B				B		

Chardonnay

2 AWARDS

L.A.	Orange	Riverside	San Fran	West Coast	State Fair	New World	Pacific Rim	San Diego	Chardonnay
				B			S		**MC ILROY WINES** '00, Russian River Vly., Signature Edition $34
		S				S			**MICHEL-SCHLUMBERGER** '00, Dry Creek Vly. $22
			B		S				**ROBERT MONDAVI COASTAL** '00, Central Coast $11
				G			B		**MONTPELLIER VINEYARDS** '00, California $7
	B					B			**MURPHY-GOODE** '00, Sonoma Co. $15
		B				B			**NAPA RIDGE** '98, North Coast $9
					B		S		**NAPA RIDGE** '00, North Coast
B								B	**OAK GROVE VINEYARDS** '00, Private Rsv., California $10
	G			B					**PELICAN RANCH** '00, Napa Carneros, Mitsuko's Vnyd. $19
	B		B						**RANCHO SISQUOC** '00, Santa Barbara, Flood Family Vnyd. $18
	S				S				**RIOS-LOVELL WINERY** '01, Livermore Vly., Estate $14
S			B						**SAN SABA VINEYARD** '01, Bocage, Monterey California $10
		B				B			**V. SATTUI WINERY** '00, Carneros $17.75
				B			B		**SEBASTIANI VINEYARDS & WINERY** '99, Russian River Vly., Dutton Ranch $25
						Σ	B		**SEQUOIA GROVE VINEYARDS** '00, Napa Vly., Carneros $18
		B			S				**SILVER RIDGE VINEYARDS** '00, California Barrel Fermented $10
	S							B	**SILVER ROSE CELLARS** '99, Napa Vly., D'argent $30
	B			S					**SILVER STONE** '99, California $9

Chardonnay

2 AWARDS

Wine	L.A.	Orange	Riverside	San Fran	West Coast	State Fair	New World	Pacific Rim	San Diego
SIMI '00, Sonoma Co. $17			B					B	
STERLING VINEYARDS '00, Napa Vly. $17					B			B	
STRYKER SONOMA WINERY & '00, Russian River Vly. $22					G		S		
SYLVESTER '00, Paso Robles, Kiara Rsv. $15			B	B					
TOAD HOLLOW '00, North Coast, Francines Selection $14	B			S					
TOLOSA '00, Edna Vly., Edna Ranch $24		B		B					
TRELLIS VINEYARDS '00, Russian River Vly. $14		B						S	
VAN RUITEN-TAYLOR WINERY '00, Lodi Rsv. $10		S		B					
VENTANA VINEYARDS '99, Monterey Rsv. $18			B			B			
VILLA MT. EDEN '99, Santa Maria, Bien Nacido Vnyd. Signature $32					S		S		
WENTE VINEYARDS '00, Livermore Vly., Vineyard Selection $11	S	S							
WINDSOR VINEYARDS '99, Alexander Vly. Simoneau Ranch $16.50			B					B	
WOODBRIDGE WINERY '00, California $9		B		S					
ZACA MESA '00, Santa Barbara Co.	S					B			

PlumpJack
Chardonnay
CHAR

SONOMA COUNTY
PORTER CREEK
DAVIS BYNUM
J. ROCHIOLI
HOP KILN
BELVEDERE
ARMIDA
RABBIT RIDGE
MILL CREEK
GARY FARRELL

Gewurztraminer

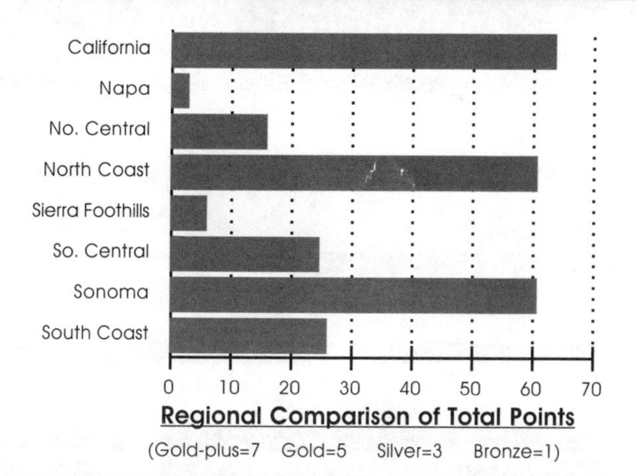

Highest Individual Wine Totals

Points	Wine
24	**FETZER** '01, Echo Ridge, California, $8.00
21	**VAN ROEKEL VINEYARDS** '01, Temecula, $11.00
20	**HUSCH VINEYARDS** '01, Anderson Vly., Estate, $12.00
20	**NAVARRO VINEYARDS** '00, Estate, Anderson Vly., $14.00
19	**GEYSER PEAK** '01, California, $9.00
19	**SUTTER HOME** '01, California, $8.00
15	**CHATEAU ST. JEAN** '01, Sonoma Co., $15.00
11	**MILL CREEK VINEYARDS** '00, Dry Creek Vly. Estate, $13.00
10	**ADLER FELS** '01, Russian River Vly., $12.00
10	**GUNDLACH-BUNDSCHU WINERY** '01, Sonoma Vly., Rhinefarm Vnyd., $18.00
9	**MERIDIAN VINEYARDS** '00, Santa Barbara Co., $8.00

Dry Gewurztraminer

Wine	L.A.	Orange	Riverside	San Fran	West Coast	State Fair	New World	Pacific Rim	San Diego
9 AWARDS									
GEYSER PEAK '01, California $9	B	B	B	B	S	S	S	B	G
8 AWARDS									
FETZER '01, Echo Ridge, California $8	S		B	B	S	S	S	Σ	S
7 AWARDS									
SUTTER HOME '01, California $8	S		B	Σ	S	B		B	S
6 AWARDS									
NAVARRO VINEYARDS '00, Estate, Anderson Vly. $14	B	G	S		S		Σ	B	
5 AWARDS									
CHATEAU ST. JEAN '01, Sonoma Co. $15	B	G	S		S				S
MILL CREEK VINEYARDS '00, Dry Creek Vly. Estate $13	S	B	S		B		S		
VAN ROEKEL VINEYARDS '01, Temecula $11		S				Σ	S	S	G
4 AWARDS									
ADLER FELS '01, Russian River Vly. $12		B	B			G	S		
ALEXANDER VALLEY VINEYARDS '01, North Coast, Mendocino Co. $9			B		S			B	B
FIRESTONE VINEYARD '00, Santa Barbara Co. $10			B	B	S		S		
GUNDLACH-BUNDSCHU WINERY '01, Sonoma Vly., Rhinefarm Vnyd. $18	B	G	S						B
HUSCH VINEYARDS '01, Anderson Vly., Estate $12			G	G		G			G
LOUIS M. MARTINI '00, Russian River Vly., Del Rio Vnyd. $15	B	S				B	B		
VENTANA VINEYARDS '01, Monterey, Arroyo Seco, Estate $10	B	S		B		B			
3 AWARDS									
DE LOACH VINEYARDS '00, Russian River Vly. Early Harvest $12		B	B					B	

Dry Gewurztraminer

L.A.	Orange	Riverside	San Fran	West Coast	State Fair	New World	Pacific Rim	San Diego	Wine
3 AWARDS									
	B	S			B				**FILSINGER VINEYARDS** '01, Temecula Estate $8
		B	B			Σ			**MERIDIAN VINEYARDS** '00, Santa Barbara Co. $8
2 AWARDS									
					B			B	**ALPEN CELLARS** '01, Trinity Co. $7.50
						S	B		**BAYWOOD** '00, Monterey Vyd., Select $15
	G				S				**FIRESTONE VINEYARD** '01, Santa Barbara Co. $10
				S		S			**HANDLEY** '00, Anderson Vly. $14
B				B					**VENTANA VINEYARDS** '00, Monterey, Arroyo Seco, Estate $10
B							B		**WINDSOR VINEYARDS** '00, Alexander Vly. $9.50

Dry Riesling

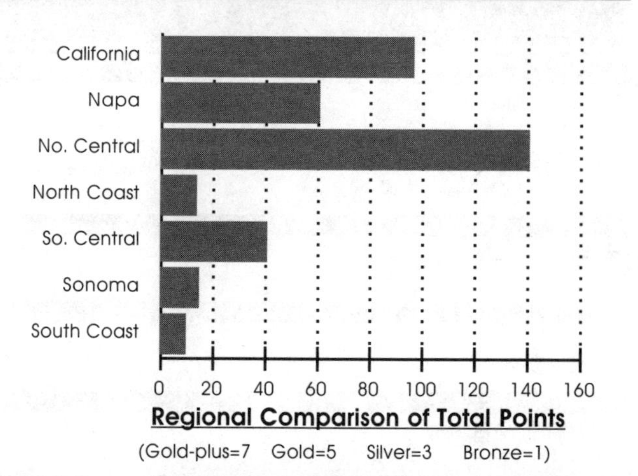

Regional Comparison of Total Points

(Gold-plus=7 Gold=5 Silver=3 Bronze=1)

Highest Individual Wine Totals

30 **FETZER**
'01, Echo Ridge, California, $8.00

26 **JEKEL VINEYARDS**
'00, Monterey Co., Sanctuary Est., $10.00

25 **GEYSER PEAK**
'01, California, $9.00

25 **J. LOHR ESTATE**
'01, Monterey Co., Bay Mist, $8.00

22 **SMITH-MADRONE**
'01, Napa Vly., $17.00

20 **TREFETHEN**
'01, Napa Vly. Estate, $15.00

19 **BERINGER**
'00, California, $7.00

16 **HAGAFEN CELLARS**
'01, Napa Vly., $15.00

15 **ANAPAMU**
'00, Monterey Co., $16.00

15 **THE GAINEY VINEYARD**
'01, Santa Ynez Vly., $12.00

Dry Riesling

Wine	L.A.	Orange	Riverside	San Fran	West Coast	State Fair	New World	Pacific Rim	San Diego
9 AWARDS									
GEYSER PEAK '01, California $9	B	B	S	B	B	B	Σ	S	Σ
J. LOHR ESTATE '01, Monterey Co., Bay Mist $8	G	S	B	B	S	S	S	G	B
8 AWARDS									
FETZER '01, Echo Ridge, California $8	S	S	S	Σ		S	Σ	B	S
7 AWARDS									
BERINGER '00, California $7	G	S		B	B	S	G	B	
6 AWARDS									
JEKEL VINEYARDS '00, Monterey Co., Sanctuary Est. $10			G	S	S		G	Σ	S
MADDALENA VINEYARD '01, Monterey Co. $10	B	B		Σ	B	S			B
SMITH-MADRONE '01, Napa Vly. $17	G	G		G	S	S			B
TREFETHEN '01, Napa Vly. Estate $15	B	G		S	S	B			Σ
5 AWARDS									
ANAPAMU '00, Monterey Co. $16	S	S		G			S	B	
THE GAINEY VINEYARD '01, Santa Ynez Vly. $12		S	Σ	B		S		B	
4 AWARDS									
CHATEAU ST. JEAN '01, Sonoma Co. $15	G	G		B	S				
GREENWOOD RIDGE VINEYARDS '01, Mendocino Ridge Estate	B	S				B		B	
HAGAFEN CELLARS '01, Napa Vly. $15		G		Σ		S		B	
KENDALL-JACKSON WINERY '01, Vintner's Rsv., California $10		S		S	S				G
3 AWARDS									
CASA DE CABALLOS '00, Paso Robles $15			S				Σ	B	

Dry Riesling

L.A.	Orange	Riverside	San Fran	West Coast	State Fair	New World	Pacific Rim	San Diego	Dry Riesling
									3 AWARDS
		S	B		S				**CONCANNON VINEYARD** '01, Monterey Johannisberg Limited Bottling $10
	G		B		G				**VENTANA VINEYARDS** '01, Monterey, Arroyo Seco, Estate $10
		S				B	B		**WINDSOR VINEYARDS** '00, Monterey Co. $8.25
									2 AWARDS
	B	B							**BAILY VINEYARD & WINERY** '01, Temecula $15
		S				S			**GREENWOOD RIDGE VINEYARDS** '00, Mendocino Ridge Estate $12
	G				G				**JEKEL VINEYARDS** '01, Monterey Co., Sanctuary Est. $10
	S				B				**ROBERT MONDAVI COASTAL** '01, Central Coast $9
		B				B			**NAVARRO VINEYARDS** '00, Anderson Vly. $14
	B		B						**V. SATTUI WINERY** '01, Dry Napa $15
	G				S				**STONY RIDGE WINERY** '00, Monterey Co. Rsv. $10.50
	S	B							**WILSON CREEK WINERY & VINEYARD** '01, Temecula $16
	B		B						**WINDSOR VINEYARDS** '01, Monterey Co. $8.25

Merlot

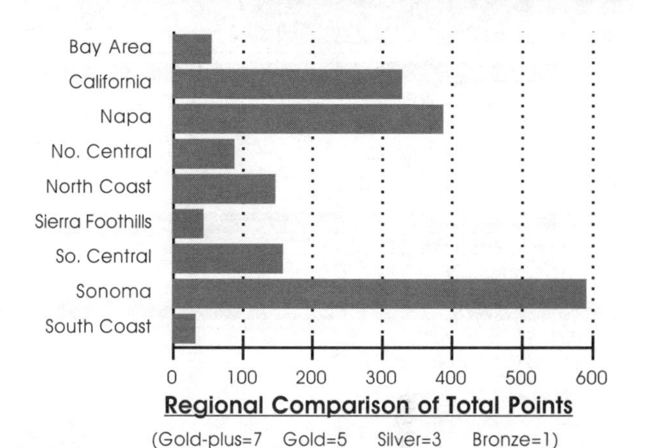

Highest Individual Wine Totals

26 **CECCHETTI SEBASTIANI CELLAR**
'99, North Coast, $13.00

25 **KENDALL-JACKSON WINERY**
'99, Grand Rsv., California, $30.00

22 **FLORA SPRINGS**
'99, Napa Vly., Rutherford, Windfall Vnyd., $40.00

22 **RAYMOND**
'99, Napa Vly. Rsv., $24.50

21 **CARMENET VINEYARD**
'00, Dynamite, North Coast, $17.25

21 **KENDALL-JACKSON WINERY**
'98, Great Estates, Sonoma Co., $35.00

20 **MERIDIAN VINEYARDS**
'99, California, $11.00

20 **STERLING VINEYARDS**
'99, Napa Vly., Three Palms, $58.00

19 **GREENWOOD RIDGE VINEYARDS**
'99, Mendocino Ridge Estate, $24.00

Merlot	L.A.	Orange	Riverside	San Fran	West Coast	State Fair	New World	Pacific Rim	San Diego
9 AWARDS									
KENDALL-JACKSON WINERY '99, Grand Rsv., California $30	S	S	B	S	S	S	G	S	B
KENDALL-JACKSON WINERY '98, Great Estates, Sonoma Co. $35	S	B	B	S	S	S	S	S	B
8 AWARDS									
CECCHETTI SEBASTIANI CELLAR '99, North Coast $13	Σ	S	G		S	S	B	B	S
7 AWARDS									
CARMENET VINEYARD '00, Dynamite, North Coast $17.25	S	S	G	B	S			G	B
KENDALL-JACKSON WINERY '99, Vintner's Rsv., California $16		S	B		S	S	B	S	B
MIDNIGHT CELLARS '99, Eclipse, Paso Robles $20	B	B	B	B	G	S		G	
6 AWARDS									
AMBERHILL '99, California $12	S	S	S	S			B		B
BONTERRA '99, Mendocino Co. $16	S	S	S		S	S	B		
CHATEAU ST. JEAN '99, Sonoma Co. $25	S		B	B	G	S		S	
ECHELON '00, Central Coast $13.50	Σ	S	S	B	S	B			
FLORA SPRINGS '99, Napa Vly., Rutherford, Windfall Vnyd. $40	G		S	S	S	S	G		
FREI BROTHERS WINERY '00, Dry Creek Vly. Rsv. $17	B		B	B	S			S	B
GUNDLACH-BUNDSCHU WINERY '99, Sonoma Vly., Rhinefarm Vnyd. $28	S	B	S	S	S				S
ROBERT KEENAN '99, Napa Vly. $30	B	S	B	B		G		B	
KENDALL-JACKSON WINERY '97, Alexander Vly. Single Vnyd. Series Buckeye $32			B	B	B	G	B	S	
LOUIS M. MARTINI '98, Napa Vly., Ghost Pines Cuvee $27		B		B	S	B	S		S

Merlot

L.A.	Orange	Riverside	San Fran	West Coast	State Fair	New World	Pacific Rim	San Diego	Merlot
6 AWARDS									
G	S	G		B		B	G		**MERIDIAN VINEYARDS** '99, California $11
	S	B		S	G	B	G		**MILL CREEK VINEYARDS** '99, Dry Creek Vly. Estate $18.50
Σ	S	S		S		B		G	**RAYMOND** '99, Napa Vly. Rsv. $24.50
B	B	S		S	B		B		**ST. SUPÉRY** '99, Napa Vly. $21
B	B	S				S	B	S	**STONEGATE** '99, Napa Vly. $28
G	B		S	B	S		B		**TRELLIS VINEYARDS** '99, Sonoma Co. $17
	G	B		B	S	Σ		B	**TRENTADUE** '99, Alexander Vly., Estate $18
G		B		B	S	S		B	**WINDSOR VINEYARDS** '98, Sonoma Co., Signature Series $25.25
5 AWARDS									
G	G			B	B	S			**ANTERRA** '98, Napa Vly. Rsv. $30
		B	B	S		S	S		**BAREFOOT CELLARS** '99, Knights Vly. Rsv. $15
B		B		S			G	B	**BARTHOLOMEW PARK** '99, Sonoma Vly., Frank's Vnyd. $27
S		B		S		S	S		**CHATEAU SOUVERAIN** '99, Alexander Vly. $17
	B	G	S	B			G		**COASTAL RIDGE WINERY** '99, California $7
B		S		S	S			S	**FENESTRA** '99, Livermore Vly. $19
	G	B	B	B		S			**FIRESTONE VINEYARD** '99, Santa Ynez Vly. 25th Anniversary $16
		G		S	S	S	B		**GEYSER PEAK** '99, Sonoma Co. $17
	B	B			G	G	S		**GEYSER PEAK** '99, Sonoma Co. Rsv. $32
		Σ		S	S		G	B	**GREENWOOD RIDGE VINEYARDS** '99, Mendocino Ridge Estate $24

Merlot

	L.A.	Orange	Riverside	San Fran	West Coast	State Fair	New World	Pacific Rim	San Diego
5 AWARDS									
GRGICH HILLS '99, Napa Vly. $38	S		B		S	S		S	
HUNTINGTON '99, Sonoma Co. $18			G	Σ		B	B	S	
INDIAN SPRINGS VINEYARDS '99, Nevada Co. $18		S		S	S	B		B	
LAMBERT BRIDGE WINERY '99, Sonoma Co. $24	S			G	S		B	B	
NAPA RIDGE '00, Napa Vly. $12		B		S	S	S			B
ORFILA VINEYARDS '99, San Diego Co. Rsv. $27	B		S		B	S		S	
PEPPERWOOD GROVE '00, California $9		S		B	G	G			B
V. SATTUI WINERY '99, Napa Vly. Lot 1 $24		B	S	S	S			B	
STERLING VINEYARDS '99, Napa Vly. $22	G				S		B	Σ	B
RODNEY STRONG '99, Sonoma Co. $16		G	S			B	B	S	
RODNEY STRONG '97, Alexander Vly., Northern Sonoma $26	S		B			S		B	G
TREFETHEN '99, Napa Vly. Estate $26	B	S		B	S	S			
WHITE OAK VINEYARDS '00, Alexander Vly. Estate $28	B	G		S	S		B		
WINDSOR VINEYARDS '99, Sonoma Co., Signature Series $25.25	S			B	S		Σ	S	
4 AWARDS									
BARTHOLOMEW PARK '99, Sonoma Vly., Desnudos Vnyd. $33	B	S		B	S				
BERINGER '99, Founders Estate, California $12	B	S			B			S	
BOGLE '00, California $9		S		B	S	S			
BRUTOCAO '99, Mendocino Co., Brutocao Vnyd. $20			B		B		B		S

L.A.	Orange	Riverside	San Fran	West Coast	State Fair	New World	Pacific Rim	San Diego	Merlot
									4 AWARDS
	B		B	S				B	**CANYON ROAD WINERY** '00, California $10
	B	Σ			S		S		**CARMODY MCKNIGHT** '99, Paso Robles, Estate $20
	S				G	S	S		**CASA NUESTRA** '99, Napa Vly., Estate $38
B	B				Σ	B			**DOCE ROBLES WINERY** '99, Paso Robles $17
	B	B		S				B	**DOMAINE ST. GEORGE WINERY** '00, California Barrel Rsv. $8
B		S	G					S	**FRATELLI PERATA** '98, Paso Robles $18
B	B		B		B				**FREY VINEYARDS** '01, Redwood Vly., Biodynamic $19
	B		B	S			B		**HAHN ESTATES** '98, Santa Lucia Highlands $12
B		S			G			Σ	**HAWLEY WINES** '99, Bradford Mtn. $25
B				S	S		S		**IMAGERY SERIES** '99, Sonoma Vly., Sunny Slope Vyd. $35
	S	B					S	S	**JANKRIS VINEYARD** '00, Mystere, Paso Robles $13
	B		S	S	G				**KIRKLAND RANCH WINERY** '99, Napa Vly. $30
G	B			S				S	**MC CRAY RIDGE** '99, Two Moon Vnyd., Dry Creek Vly. $28
Σ		B			G	S			**MICHAEL-DAVID PHILLIPS** '00, Lodi $20
G	B	B			S				**MICHEL-SCHLUMBERGER** '99, Dry Creek Vly. $22
S			B	S	B				**RIVER GROVE WINERY** '00, Clarksburg $14
B				G	S		B		**SALMON CREEK CELLARS** '00, California $7
B	S	B	B						**SEVEN PEAKS** '99, Central Coast $14

Merlot	L.A.	Orange	Riverside	San Fran	West Coast	State Fair	New World	Pacific Rim	San Diego
4 AWARDS									
SILVER RIDGE VINEYARDS '00, California Barrel Select $10		B			S		S		B
SILVER ROSE CELLARS '99, Napa Vly. Jupilles $38	B	B	G	B					
STERLING VINEYARDS '99, Napa Vly., Three Palms $58	S				G	Σ		G	
M. TRINCHERO WINERY '99, Family Selection, California $14			B	B	G			B	
M. TRINCHERO WINERY '99, Napa Vly., Chicken Ranch $25			S		B	S		B	
TRINITY OAKS '99, California $10	S	S			S			B	
VENDANGE 'NV, California $5	B	B	S		B				
WHITE OAK VINEYARDS '00, Napa Vly. $24	S			B	S	B			
3 AWARDS									
ARMIDA WINERY '99, Russian River Vly. $24	S				S				B
BARON HERZOG WINE CELLARS '00, Paso Robles $13		B	B				S		
BUENA VISTA '99, Carneros Estate $22	B			B		S			
CAMELOT WINERY '99, California $9	G	G			S				
CASTLE VINEYARDS '98, Los Carneros, Sangiacomo-Durell Vnyds. $25	S			S		S			
CHARLES CREEK VINEYARDS '00, Miradero, Sonoma Co. $18					S	S			B
CINNABAR '00, Paso Robles $20	B			G					B
CLOS DU BOIS '99, Sonoma Co. $18	B	B		B					
CONCANNON VINEYARD '99, Central Coast $18				B	S				B

Merlot

3 AWARDS

L.A.	Orange	Riverside	San Fran	West Coast	State Fair	New World	Pacific Rim	San Diego	Merlot
B		B		S					**CONN CREEK** '99, Napa Vly., Limited Release $25
	S	S			B				**THOMAS COYNE** '99, El Dorado Quartz Hill Vnyd. $16
		B			S		B		**THOMAS COYNE** '99, Livermore Vly., Detjens Farms $20
B	B					B			**DEERFIELD RANCH** '99, Russian River Vly. $35
		B			B			B	**DELICATO** '00, California $8
					B		B	B	**DRY CREEK VINEYARD** '98, Dry Creek Vly. Rsv. $35
B		S		S					**FETZER** '99, Central Coast 5 Rivers Ranch $13
		Σ				B	B		**FETZER** '99, Sonoma Co., Barrel Select $14
			B	B	B				**FETZER** '00, Eagle Peak California $9
				B	B			B	**FOPPIANO VINEYARDS** '98, Sonoma Co. $18
B				B	B				**FOPPIANO VINEYARDS** '97, Russian River Vly., Rsv. Estate $31
	B				S		B		**FOXHOLLOW VINEYARDS** '00, California, Barrel Select $9
	G				S		S		**THE GAINEY VINEYARD** '99, Santa Ynez Vly. $16
				S		G		B	**GALLO OF SONOMA** '99, Sonoma Co. $11
B			B	G					**GEYSER PEAK** '99, Alexander Vly. Rsv. $40
B						B		S	**GEYSER PEAK** '98, Sonoma Vly., Shorenstein Vnyd. Block Collection $26
		B					B	B	**HART WINERY** '00, Estate, Temecula $24
B		B				S			**INDIGO HILLS** '99, San Francisco Bay Livermore Vly. $14

Merlot

3 AWARDS	L.A.	Orange	Riverside	San Fran	West Coast	State Fair	New World	Pacific Rim	San Diego
JEKEL VINEYARDS '99, Monterey Co. $15			B	B				B	
KENDALL-JACKSON WINERY '98, Grand Rsv., California $30			B				S	B	
KENWOOD VINEYARDS '99, Sonoma Vly. Jack London Vnyd. $30	B		S		S				
LOCKWOOD VINEYARD '99, Monterey Co. Estate $17	S	B	B						
MARKHAM '99, Napa Vly. $21			S		S			B	
MERRYVALE '99, Napa Vly. Rsv. $39		S		S		S			
MONTERRA WINERY '00, Monterey Co. $13	B		B			S			
MONTPELLIER VINEYARDS '00, Calfornia $7			B		B	S			
PEIRANO ESTATE VINEYARDS '98, Lodi Six-Clones $10			B	B				S	
PEPPERWOOD GROVE '99, California $7			B				B	B	
RIOS-LOVELL WINERY '00, Livermore Vly., Estate Rsv. $22	B		B						B
RUTHERFORD RANCH '99, Napa Vly. $14			B		S			B	
RUTHERFORD VINTNERS '00, Stanislaus Co., Barrel Select $9		B			S	B			
SEBASTIANI VINEYARDS & WINERY '98, Sonoma Co. $22					G			S	G
ROBERT STEMMLER '99, Sonoma Co. $28	G		B		S				
STONE CELLARS '99, California $8					B			S	B
STONE CREEK '99, North Coast, Chairman's Rsv. $17		B		S		Σ			
STUART CELLARS '00, Limited Estate, South Coast $27		B	B						B

L.A.	Orange	Riverside	San Fran	West Coast	State Fair	New World	Pacific Rim	San Diego	Merlot
									3 AWARDS
	S			S	S				**WHITEHALL LANE** '99, Napa Vly. $26
	B	B			S				**WILSON WINERY** '99, Dry Creek Vly. Sydney Vnyd. $24
B		Σ						S	**WINDSOR VINEYARDS** '00, Mendocino Co. Private Rsv. $15.75
G		B		S					**YORKVILLE CELLARS** '98, Yorkville Highlands, Rennie Vnyd. $18
									2 AWARDS
				S				B	**ALBERTONI VINEYARDS** '00, California $13
				S				G	**ALEXANDER VALLEY VINEYARDS** '00, Alexander Vly. Estate $20
	B							S	**ARROW CREEK WINERY** '99, California $10
			S		B				**BAILY VINEYARD & WINERY** '99, Temecula $21
		B				B			**BARGETTO** '99, Santa Cruz Mtns. $20
B							B		**BEAULIEU** '00, California Coastal
	B				B				**BEL ARBOR** '00, California $6
		B		S					**BERINGER** '99, Napa Vly. $26
			B			B			**BLACKSTONE WINERY** '00, Napa $18
					S			B	**BUTTERFIELD STATION** '00, California $8
G			S						**CALLAWAY COASTAL** '99, California $11
			S				S		**CAPELLO WINERY** '99, California $9
		S					S		**CASTORO CELLARS** '99, Paso Robles $13
			S	G					**CEDAR MOUNTAIN WINERY** '98, Livermore Vly. $22

Merlot

2 AWARDS

Winery / Wine	L.A.	Orange	Riverside	San Fran	West Coast	State Fair	New World	Pacific Rim	San Diego
CORBETT CANYON VINEYARDS '99, California Rsv. $7		S						B	
CYPRESS VINEYARD '99, California $10			B		G				
DE LOACH VINEYARDS '99, Russian River Vly. Estate $20			B	B					
DE LORIMIER WINERY '99, Alexander Vly. $20		B						S	
FETZER '00, Sonoma Co., Barrel Select $14				G	B				
FOREST GLEN WINERY '00, Oak Barrel Selection $10			B		S				
FRENCH HILL WINERY '00, El Dorado, Gold Hill Vnyd. $28	B	B							
FREY VINEYARDS '01, Redwood Vly., Organic $17	S			B					
HACIENDA WINERY '00, California Clair de Lune $7	S		S						
HANNA '99, Alexander Vly. $25					S		G		
HARMONY CELLARS '00, Paso Robles $15				B		S			
HELLER ESTATE '99, Carmel Vly./Monterey, Durney Vnyd. $26				S		G			
JEPSON '98, Mendocino Co. $18	G								B
KENWOOD VINEYARDS '99, Sonoma Co. $17		B	B						
KIRKLAND RANCH WINERY '99, Napa Vly. Estate $35		G			S				
LEDSON WINERY & VINEYARDS '99, Sonoma Vly. $36		B					G		
J. LOHR ESTATE '99, Paso Robles, Los Osos $15					S				S
MARCELINA VINEYARDS '99, Napa Vly. $30					S			S	

L.A.	Orange	Riverside	San Fran	West Coast	State Fair	New World	Pacific Rim	San Diego	Merlot
									2 AWARDS
		B		S					**LOUIS M. MARTINI** '99, Russian River Vly., Del Rio Vnyd. $22
			B		S				**MC MANIS FAMILY VINEYARDS** '01, California $9
B		S							**MC MANIS FAMILY VINEYARDS** '00, California $9
	G				Σ				**MERIDIAN VINEYARDS** '99, Paso Robles $18
		B		B					**MIDNIGHT CELLARS** '99, Paso Robles Estate $22
				B		B			**MIRASSOU** '99, Monterey Co., Coastal Selection $10
						B		B	**MIRASSOU** '98, Monterey Co., Harvest Rsv. $15
		B		S					**NAPA RIDGE** '97, Napa Vly. Rsv. $20
	S				B				**OAKSTONE** '99, Fair Play, De Cascabel Vnyd. $16
							B	S	**ORFILA VINEYARDS** '98, California Coastal $16
B	B								**PARDUCCI WINE CELLARS** '99, Mendocino Co., Vintner Select $9
		S	B						**J. PEDRONCELLI** '99, Dry Creek Vly. Bench Vnyd. $14
B								B	**PEPPER LANE WINERY** '00, California $12
		B					S		**PERRY CREEK VINEYARDS** '99, El Dorado Estate $12
		B		S					**ROSENBLUM CELLARS** '99, Russian River Vly. Lone Oak Vnyd. $21
B	B								**SAWYER CELLARS** '99, Napa Vly., Rutherford, Estate $34
	S						B		**SEBASTIANI VINEYARDS & WINERY** '98, Sonoma Vly $22
S		B							**SILVER ROSE CELLARS** '99, Napa Vly. $29

Merlot

	L.A.	Orange	Riverside	San Fran	West Coast	State Fair	New World	Pacific Rim	San Diego
2 AWARDS									
SIMI '99, Alexander Vly.	B							S	
STELTZNER VINEYARDS '99, Napa Vly., Stags Leap District	B					G			
STONEHEDGE '00, Napa Vly. $30	B						S		
SUMMERS WINERY '99, Knights Vly. $22		S	S						
SUNSTONE VINEYARDS & WINERY '99, Santa Ynez Vly. Rsv. $30				B		S			
SWANSON '99, Napa Vly. $30		S		S					
SYLVESTER '99, Paso Robles, Kiara Rsv. $14							B	B	
SYLVESTER '00, Paso Robles, Kiara Rsv. $14		B		B					
TAFT STREET '99, Central Coast $12					S			B	
TAFT STREET '99, Sonoma Co. $17		B	S						
TURNING LEAF '00, California Rsv. $10				B					B
TURNING LEAF '00, Coastal Rsv., Sonoma Co. $10				B					G
VENTANA VINEYARDS '00, Monterey, Arroyo Seco, Estate $18	G			B					
WENTE VINEYARDS '99, Livermore Vly. Crane Ridge Rsv. $19			B			S			
WILD HORSE '00, Paso Robles $18		B				S			
WILSON CREEK WINERY & VINEYARD '00, Temecula Rsv. $29	B						G		
WINDSOR VINEYARDS '99, 40th Anniversary, Dry Creek Vly. $40					B		S		

Crushers, Clos du Bois Winery, Sonoma County

Petite Sirah

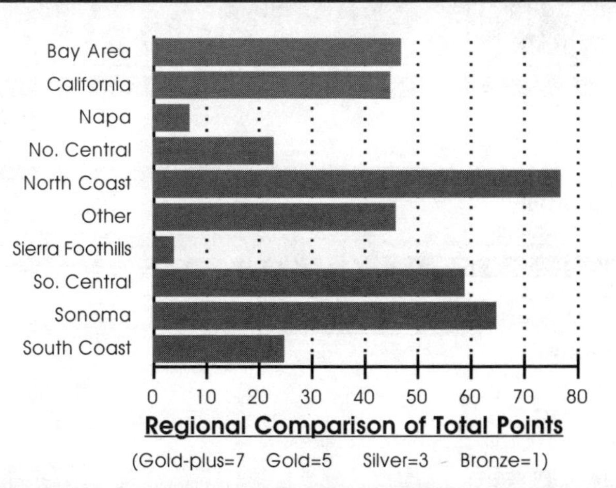

Regional Comparison of Total Points

(Gold-plus=7 Gold=5 Silver=3 Bronze=1)

Highest Individual Wine Totals

26 **BOGLE**
'00, California, $10.00

23 **TRENTADUE**
'00, Alexander Vly., Estate, $20.00

22 **JEFF RUNQUIST WINES**
'00, Clarksburg, Salman Vnyd., $24.00

19 **GUENOC**
'99, North Coast, $19.00

18 **FENESTRA**
'99, Lodi, $17.00

18 **GUENOC**
'98, Guenoc Vly. Serpentine Meadow, $36.00

18 **KEMPTON CLARK**
'99, Dunnigan Hills, $10.00

18 **MERIDIAN VINEYARDS**
'99, Paso Robles, Limited Release, $18.00

17 **RIOS-LOVELL WINERY**
'00, Livermore Vly., Estate, $18.00

14 **DAVID BRUCE WINERY**
'00, Central Coast, $16.00

14 **VICTOR HUGO**
'00, Paso Robles, $17.00

Petite Sirah

Wine	L.A.	Orange	Riverside	San Fran	West Coast	State Fair	New World	Pacific Rim	San Diego
8 AWARDS									
BOGLE '00, California $10	B	B	G	B	G		Σ	S	S
7 AWARDS									
TRENTADUE '00, Alexander Vly., Estate $20	S	S	S	G	B			B	Σ
6 AWARDS									
EDMEADES '99, Mendocino Co., Eaglepoint Ranch $25	B		B	S		B	B		B
FENESTRA '99, Lodi $17	G	S	B		S	S			S
GUENOC '98, Guenoc Vly. Serpentine Meadow $36	S	B	B		S	S	Σ		
IMAGERY SERIES '99, Artist Collection, Paso Robles $35	S			B	G	B		B	B
KEMPTON CLARK '99, Dunnigan Hills $10	S		G	G			B	S	B
MERIDIAN VINEYARDS '99, Paso Robles, Limited Release $18	S			B	S		Σ	B	S
JEFF RUNQUIST WINES '00, Clarksburg, Salman Vnyd. $24	Σ		B	S	S	G	S		
5 AWARDS									
CHRISTOPHER CREEK '00, Russian River Vly. Estate $28			B	B			S	B	B
GUENOC '99, North Coast $19	B		Σ	B	Σ	S			
GUENOC '98, North Coast $19	S			S	B	B	S		
RIOS-LOVELL WINERY '00, Livermore Vly., Estate $18	G		S	S	B				G
4 AWARDS									
DAVID BRUCE WINERY '00, Central Coast $16	B			S		Σ		S	
CONCANNON VINEYARD '98, Rsv., San Francisco Bay $25			B		B		S		B
GEYSER PEAK '99, Alexander Vly., Winemaker's Selection $20				B	S		B		B

L.A.	Orange	Riverside	San Fran	West Coast	State Fair	New World	Pacific Rim	San Diego	Petite Sirah
									4 AWARDS
G			B		G			S	**VICTOR HUGO** '00, Paso Robles $17
		B	S		S			S	**SAN SIMEON CELLARS** '00, Paso Robles $20
B		S	B			B			**WINDSOR VINEYARDS** '98, Mendocino Co. $12.50
									3 AWARDS
		S		S		S			**CILURZO VINEYARD & WINERY** '99, Temecula Estate $25
		B				Σ		B	**CONCANNON VINEYARD** '98, Central Coast Selected Vnyd. $11.50
				B		B	G		**FOPPIANO VINEYARDS** '99, Sonoma Co. Estate $20.50
G	B		B						**FOPPIANO VINEYARDS** '00, Sonoma Co. Estate $23
S						S		B	**FREY VINEYARDS** '00, Mendocino Co., Organic $12.25
B		B					Σ		**KENDALL-JACKSON WINERY** '00, Vintner's Rsv., California $16
	B	G						B	**PARDUCCI WINE CELLARS** '99, California, Vintner Select $10
	S	B		S					**ROSENBLUM CELLARS** '00, Dry Creek Vly. Rockpile Road Vnyd. $30
		S	S				B		**ROSENBLUM CELLARS** '00, Napa Vly. Picket Road $28
									2 AWARDS
	B				B				**DAVID BRUCE WINERY** '00, Paso Robles, Shell Creek Vnyd. $25
G						G			**CILURZO VINEYARD & WINERY** '00, Temecula Rsv. Late Harvest $11
	B						B		**GRANITE SPRINGS** '99, El Dorado $12.50

Pinot Gris

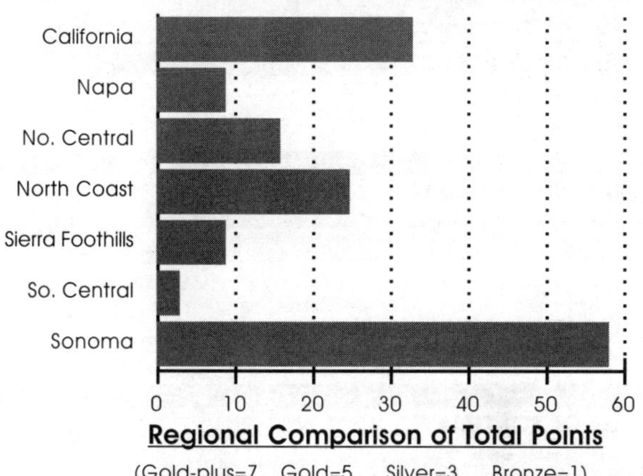

Regional Comparison of Total Points

(Gold-plus=7 Gold=5 Silver=3 Bronze=1)

Highest Individual Wine Totals

18 **RANCHO ZABACO**
'01, Sonoma Coast, $16.00

15 **HANDLEY**
'01, Anderson Vly., $16.00

14 **GALLO OF SONOMA**
'01, Sonoma Coast, $13.00

11 **BARGETTO**
'01, Pinot Grigio, $16.00

11 **ROBERT PEPI WINERY**
'00, Willamette Vly. Pinot Grigio, $12.00

10 **MADONNA ESTATE**
'01, Carneros Pinot Grigio, $22.00

9 **ALBERTONI VINEYARDS**
'00, California Pinot Grigio, $13.00

8 **GALLO OF SONOMA**
'00, Sonoma Coast, $13.00

8 **MADDALENA VINEYARD**
'00, Monterey Co., Loma Vista Pinot Grigio, $10.00

7 **TALUS**
'01, California Pinot Grigio, $9.00

Pinot Gris

Wine	L.A.	Orange	Riverside	San Fran	West Coast	State Fair	New World	Pacific Rim	San Diego
6 AWARDS									
RANCHO ZABACO '01, Sonoma Coast $16	B	S	G		S	B			G
5 AWARDS									
ALBERTONI VINEYARDS '00, California Pinot Grigio $13		B	B		S		S	B	
HANDLEY '01, Anderson Vly. $16	S		S	S	G			B	
ROBERT PEPI WINERY '00, Willamette Vly. Pinot Grigio $12			B		S		B	S	S
4 AWARDS									
GALLO OF SONOMA '01, Sonoma Coast $13		S	G	B		G			
GALLO OF SONOMA '00, Sonoma Coast $13			B		G		B	B	
3 AWARDS									
BARGETTO '01, Pinot Grigio $16				S	B		Σ		
BOEGER '01, El Dorado, Johnson Vnyd. Pinot Grigio $12	B	B				B			
ECHELON '01, Central Coast Pinot Grigio $11	B	S		B					
MONTEVINA '01, Amador Co. Pinot Grigio $10		S	B		B				
TALUS '01, California Pinot Grigio $9		B	S		S				
2 AWARDS									
BEAULIEU '99, California Winemaker's Collection $14				B			S		
FLORA SPRINGS '01, Napa Vly., Crossroads Vnyd. Pinot Grigio	B					B			
MADDALENA VINEYARD '00, Monterey Co., Loma Vista Pinot Grigio $10	S				G				
MADONNA ESTATE '01, Carneros Pinot Grigio $22	Σ		S						

Pinot Gris

L.A.	Orange	Riverside	San Fran	West Coast	State Fair	New World	Pacific Rim	San Diego	Wine
2 AWARDS									
			S		S				**NAVARRO VINEYARDS** '01, Anderson Vly. $16
		B					B		**PEPPERWOOD GROVE** '00, California Pinot Grigio $7
						S	B		**RANCHO ZABACO** '00, Sonoma Coast $16
B	G								**SWANSON** '01, Napa Vly. Pinot Grigio $20
						B	B		**IVAN TAMÁS** '00, Monterey Co. Pinot Grigio $10

Pinot Noir

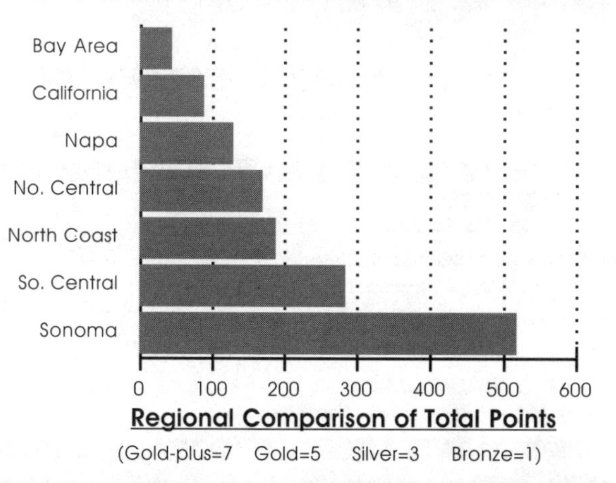

Regional Comparison of Total Points

(Gold-plus=7 Gold=5 Silver=3 Bronze=1)

Highest Individual Wine Totals

29 **FETZER**
'00, Santa Maria Vly., Bien Nacido Vnyd. Rsv., $40.00

25 **KENDALL-JACKSON WINERY**
'99, Great Estates, Monterey Co., $32.00

25 **LA CREMA**
'00, Sonoma Coast, $22.00

23 **FREI BROTHERS WINERY**
'00, Russian River Vly. Rsv., $24.00

22 **KENDALL-JACKSON WINERY**
'00, Vintner's Rsv., California, $14.00

21 **CHATEAU ST. JEAN**
'00, Sonoma Co., $19.00

21 **ECHELON**
'00, Central Coast, $14.00

21 **EDMEADES**
'99, Anderson Vly., $20.00

21 **ORFILA VINEYARDS**
'99, San Luis Obispo/Edna Vly., $35.00

Pinot Noir	L.A.	Orange	Riverside	San Fran	West Coast	State Fair	New World	Pacific Rim	San Diego
9 AWARDS									
KENDALL-JACKSON WINERY '99, Great Estates, Monterey Co. $32	S	S	B	S	S	G	B	B	G
8 AWARDS									
GALLO OF SONOMA '00, Sonoma Co. Rsv., Barrel Aged $15	B	B	B	S	B	B	S		Σ
KENDALL-JACKSON WINERY '00, Vintner's Rsv., California $14	S	G	S	B		B	S	G	B
MERIDIAN VINEYARDS '00, Santa Barbara Co. $11		B	B	S	B	B	S	B	G
NAVARRO VINEYARDS '00, Anderson Vly. Methode Ancienne $19	B	S	B	B	B	B	B	S	
7 AWARDS									
BERINGER '99, Appellation Collection, North Coast $16	S	B		B	S	B	Σ		B
CHATEAU ST. JEAN '00, Sonoma Co. $19	S	G	S	S			B	G	B
ECHELON '00, Central Coast $14	S	B	S	G			S	B	G
EDMEADES '99, Anderson Vly. $20	G	S	B	B	S		G	S	
EDNA VALLEY VINEYARD '00, Edna Vly., Paragon Vyd. $20	B		B	S	S	B	S	S	
FETZER '00, Santa Maria Vly., Bien Nacido Vnyd. Rsv. $40	Σ	G	B	B	S	Σ		G	
FETZER '00, Sonoma Co., Barrel Select $20	B		B	G	S	B	B	Σ	
FREI BROTHERS WINERY '00, Russian River Vly. Rsv. $24	B	S	S		S		Σ	B	G
LA CREMA '99, Russian River Vly. $35	B		S	S	S	S	S		S
LA CREMA '00, Sonoma Coast $22	S	S	S		S		G	G	S
6 AWARDS									
BARGETTO '00, Santa Cruz Mtns, Regan Vnyd. $30	B	B	S		G	S	B		

Pinot Noir

6 AWARDS

L.A.	Orange	Riverside	San Fran	West Coast	State Fair	New World	Pacific Rim	San Diego	Pinot Noir
B				Σ	B	G	S	B	**BERINGER** '00, Founders Estate, California $12
	B	S	G	B		B		S	**BOUCHAINE** '99, Carneros $34
S	B	B	B			S	S		**JEKEL VINEYARDS** '00, Monterey Co., Sanctuary Est. $15
G		B	S		B	S	S		**MIRASSOU** '99, Monterey Co., Harvest Rsv. $15
	B		S	B	S		S	B	**J. PEDRONCELLI** '00, Dry Creek Vly., F. Johnson Vnyd. $14
B	B		S	S	B	B			**V. SATTUI WINERY** '00, Carneros, Henry Ranch $35

5 AWARDS

L.A.	Orange	Riverside	San Fran	West Coast	State Fair	New World	Pacific Rim	San Diego	Pinot Noir
		Σ	B	S		S	S		**ACACIA WINERY** '00, Carneros, Napa Vly. $27
	B	S			S	B	B		**DE LOACH VINEYARDS** '00, OFS, Russian River Vly., Estate $40
Σ	B				B	G		S	**DOMAINE ALFRED** '99, Califa Chamisal Vnyd., Edna Vly. $42
	B	G	B	B			S		**GLORIA FERRER** '00, Carneros, Sonoma $24
B		B	B		B			G	**FETZER** '00, Santa Maria Vly. 5 Rivers Ranch $13
			B	S		S	B	S	**GREENWOOD RIDGE VINEYARDS** '00, Anderson Vly. $24
G		S	Σ			S	B		**INDIGO HILLS** '99, Central Coast $12
B	B	Σ			B	G			**KENWOOD VINEYARDS** '00, Russian River Vly. $17
S			B	B	B			B	**MIRASSOU** '99, Monterey Co., Showcase Selection $30
	G	Σ	S	B	G				**ORFILA VINEYARDS** '99, San Luis Obispo/Edna Vly. $35
S	S		B		B	S			**SANTA BARBARA WINERY** '99, Santa Barbara Co. $18
S		G		S			B	B	**ROBERT STEMMLER** '00, Sonoma Co. $28

Pinot Noir	L.A.	Orange	Riverside	San Fran	West Coast	State Fair	New World	Pacific Rim	San Diego
5 AWARDS									
TOLOSA '00, Edna Vly., Edna Ranch $30		B		B		S	S		S
WINDSOR VINEYARDS '99, Sonoma Co. Private Rsv. $16.75		B		B			B	B	B
4 AWARDS									
ALEXANDER VALLEY VINEYARDS '00, Alexander Vly. Estate $20		S			S		G		G
BAILEYANA VINEYARD '99, Edna Vly., Firepeak Vnyd. $38		S	B					B	Σ
BAREFOOT CELLARS '00, Sonoma Co. Rsv. $13	Σ		S	B				G	
BENZIGER '99, Sonoma Co. $22	G	S		S		B			
DAVID BRUCE WINERY '00, Central Coast $20	S	B					S	G	
DAVID BRUCE WINERY '00, Russian River Vly. $35				S		G	G	G	
DAVID BRUCE WINERY '00, Sonoma Co. $25	S	S		S			S		
CAMELOT WINERY '00, California $9			B				B	B	B
CASTORO CELLARS '00, Central Coast Rsv. $18		B	B				S	B	
COSENTINO WINERY '00, Carneros, Punched Cap Ferm. $30	S	B		S		S			
DOMAINE CHANDON '00, Carneros $29	S			S		Σ	B		
ELKHORN PEAK '99, Napa Vly., Fagan Creek Vyd. $30	S	S				B		S	
FOLEY ESTATES '00, Santa Barbara Co. Barrel Select $50	B	B		S		G			
HANDLEY '99, Anderson Vly. $25				B	B		B	S	
J WINE COMPANY '99, Russian River Vly. Estate $20	S	B		B		S			
J WINE COMPANY '98, Russian River Vly., Nicole's Vnyd. $35	S	S		B		B			

Pinot Noir

L.A.	Orange	Riverside	San Fran	West Coast	State Fair	New World	Pacific Rim	San Diego	Wine
									4 AWARDS
G	S	B		S					**KENWOOD VINEYARDS** '99, Russian River Vly. Rsv. Olivet $30
G	G		G		B				**LA CREMA** '00, Carneros Napa $26
S	B		Σ		B				**LAFOND** '00, Santa Ynez Vly., Santa Rita Hills $18
B						B	B	S	**MIRASSOU** '99, Monterey Co., Coastal Selection $11
		B		B	S	B			**NAPA RIDGE** '00, North Coast $9
B	B	B		G					**NAVARRO VINEYARDS** '00, Mendocino $15
	B	B		S				S	**PELICAN RANCH** '99, Santa Lucia Highlands, Sleepy Hollow Vnyd. $24
B				S		B	S		**PEPPERWOOD GROVE** '00, California $9
	S	B		S				B	**JEFF RUNQUIST WINES** '00, Carneros, Sisters Vnyd. $28
				G		S	S	B	**STERLING VINEYARDS** '00, Carneros, Winery Lake $25
B	B		S		B				**RODNEY STRONG** '99, Russian River Vly. Rsv. $30
B		B				B		G	**TURNING LEAF** '00, Coastal Rsv., North Coast $10
								3 AWARDS
		B				S	S		**BAILEYANA VINEYARD** '99, Edna Vly. $23
S	B				B				**BAILEYANA VINEYARD** '00, Edna Vly. $23
				B			B	B	**BARTHOLOMEW PARK** '99, Sonoma Vly., Frank's Vnyd. $26
				B		B	S		**BEAULIEU** '00, California Coastal $11
	B	G			S				**BELVEDERE** '00, Russian River Vly. $30

Pinot Noir

3 AWARDS

Winery	L.A.	Orange	Riverside	San Fran	West Coast	State Fair	New World	Pacific Rim	San Diego
DAVID BRUCE WINERY '00, Santa Cruz Mtns. $35		B		B		S			
BUENA VISTA '99, Carneros Estate Sonoma $22	B	S		B					
BYRON '00, Santa Maria Vly. $28		S		B		B			
CASTLE VINEYARDS '99, Los Carneros, Durell Vnyd. $35	S	S		B					
CECCHETTI SEBASTIANI CELLAR '99, Central Coast $12			G				B		B
CINNABAR '99, Santa Cruz Mtns. $38	S			B					G
CLAUDIA SPRINGS '99, Anderson Vly. $25			S				G	G	
CLONINGER CELLARS '00, Monterey, Santa Lucia Highlands $23		G					S	B	
DOMAINE DANICA '99, Carneros $35	B			S	B				
GUNDLACH-BUNDSCHU WINERY '00, Sonoma Vly., Rhinefarm Vnyd. $27			B			B		S	
HANDLEY '99, Anderson Vly. Rsv. $48	B	B		B					
LA CREMA '00, Anderson Vly. $26	S	G		B					
LAETITIA '00, Arroyo Grande Vly. $25	B							B	G
LINCOURT '00, Santa Barbara Co. $22	B			S		B			
MC ILROY WINES '00, Russian River Vly., Aquarius Ranch $24		B	B					B	
NAVARRO VINEYARDS '99, Anderson Vly., Deep End Blend $38				B			S	S	
RANCHO SISQUOC '00, Santa Barbara, Flood Family Vnyd. $30		S		S		G			
RAYE'S HILL '98, Anderson Vly. $24			B				S		S

L.A.	Orange	Riverside	San Fran	West Coast	State Fair	New World	Pacific Rim	San Diego	Pinot Noir
3 AWARDS									
	B		Σ	S					**SAPPHIRE HILL VINEYARDS** '00, Russian River Vly. Estate $36
	B	S					B		**SCHUG** '00, Carneros $19.50
G	G			S					**SEVEN LIONS WINERY** '00, Russian River, Buena Tierra Vnyd. $75
B	S			G					**SEVEN LIONS WINERY** '00, Russian River, Wes Cameron Vnyd. $65
G		S				B			**ROBERT STEMMLER** '98, Sonoma Co. $25
		B		B			G		**ROBERT STEMMLER** '00, Carneros, Sonoma Co. $38
	S		B					B	**STEPHEN'S** '99, York Mtn. $24
	B			S		Σ			**STONEHEDGE** '00, California $10
B		B					B		**RODNEY STRONG** '00, Russian River Vly., Estate Vnyd. $18
B				B		B			**VILLA MT. EDEN** '00, California Coastal $10
S	G				B				**WILD HORSE** '00, Central Coast $21
		B		B	B				**WINDSOR VINEYARDS** '00, North Coast Private Rsv. $16.75
S		B		B					**WINDSOR VINEYARDS** '00, Sonoma Co., Signature Series $18.75
S	S		S						**WOODENHEAD VINTNERS** '00, Humboldt Co., Elk Prairie Vnyd. $42
2 AWARDS									
B	B								**ARMIDA WINERY** '99, Russian River Vly. $22
	S				S				**BANNISTER** '99, Anderson Vly., Floodgate Vnyd. $30
	S					S			**BEAULIEU** '00, Carneros $18
			B		B				**BOEGER** '99, El Dorado Rsv. $25

Pinot Noir

2 AWARDS

Wine	L.A.	Orange	Riverside	San Fran	West Coast	State Fair	New World	Pacific Rim	San Diego
BROPHY CLARK '00, Santa Maria Vly. $22		B				S			
DAVID BRUCE WINERY '00, Carneros, Truchard Vnyd. $35	G			S					
CAMELOT WINERY '01, California $9	B				S				
CASTLE VINEYARDS '99, Los Carneros $25				S		S			
CECCHETTI SEBASTIANI CELLAR '00, Central Coast $13	S	B							
CHUMEIA VINEYARDS '00, Santa Lucia Highlands $28		G		B					
CLAUDIA SPRINGS '99, Mendocino Co. $20							S	B	
CLOS DU BOIS '00, Sonoma Co. $17	B	G							
GARY FARRELL '00, Russian River Vly., Olivet Lane $38	G	B							
FETZER '99, Santa Maria Vly., Bien Nacido Vnyd. Rsv. $28							Σ	S	
FLOODGATE VINEYARD '00, Anderson Vly. $30		B		S					
FOLEY ESTATES '00, Santa Maria Hills Vnyd. $38		S				B			
FOXHOLLOW VINEYARDS '00, California, Barrel Select $9		B					B		
HACIENDA WINERY '99, California Clair de Lune	S						S		
KIRKLAND RANCH WINERY '00, Napa Vly. $30					B				S
KOEHLER WINERY '00, Monterey Co. $26	S			B					
MADONNA ESTATE '00, Carneros $26	S		G						
MONTICELLO CORLEY FAMILY '00, Napa Vly., Estate $34		S							S

Pinot Noir

2 AWARDS

L.A.	Orange	Riverside	San Fran	West Coast	State Fair	New World	Pacific Rim	San Diego	Wine
	B				B				**PARAISO SPRINGS VINEYARDS** '98, Monterey, Santa Lucia Highlands $16
	S		B						**RENAISSANCE** '00, Sierra Foothills $28
	S				S				**RUSACK VINEYARDS** '00, Santa Maria Vly. $29
	G				S				**SAN SIMEON CELLARS** '00, Monterey Co. $18
S					B				**SANTA BARBARA WINERY** '00, Santa Barbara Co.
B								B	**TOAD HOLLOW** '99, Russian River Vly., Goldies Vines $22
	S			Σ					**TROUT GULCH VINEYARDS** '00, Santa Cruz Mtns. $22
			B				B		**TURNING LEAF** '00, California $8
			B		B				**VILLA MT. EDEN** '00, Russian River Vly. Rsv. $22

Red Meritage

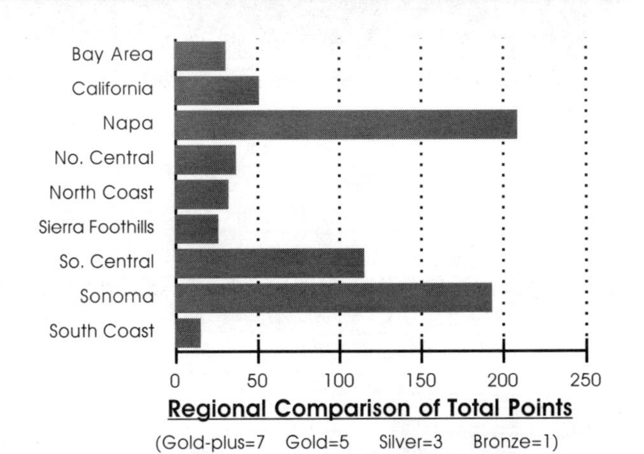

Regional Comparison of Total Points

(Gold-plus=7 Gold=5 Silver=3 Bronze=1)

Highest Individual Wine Totals

25 **ST. SUPÉRY**
'98, Napa Vly., $50.00

24 **TRENTADUE**
'99, La Storia, Alexander Vly., $45.00

22 **COSENTINO WINERY**
'99, M. Coz, Napa Vly., $100.00

22 **GEYSER PEAK**
'99, Rsv. Alexandre, Alexander Vly., $45.00

22 **KENDALL-JACKSON WINERY**
'97, Grand Rsv., California, $40.00

20 **CONCANNON VINEYARD**
'99, Assemblage, Rsv., San Francisco, $19.00

20 **NORMAN VINEYARDS**
'99, No Nonsense, Paso Robles, $18.00

20 **SILVER ROSE CELLARS**
'99, Napa Vly., Dentelle, $44.00

18 **DE LORIMIER WINERY**
'99, Mosaic, Alexander Vly., $30.00

18 **MIDNIGHT CELLARS**
'98, Mare Nectaris, Paso Robles, $32.00

17 **DARK STAR CELLARS**
'99, Ricordati, Paso Robles, $24.00

Red Meritage Type

Winery / Wine	L.A.	Orange	Riverside	San Fran	West Coast	State Fair	New World	Pacific Rim	San Diego
7 AWARDS									
GODWIN '99, Alexander Vly., Moss Oak Vnyd. $35	B		B	B	B		Σ	B	B
GUENOC '98, Langtry, Napa/Lake Co. $49	B	S	B	B		S	B	S	
ST. SUPÉRY '98, Napa Vly. $50	G	B		S	G	S	Σ	B	
6 AWARDS									
BERINGER '98, Alluvium, Knights Vly. $30	B			B	B		S	B	B
CE2V '99, Napa Vly. Estate $75	S	S	S	B		S		S	
DE LORIMIER WINERY '99, Mosaic, Alexander Vly. $30	B		S	G		S		G	B
GEYSER PEAK '99, Rsv. Alexandre, Alexander Vly. $45	B	G		B		Σ	S		G
HAHN ESTATES '99, Santa Lucia Highlands $18		B	B	S	B			S	G
VICTOR HUGO '99, Opulence Paso Robles $22	B	S	S	B		S		S	
KENDALL-JACKSON WINERY '97, Grand Rsv., California $40	Σ		S	B		S	S	G	
MIDNIGHT CELLARS '98, Mare Nectaris, Paso Robles $32	B	S	S		S	S		G	
NORMAN VINEYARDS '99, No Nonsense, Paso Robles $18	B	B	G				Σ	S	S
SILVER ROSE CELLARS '99, Napa Vly., Dentelle $44	B	G	B	Σ		G			B
ST. SUPÉRY '99, Napa Vly., Rutherford $60		S	S	B	B	B		Σ	
TRENTADUE '99, La Storia, Alexander Vly. $45	S		B	S	G	Σ	G		
5 AWARDS									
BEAULIEU '98, Tapestry Rsv., Napa Vly. $45	B	G			S		B	B	
BUTTONWOOD FARM '97, Trevin, Santa Ynez Vly. $30	S	B		B		B		G	

Red Meritage Type

L.A.	Orange	Riverside	San Fran	West Coast	State Fair	New World	Pacific Rim	San Diego	Wine
5 AWARDS									
		S			Σ	B	B	B	**CARMODY MCKNIGHT** '99, Cadenza, Paso Robles, Conway Vnyd. $25
S	B		S	S				Σ	**DARK STAR CELLARS** '99, Ricordati, Paso Robles $24
B		B		B		S		G	**GEYSER PEAK** '98, Rsv. Alexandre, Alexander Vly. $45
S	S		B		S		S		**WINDSOR VINEYARDS** '98, Sonoma Co. Private Rsv. $18
S		G				B	S	B	**WINDSOR VINEYARDS** '97, Sonoma Co., Signature Series $23.75
4 AWARDS									
		B	S				S	B	**ALEXANDER VALLEY VINEYARDS** '98, Cyrus, Alexander Vly. $50
S			S			Σ		B	**ALLORA VINEYARDS** '99, Tresca, Stag's Leap District / Howell Mtn., Allora Vnyds. $60
	G		S			B	G		**CASA NUESTRA** '99, Napa Vly. $45
S	S		Σ	Σ					**CONCANNON VINEYARD** '99, Assemblage, Rsv., San Francisco $19
S		Σ	G		Σ				**COSENTINO WINERY** '99, M. Coz, Napa Vly. $100
B			S		S	S			**DRY CREEK VINEYARD** '99, Dry Creek Vly. $28
		S	B				S	B	**FLORA SPRINGS** '99, Trilogy, Napa Vly. $65
B		G	B	G					**JEKEL VINEYARDS** '98, Monterey Co., Sanctuary Est. $28
		G		S		S	B		**KENDALL-JACKSON WINERY** '00, Collage Cabernet Sauvignon/Merlot $10
B		B			B		B		**MOUNT PALOMAR WINERY** '97, Estate, Temecula $18
B	B		B		B				**MURRIETA'S WELL** '98, Red Vendimia, Livermore Vly. $35
		B				B	B	S	**THORNTON** '99, Cabernet/Merlot, South Coast $14

Red Meritage Type

Wine	L.A.	Orange	Riverside	San Fran	West Coast	State Fair	New World	Pacific Rim	San Diego
4 AWARDS									
YORKVILLE CELLARS '98, Richard The Lion-Heart, Rennie Vnyd. $25			B	S			G		B
3 AWARDS									
BAILY VINEYARD & WINERY '98, Temecula $35	S	B				B			
BARTHOLOMEW PARK '99, Sonoma Vly., Mayacamas Cuvee $21	B		S						S
CATACULA LAKE WINERY '99, Napa Vly. Rancho Cuvee $35	S	S	S						
CLOS DU BOIS '98, Marlstone Vnyd, Alexander Vly. $39	B			S		S			
CONN CREEK '98, Anthology, Napa Vly. $54	S						B	S	
COSENTINO WINERY '99, The Poet, Napa Vly. $65	B			S		S			
THOMAS COYNE '99, Confluence, California $20		B	B			S			
GRAESER '99, Red Table Wine, Diamond Mtn.	S					S			S
MAZZOCCO '97, Dry Creek Vly. Matrix Estate $40		B	Σ			B			
NEVADA CITY WINERY '99, Sierra Foothills Vin Cing $14			B			S		S	
2 AWARDS									
BOEGER '99, Rsv. Meritage El Dorado $23				B		G			
CASA DE CABALLOS '99, Forgetmenot Paso Robles $24			S	B					
CONCANNON VINEYARD '98, Central Coast, Rsv. $19			B					B	
CORLEY FAMILY NAPA VALLEY '99, Napa Vly. $45		S				S			
COULSON EL DORADO '98, El Dorado, Von Huene Vyd.						S		G	

Red Meritage Type

2 AWARDS

L.A.	Orange	Riverside	San Fran	West Coast	State Fair	New World	Pacific Rim	San Diego	Wine
B		S							**GUENOC** '98, Napa & Lake Co. Victorian Claret $20.50
	B						B		**JUSTIN** '99, Isoceles, Paso Robles, Estate $48
S	S								**LOCKWOOD VINEYARD** '97, Monterey Co. Rsv. $45
		B				B			**MURRIETA'S WELL** '97, Red Vendimia, Livermore Vly. $35
			S		S				**NOB HILL TRADING CO.** '00, Meritage Alexander Vly. $25
		B	B						**PHOENIX VINEYARDS** '99, Napa Vly. Rancho Napa $37
			B		Σ				**RANCHO SISQUOC** '99, Santa Barbara, Flood Family Vnyd. $40
G	B								**SAWYER CELLARS** '99, Bradford, Napa Vly., Rutherford, Estate $42
	S	B							**SUMMERS WINERY** '99, North Coast Chevalier Noir $32
S						G			**VALLEY OF THE MOON** '98, Cuvee De La Luna, Sonoma Co. $25

Sangiovese

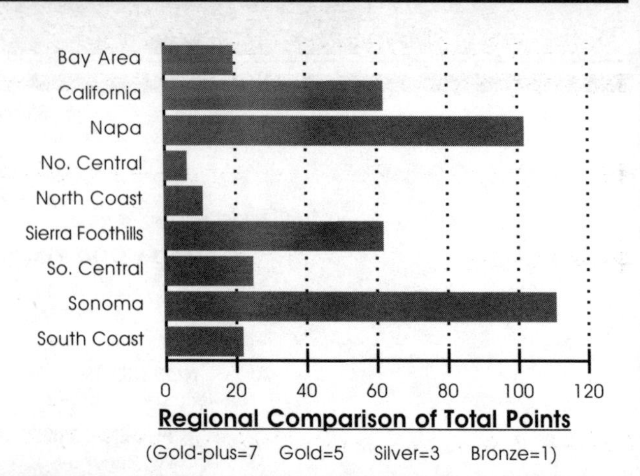

Regional Comparison of Total Points

(Gold-plus=7 Gold=5 Silver=3 Bronze=1)

Highest Individual Wine Totals

28 **KENDALL-JACKSON WINERY**
'99, Vintner's Rsv., California, $15.00

19 **GALLO OF SONOMA**
'99, Alexander Vly., $13.00

17 **EBERLE**
'00, Paso Robles, Filipponi and Thompson Vyds, $16.00

17 **FOLIE A'DEUX**
'99, Napa Vly., $22.00

14 **ATLAS PEAK VINEYARD**
'99, Napa Vly., Atlas Peak Rsv., $30.00

14 **EMILIO GUGLIELMO WINERY**
'00, Napa Vly. Private Rsv., $12.00

13 **VINO NOCETO**
'99, Shenandoah Vly. Rsv., $22.00

12 **CE2V**
'00, Napa Vly., Pope Vly. Vnyd., $30.00

12 **RIOS-LOVELL WINERY**
'01, Livermore Vly., Estate, $18.00

12 **STELTZNER VINEYARDS**
'99, Napa Vly., Stags Leap District, $22.00

12 **THORNTON**
'99, South Coast, Temecula Vly. Vnyds., $12.00

Sangiovese

L.A.	Orange	Riverside	San Fran	West Coast	State Fair	New World	Pacific Rim	San Diego	Wine
									8 AWARDS
S	S	B	B	Σ	G		B	Σ	**KENDALL-JACKSON WINERY** '99, Vintner's Rsv., California $15
									7 AWARDS
Σ		B	S	S	B	B	S		**GALLO OF SONOMA** '99, Alexander Vly. $13
									6 AWARDS
S		B	B			B	B	B	**FOPPIANO VINEYARDS** '00, Alexander Vly. $18
B		S	B	B		B	S		**MONTEVINA** '99, Terra D'oro, Amador Co. $18
B		B	B	S		S		B	**ORFILA VINEYARDS** '98, San Pasqual Vly., Di Collina $20
B	S	B	B	S				S	**RIOS-LOVELL WINERY** '01, Livermore Vly., Estate $18
B		S		S	S		B	B	**THORNTON** '99, South Coast, Temecula Vly. Vnyds. $12
									5 AWARDS
B			S	S	G	G			**EBERLE** '00, Paso Robles, Filipponi and Thompson Vyds $16
B	S		B		G	Σ			**FOLIE A'DEUX** '99, Napa Vly. $22
S	S	B		S				B	**ROBERT PEPI WINERY** '99, California $12
B	B				B	Σ		S	**VINO NOCETO** '99, Shenandoah Vly. Rsv. $22
									4 AWARDS
B	B				S			B	**ALBERTONI VINEYARDS** '01, California $13
S	S		B		B				**ATLAS PEAK VINEYARD** '99, Napa Vly. $16
G	G		B		S				**ATLAS PEAK VINEYARD** '99, Napa Vly., Atlas Peak Rsv. $30
B	S		B		S				**BENESSERE VINEYARDS** '99, Napa Vly. $29
S		B	S		G				**CE2V** '00, Napa Vly., Pope Vly. Vnyd. $30

Sangiovese

Winery / Wine	L.A.	Orange	Riverside	San Fran	West Coast	State Fair	New World	Pacific Rim	San Diego
4 AWARDS									
EMILIO GUGLIELMO WINERY '00, Napa Vly. Private Rsv. $12	S	B		S		Σ			
JEFF RUNQUIST WINES '00, Amador Co., Pioneer Hill Vnyd. $20	S		B			B			S
STELTZNER VINEYARDS '99, Napa Vly., Stags Leap District $22		B	Σ			B		S	
3 AWARDS									
ALEXANDER VALLEY VINEYARDS '00, Alexander Vly. Estate $20		G	B		G				
ALTERRA '98, Sonoma Co. $18	B		B	G					
BAYWOOD '99, Alexander Vly., Rsv. $45						S	S	S	
CAMELLIA CELLARS '00, Dry Creek Vly., Merlo Vnyds. $28	S			S		G			
FIELD STONE WINERY '99, North Coast $18	S		B		S				
FOREST GLEN WINERY '99, Oak Barrel Selection, California $10	B				B				S
MIDNIGHT CELLARS '99, Starlight, Paso Robles $20					S	S	B		
PIETRA SANTA '99, Cienega Vly. $24	B		S						B
MICHAEL POZZAN WINERY '99, Napa Vly., Special Rsv. $8		B					S	S	
VALLEY OF THE MOON '99, Sonoma Co. $15	S				B		G		
2 AWARDS									
ALBERTONI VINEYARDS '99, California $13			B				S		
CAMELLIA CELLARS '99, Dry Creek Vly., Merlo Vnyds. $28	S								S
CHATOM VINEYARDS '99, Calavares Co., Gitano $12						S	Σ		
DEERFIELD RANCH '00, Windsor Oaks Vnyd, Chalk Hill $28	B						S		

Sangiovese

L.A.	Orange	Riverside	San Fran	West Coast	State Fair	New World	Pacific Rim	San Diego	Sangiovese
									2 AWARDS
			S		S				**IMAGERY SERIES** '99, Artist Collection Sonoma $25
		B		B					**JODAR** '00, El Dorado $16
Σ		B							**LOUIS M. MARTINI** '99, Dunnigan Hills $15
				S		B			**MONTEVINA** '98, Amador Co. $12
G			B						**SAUSAL WINERY** '98, Alexander Vly. $15
				B		S			**STRYKER SONOMA WINERY &** '99, Alexander Vly. $22
			B					G	**VIANSA** '99, Napa-Sonoma, Thalia $38
S					B				**VINO NOCETO** '99, Shenandoah Vly.

Sauvignon Blanc

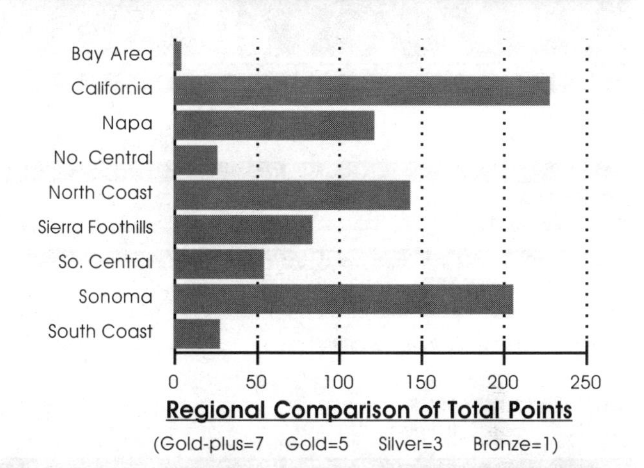

Highest Individual Wine Totals

43 **ST. SUPÉRY**
'01, Napa Vly., $15.00

28 **CANYON ROAD WINERY**
'01, California, $9.00

26 **GEYSER PEAK**
'01, California, $10.00

25 **SONORA WINERY & PORT WORKS**
'01, Amador Co., $13.00

25 **WHITE OAK VINEYARDS**
'01, North Coast, 20th Edition, $13.00

22 **RANCHO ZABACO**
'01, Russian River Vly., Rsv., $18.00

19 **FLORA SPRINGS**
'00, Soliloquy, Napa Valley-Oakville, $22.50

17 **MAURICE CAR'RIE WINERY**
'00, Temecula, $8.00

17 **SIERRA VISTA**
'01, El Dorado Fume Blanc, $12.00

Sauvignon Blanc

Wine	L.A.	Orange	Riverside	San Fran	West Coast	State Fair	New World	Pacific Rim	San Diego
9 AWARDS									
ST. SUPÉRY '01, Napa Vly. $15	G	G	G	G	G	Σ	S	Σ	B
8 AWARDS									
GEYSER PEAK '01, California $10	S	S	S	B	G	G		S	S
7 AWARDS									
NAVARRO VINEYARDS '01, Mendocino, Cuvee 128 $14	B	S	B	B	G	B		B	
SONORA WINERY & PORT WORKS '01, Amador Co. $13	B	G		S	G	S		S	G
WHITE OAK VINEYARDS '01, North Coast, 20th Edition $13	G	S	Σ	B	G	S			B
6 AWARDS									
CANYON ROAD WINERY '01, California $9				B	G	Σ	Σ	G	S
DRY CREEK VINEYARD '00, Dry Creek Vly. Rsv. Fume $18	B	B	B			S	Σ		B
FIRESTONE VINEYARD '00, Santa Ynez Vly. $12	B	S		S			G	B	S
KENDALL-JACKSON WINERY '00, Fume Blanc Vintner's Rsv., California $10		B	S	S			S	B	S
KENDALL-JACKSON WINERY '00, Grand Rsv., California $16			S	B	S	B		B	G
KENDALL-JACKSON WINERY '00, Vintner's Rsv., California $10	Σ	B	S		S		B	B	
PEIRANO ESTATE VINEYARDS '99, Lodi Estate $9			S	B	B		B	S	B
ROBERT PEPI WINERY '00, Two Heart Canopy, California $12		B	B		S	B	B		B
RANCHO ZABACO '01, Russian River Vly., Rsv. $18	G	B	B	B	Σ	Σ			
WATTLE CREEK '01, Mendocino Co. $18	S			B	G	B		B	B
5 AWARDS									
AMBERHILL '00, California $6	B	B	B		S		S		

Sauvignon Blanc

L.A.	Orange	Riverside	San Fran	West Coast	State Fair	New World	Pacific Rim	San Diego	Wine
									5 AWARDS
B		S		S			B	S	**BOGLE** '01, California $8
G		G				S	B	S	**MAURICE CAR'RIE WINERY** '00, Temecula $8
S		B		B			B	B	**CHATEAU SOUVERAIN** '00, Alexander Vly. $12
			B	S	S	G	B		**FETZER** '01, Echo Ridge Sauvignon Blanc $9
	G	G		G		B		S	**FLORA SPRINGS** '00, Soliloquy, Napa Valley-Oakville $22.50
G	S		G		B	S			**SIERRA VISTA** '01, El Dorado Fume Blanc $12
S			B	S	S			B	**RODNEY STRONG** '01, Sonoma, Charlotte's Home Vnyds. $12
B	S			B		S		B	**WATTLE CREEK** '00, Alexander Vly. $18
									4 AWARDS
		S	B	S			B		**CAMELOT WINERY** '00, California $9
			B			Σ	B	S	**CHATOM VINEYARDS** '00, Calaveras Co. $10
			B		Σ	B	B		**DE LOACH VINEYARDS** '00, Fume Blanc, Russian River Vly. $14
		B			B		S	B	**DE LORIMIER WINERY** '99, Alexander Vly. Estate $10
S	B			G	S				**DRY CREEK VINEYARD** '01, Dry Creek Vly., DCV3 Estate $16
B	G	B		S					**DRY CREEK VINEYARD** '01, Fume Blanc, Sonoma Co. $12.75
B		S				S		S	**THE GAINEY VINEYARD** '00, Santa Ynez Vly. $14
G		B		S				S	**GREENWOOD RIDGE VINEYARDS** '00, Anderson Vly. $13.50
	B	B		S				B	**GUENOC** '01, California $10
	B	B		S				S	**GUENOC** '00, North Coast $14

Sauvignon Blanc

	L.A.	Orange	Riverside	San Fran	West Coast	State Fair	New World	Pacific Rim	San Diego
4 AWARDS									
HANDLEY '00, Anderson Vly., Ferrington Vnyd. $14	B	S		S			S		
HUNTINGTON '01, Earthquake, Napa Vly. $12	B			B	S			S	
HUSCH VINEYARDS '01, Mendocino Co., La Ribera Vnyd. $13	S	B		B				B	
KENWOOD VINEYARDS '00, Sonoma Co. $12		S	S		B				S
KENWOOD VINEYARDS '00, Sonoma Co. Rsv. $15	Σ	S	S						S
MERIDIAN VINEYARDS '00, California $8	S		B			B	S		
STONE CELLARS '01, California $8	S	G	B			B			
WHITE OAK VINEYARDS '01, Napa Vly. $18	S			B	S	B			
3 AWARDS									
BAILEYANA VINEYARD '01, Edna Vly., Paragon Vnyd. $13	B			S					S
BARON HERZOG WINE CELLARS '01, California $9	B	S		B					
BERINGER '00, Founders Estate, California $11				B	S	B			
CHATEAU ST. JEAN '00, Fume Blanc, Sonoma Co. $13			S		S	B			
GRGICH HILLS '00, Fume Blanc, Napa Vly. $18		B		B	S				
HANNA '01, Russian River, Slusser Road Vnyd. $16	Σ			B		S			
LATCHAM VINEYARDS '01, El Dorado $12		S		S		S			
LUCAS & LEWELLEN '01, Virgin, Central Coast $13	B		S		B				
QUIVIRA '00, Dry Creek Vly., Fig Tree Vnyd. $17			S	B	S				
STERLING VINEYARDS '01, North Coast $12	B	B			S				

L.A.	Orange	Riverside	San Fran	West Coast	State Fair	New World	Pacific Rim	San Diego	Sauvignon Blanc
									3 AWARDS
		B		B	B				**M. TRINCHERO WINERY** '00, Napa Vly. Mary's Vnyd. $20
		S		S			S		**VENTANA VINEYARDS** '00, Monterey, Arroyo Seco, Estate $12
		G		B		B			**WINDSOR VINEYARDS** '00, Fume Blanc, North Coast $11.75
									2 AWARDS
		B			B				**ADLER FELS** '00, Russian River Fume Blanc $14
	G				B				**AMADOR FOOTHILL WINERY** '00, Shenandoah Vly. $10
						Σ	B		**BAILEYANA VINEYARD** '00, Edna Vly. $13
	B			B					**BEAULIEU** '00, Napa Vly. $13
				S	B				**BERINGER** '00, Napa Vly. $12
B	S								**BUENA VISTA** '00, California $10
		B						S	**BUTTONWOOD FARM** '00, Santa Ynez Vly. $12
S	G								**CLOS DU BOIS** '00, North Coast $10
		B						B	**COASTAL RIDGE WINERY** '99, California $7
	B	S							**FALKNER WINERY** '00, South Coast $10
B			B						**GARY FARRELL** '01, Sonoma Co., Redwood Ranch $20
		B					B		**GRGICH HILLS** '99, Fume Blanc, Napa Vly. $18
		S		S					**INGLENOOK ESTATE CELLARS** 'NV, California $8
S	B								**KUNDE ESTATE WINERY** '01, Sonoma Vly., Magnolia Lane
	B	G							**MILL CREEK VINEYARDS** '00, Dry Creek Vly. Estate $14

Sauvignon Blanc

2 AWARDS	L.A.	Orange	Riverside	San Fran	West Coast	State Fair	New World	Pacific Rim	San Diego
MONTEVINA '00, Fume Blanc, Amador Co. $7			G						B
MURPHY-GOODE '00, Fume Rsv., Alexander Vly. $17			G						B
PARADISE RIDGE '01, Sonoma Co., Grandview Vnyd. $14				S	S				
PARDUCCI WINE CELLARS '01, Lake Co. $8			B						B
J. PEDRONCELLI '00, Dry Creek Vly. East Side Vnyd. $10	S		B						
PEZZI-KING VINEYARDS '00, Fume Blanc, North Coast $13	B	B							
R. H. PHILLIPS '01, Dunnigan Hills, Estate $8	B			B					
SIMI '00, Sonoma Co. $14	S		S						
TAFT STREET '01, Russian River Vly., Poplar Vnyd.	B					B			
TRELLIS VINEYARDS '00, Dry Creek Vly. $11					S			B	
TURNBULL WINE CELLARS '00, Napa Vly., Oakville $15	S			B					
TURNING LEAF '01, California $8	S				G				
TURNING LEAF '01, California Rsv. $8			B						B
VAN ASPEREN '00, Napa Vly. $12			B		S				
VOSS VINEYARDS '01, Napa Vly. $18				Σ				G	
YORKVILLE CELLARS '00, Yorkville Highlands, Randle Hill Vnyd. $12					B				Σ

Sparkling Wine

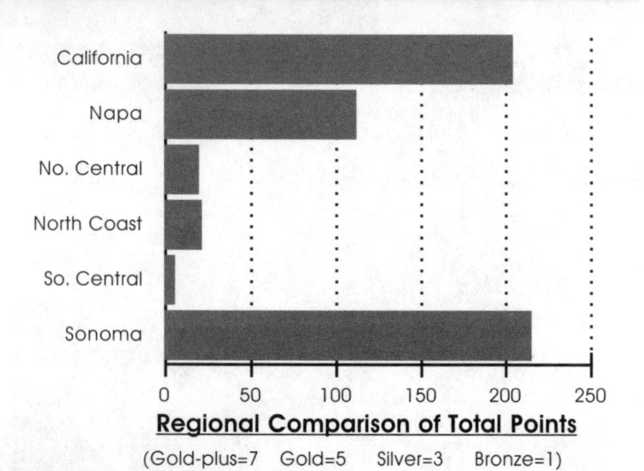

Regional Comparison of Total Points

(Gold-plus=7 Gold=5 Silver=3 Bronze=1)

Highest Individual Wine Totals

23 **GLORIA FERRER**
'94, Brut, Royal Cuvee, Carneros, $22.00

23 **GLORIA FERRER**
'NV, Brut, Sonoma Co., $18.00

22 **GLORIA FERRER**
'92, Brut, Carneros Cuvee, $32.00

20 **GLORIA FERRER**
'NV, Blanc De Noir, Sonoma Co., $18.00

20 **WINDSOR VINEYARDS**
'99, Blanc de Noir, Sonoma Co. Rsv., $22.00

19 **BALLATORE CHAMPAGNE CELLARS**
'NV, Gran Spumante, California, $6.00

18 **DOMAINE CHANDON**
'NV, Brut, Etoile, Napa & Sonoma, $35.00

17 **DOMAINE CHANDON**
'95, Brut, Sonoma-Napa Counties, $50.00

17 **KORBEL**
'99, Natural, Sonoma Co., $13.00

17 **MUMM CUVEE NAPA**
'97, Blanc De Blanc, Napa Vly., $22.00

17 **SCHRAMSBERG**
'98, Blanc De Blanc, North California Coast, $30.00

17 **THORNTON**
'NV, Cuvee De Frontignan, California, $12.00

L.A.	Orange	Riverside	San Fran	West Coast	State Fair	New World	Pacific Rim	San Diego	Sparkling Wine
									8 AWARDS
B	S	S		S	S	S	B	S	**WINDSOR VINEYARDS** '99, Blanc de Noir, Sonoma Co. Rsv. $22
									7 AWARDS
B		S		S	B	G	B	G	**BALLATORE CHAMPAGNE CELLARS** 'NV, Gran Spumante, California, R.S. 8 $6
S	B	G		Σ	S	B		S	**GLORIA FERRER** 'NV, Brut, Sonoma Co. $18
S	S	S			S	Σ	B	S	**GLORIA FERRER** '94, Brut, Royal Cuvee, Carneros $22
	B	B	B		S	S	B	S	**KORBEL** 'NV, Blanc De Noir, California $11
S	B	S		S	B	B		G	**KORBEL** '99, Natural, Sonoma Co. $13
		S	B	S	S	S	B	B	**THORNTON** 'NV, Cuvee Rouge, California $12
									6 AWARDS
S		B	S		S	G		S	**DOMAINE CHANDON** 'NV, Brut, Etoile, Napa & Sonoma $35
B	B	B	B		B			G	**DOMAINE CHANDON** 'NV, Extra Dry, Chandon Riche, California $17
B	G	S		S	G			S	**GLORIA FERRER** 'NV, Blanc De Noir, Sonoma Co. $18
B	S	S			S	Σ	G		**GLORIA FERRER** '92, Brut, Carneros Cuvee $32
B		B	B		B	S	B		**KORBEL** 'NV, Brut Rose, California $11
B		B	B	B	S			S	**TOTT'S CHAMPAGNE CELLARS** 'NV, Extra Dry, Rsv. Cuvee, California $7
									5 AWARDS
	B	S			Σ	S		B	**DOMAINE CHANDON** 'NV, Blanc De Noir, Carneros $17
S	S	G			B	S			**DOMAINE CHANDON** 'NV, Brut, Rsv., Sonoma & Napa $24
B	G	S			G	S			**DOMAINE CHANDON** '95, Brut, Sonoma-Napa Counties $50

Sparkling Wine	L.A.	Orange	Riverside	San Fran	West Coast	State Fair	New World	Pacific Rim	San Diego
5 AWARDS									
MUMM CUVEE NAPA '97, Blanc De Blanc, Napa Vly. $22	S	G					S	S	S
SCHRAMSBERG '98, Blanc De Blanc, North California Coast $30	G	G		B		S	S		
THORNTON 'NV, Cuvee De Frontignan, California $12			G			B	G	S	S
TOTT'S CHAMPAGNE CELLARS 'NV, Brut, California $7				B	B	G	S	S	
4 AWARDS									
BALLATORE CHAMPAGNE CELLARS 'NV, Rosso Red Spumante, California, R.S. 7.60 $6			S		S	G			G
DOMAINE CHANDON 'NV, Etoile Rose, Napa & Sonoma $40	S		S			S	S		
HANDLEY '96, Brut, Anderson Vly. $28	S	B	B						S
J WINE COMPANY '97, Brut Russian River Vly. $28	B	B		S		G			
MIRASSOU 'NV, Blanc De Blanc, Monterey Co. $24	G	B	S					S	
MUMM CUVEE NAPA 'NV, Blanc De Noir, Napa Vly. $18	S	S					B		G
SCHRAMSBERG 'NV, Mirabelle Brut, North California Coast $16	S			B		Σ	B		
SCHRAMSBERG '96, Brut, J Schram, Napa Vly. $75	G	S		B		S			
3 AWARDS									
DOMAINE CHANDON 'NV, Brut, Classic, California $17	S	B				S			
FOLIE A'DEUX '98, Brut, Napa Vly. Grande Folie Wrotham Pinot $35	B		S				S		
HANDLEY '98, Brut Rose, Anderson Vly. $28		B	B					B	
KORBEL 'NV, Brut, California $11			B	B	B				

L.A.	Orange	Riverside	San Fran	West Coast	State Fair	New World	Pacific Rim	San Diego	Sparkling Wine
									3 AWARDS
				S	B		B		**KORBEL** 'NV, Chardonnay Champagne, California $12
B						B		B	**KORBEL** 'NV, Extra Dry, California $11
G				S				Σ	**MUMM CUVEE NAPA** 'NV, Brut Prestige, Napa Vly. $18
B				S		G			**MUMM CUVEE NAPA** '96, Brut, DVX, Napa Vly. $50
G	S				S				**SCHRAMSBERG** '98, Blanc De Noir, Napa Vly. $30
									2 AWARDS
					B		B		**BAREFOOT CELLARS** 'NV, Barefoot Bubbly Brut, California
		B				B			**COOK'S CHAMPAGNE CELLARS** 'NV, California Brut $4.50
		S				S			**COOK'S CHAMPAGNE CELLARS** 'NV, California Spumante $5
B			B						**HACIENDA WINERY** 'NV, Brut, California $10
B		S							**KORBEL** 'NV, Sonoma Co. Muscat Rouge $13
B					B				**KORBEL** '97, Blanc De Noir, Sonoma Co., Russian River Vly.
		B						S	**THORNTON** '96, Brut, Rsv., California $21
			B					G	**WEIBEL** 'NV, Almondine Flavored, California $7
B		B							**WINDSOR VINEYARDS** '98, Brut, Sonoma Co. Rsv. $20

Syrah

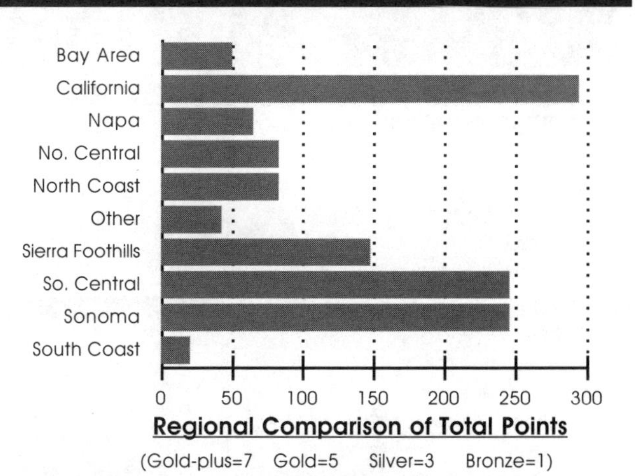

Regional Comparison of Total Points

(Gold-plus=7 Gold=5 Silver=3 Bronze=1)

Highest Individual Wine Totals

29 **FOREST GLEN WINERY**
'00, Oak Barrel Selection, California, $10.00

20 **PERRY CREEK VINEYARDS**
'99, El Dorado Estate, $16.00

20 **SAN SIMEON CELLARS**
'00, Monterey Co., $15.00

20 **ST. SUPÉRY**
'00, Napa Vly., $25.00

19 **BAILEYANA VINEYARD**
'99, Edna Vly., Firepeak Vnyd., $38.00

19 **WATTLE CREEK**
'99, Alexander Vly. Shiraz, $35.00

18 **CECCHETTI SEBASTIANI CELLAR**
'00, North Coast, $13.00

18 **GEYSER PEAK**
'00, Sonoma Co. Shiraz, $17.00

18 **MONTPELLIER VINEYARDS**
'00, California, $7.00

18 **ORFILA VINEYARDS**
'99, San Pasqual Vly., Val De La Mer, $24.00

18 **PEPPERWOOD GROVE**
'00, California, $9.00

Syrah

Syrah	L.A.	Orange	Riverside	San Fran	West Coast	State Fair	New World	Pacific Rim	San Diego
8 AWARDS									
CECCHETTI SEBASTIANI CELLAR '00, North Coast $13	G		B	B	S	S	S	B	B
FETZER '99, Valley Oaks, California $9		B	B	B	S	B	B	B	B
GEYSER PEAK '00, Sonoma Co. Shiraz $17	S	G	S	B	B		B	B	S
7 AWARDS									
BONTERRA '99, Mendocino Co. $19		B	B	S	S		S	B	B
FOREST GLEN WINERY '00, Oak Barrel Selection, California $10	G	G	B	B	G	Σ			G
GEYSER PEAK '98, Sonoma Co. Shiraz Rsv. $40	G		S	B		S	B	B	S
JEKEL VINEYARDS '99, Monterey Co. $15	S	S	S	B	B		S		S
MERIDIAN VINEYARDS '99, Paso Robles $15	S	B	B	B	G		S	B	
PEIRANO ESTATE VINEYARDS '98, Lodi Estate $11	B	B	B		G	S	B		B
WATTLE CREEK '99, Alexander Vly. Shiraz $35	B		S	B	S	S	Σ	B	
6 AWARDS									
BERINGER '99, Founders Estate, California $12	B		B	B		S	B		S
CHAMELEON CELLARS '00, Napa Vly. $29	S		S	S	B	B		S	
GEYSER PEAK '99, Sonoma Co. Shiraz Rsv. $40			B	B	G	S	S	S	
MIDNIGHT CELLARS '00, Nocturne, Paso Robles $24	S		B	G	S	B		B	
MONTEVINA '99, Terra D'oro, Amador Co. $18		S	B	S	S	B	S		
MONTPELLIER VINEYARDS '00, California $7	S	G	B		S		S	S	
PEPPERWOOD GROVE '00, California $9	B		B	Σ	S	G			B

Syrah

6 AWARDS

L.A.	Orange	Riverside	San Fran	West Coast	State Fair	New World	Pacific Rim	San Diego	Syrah
S	G	S		S			S	S	**PERRY CREEK VINEYARDS** '99, El Dorado Estate $16
B	B	S			B		S	B	**R. H. PHILLIPS** '00, EXP, Dunnigan Hills $14
S	S	S	B	S				Σ	**SAN SIMEON CELLARS** '00, Monterey Co. $15
B	S	S		B			B	B	**SEVEN PEAKS** '99, Shiraz, Paso Robles $14
G		S		B	S	G		S	**ST. SUPÉRY** '00, Napa Vly. $25
B	S		S	G	B	S			**VALLEY OF THE MOON** '99, Sonoma Co. $17
B		B	B			S	B	S	**WINDSOR VINEYARDS** '99, Dry Creek Vly. Private Rsv. $15.75

5 AWARDS

L.A.	Orange	Riverside	San Fran	West Coast	State Fair	New World	Pacific Rim	San Diego	Syrah
	S	S	S	G			B		**ALEXANDER VALLEY VINEYARDS** '00, Alexander Vly. Estate $20
Σ	B	G				G		B	**BAILEYANA VINEYARD** '99, Edna Vly., Firepeak Vnyd. $38
G		S	B		B	G			**BAYSTONE** '00, Dry Creek Vly. $24
S	B	S		G				B	**CAMELOT WINERY** '99, California $9
B		S	B	B		G			**CANYON ROAD WINERY** '00, California Shiraz $10
B	B	B			S			S	**DOCE ROBLES WINERY** '99, Paso Robles, Estate $20
G			B	S			B	S	**EBERLE** '00, Paso Robles, Steinbeck Vnyd. $20
	B	S	S	S		B			**ECHELON** '00, Clarksburg, Esperanza Vyd. $13.50
G	B	B				B	S		**FOXHOLLOW VINEYARDS** '00, California, Barrel Select $9
S		S	S	B		S			**INDIAN SPRINGS VINEYARDS** '99, Nevada Co. $18
	B		B	S	G	S			**IRONSTONE VINEYARDS** '00, California Shiraz $10

Syrah

Wine	L.A.	Orange	Riverside	San Fran	West Coast	State Fair	New World	Pacific Rim	San Diego
5 AWARDS									
JEPSON '00, Mendocino Co. Estate Select $22	B			S	B	S			G
KENDALL-JACKSON WINERY '99, Grand Rsv., California $18	B		B	B			B	B	
KENDALL-JACKSON WINERY '99, Vintner's Rsv., California $12	S				B		G	B	B
MERIDIAN VINEYARDS '99, California Shiraz $11	S			B	B		B	B	
MONTERRA WINERY '99, Monterey Co. $13	G		B			S	B		S
4 AWARDS									
BENZIGER '99, Sonoma Co. $22	B	G		B		G			
CHAMELEON CELLARS '00, California $14		B	B		S			G	
CHRISTOPHER CREEK '00, Russian River Vly. Estate $22		B		B	B	B			
COASTAL RIDGE WINERY '00, Shiraz, California $7			S			B	G		S
CONCANNON VINEYARD '99, Rhone Style, San Francisco Bay $19		B		S	G	S			
DELICATO '01, Shiraz, California $8	S	S	S			Σ			
FENESTRA '99, Livermore Vly. $20	S		B	S			B		
JADE MOUNTAIN '99, Napa Vly. $27	S		B	B			G		
J. LOHR ESTATE '99, Paso Robles, South Ridge $15	B	B	B	G					
MARIAH '99, Mendocino Ridge $30			B	B			B	S	
MICHEL-SCHLUMBERGER '99, North Coast $22	B		B			B			S
CHARLES B. MITCHELL VINEYARDS '00, El Dorado Rsv. $25	B		G					B	S
NEVADA CITY WINERY '00, Sierra Foothills $18	G		B				G	S	

Syrah

L.A.	Orange	Riverside	San Fran	West Coast	State Fair	New World	Pacific Rim	San Diego	
4 AWARDS									
		G	Σ			S	S		**ORFILA VINEYARDS** '99, San Pasqual Vly., Val De La Mer $24
		B	B		B		B		**R. H. PHILLIPS** '99, EXP, Dunnigan Hills $25
B		B	S		S				**RANCHO ZABACO** '99, Sonoma Co. $18
	S		B		S			B	**STEVENOT** '00, Calaveras Co., Canterbury Vnyds. $18
B				G		S		B	**TOPOLOS AT RUSSIAN RIVER** '00, Sonoma Co., Ladi's Vnyd. $25
B	B		B	S					**TULIP HILL WINERY** '00, San Joaquin, Mt. Oso Vnyd. $32
3 AWARDS									
B		S	B						**ALTERRA** '99, Russian River Vly. $18
S						B		S	**BELL WINE CELLARS** '99, Sierra Foothills, Canterbury Vnyd. $28
B			B					B	**BIANCHI VINEYARDS** '98, Paso Robles $14
		B					S	B	**CHRISTOPHER CREEK** '99, Russian River Vly. Estate $22
	B		G		B				**CLINE CELLARS** '00, Sonoma $16
						S	B	B	**CONCANNON VINEYARD** '98, Rhone Style, San Francisco Bay $19
		S	B		B				**CRYSTAL VALLEY CELLARS** '00, California $18
B		B	B						**EBERLE** '00, Paso Robles, Reid Vnyd. $20
G		S		S					**EDMEADES** '99, Mendocino Co., Eaglepoint Ranch $23
S		S		G					**EVERETT RIDGE VINEYARDS & WINERY** '99, Sonoma Vly. Nuns Canyon Vnyd. $26
	S		B		B				**FIRESTONE VINEYARD** '00, Santa Ynez Vly. $18
	S				S	S			**FRESNO STATE VINEYARDS** '99, John Diener Vnyd., 13.75% Alc. $13

Syrah	L.A.	Orange	Riverside	San Fran	West Coast	State Fair	New World	Pacific Rim	San Diego
3 AWARDS									
GRAND CRU VINEYARDS '00, California $7		B				S	B		
VICTOR HUGO '00, Paso Robles Estate $20	S	S							S
HUNT CELLARS '99, California, Serenade $22	Σ			B	B				
LAFOND '00, Santa Ynez Vly., Santa Rita Hills $18		S		Σ		G			
MEADOR ESTATE '98, Monterey, Arroyo Seco, Maverick $50		B		B	B				
MIRASSOU '99, Monterey Co., Harvest Rsv. $15		B	B		S				
PERRY CREEK VINEYARDS '98, El Dorado Estate $16	S		S				S		
RENAISSANCE '00, Sierra Foothills $21	S		S		B				
JEFF RUNQUIST WINES '00, Paso Robles $24			S		Σ				G
RUTHERFORD VINTNERS '99, Stanislaus Co., Barrel Select $9		S			S			B	
SIMI '00, Alexander Vly. $20	B	S	G						
STONEHEDGE '00, California $10			S		S		B		
TALUS '99, California $9			B				S	S	
WATTLE CREEK '98, Alexander Vly. Shiraz $35				B	S				B
WENTE VINEYARDS '00, Livermore Vly., Vineyard Selection $11	B			B	G				
2 AWARDS									
ABUNDANCE WINERY '99, Paso Robles, French Camp Vnyd. $18	B				B				
AHLGREN VINEYARD '99, Monterey Co., Ventana Vnyds. $24				B		B			
AMADOR FOOTHILL WINERY '00, Sierra Foothills, Hollander Vnyd. $20		B	G						

L.A.	Orange	Riverside	San Fran	West Coast	State Fair	New World	Pacific Rim	San Diego	Syrah
									2 AWARDS
B						S			**ANAPAMU** '99, Paso Robles/Central Coast $20
						G		B	**BAILEYANA VINEYARD** '99, Paso Robles $18
						B	B		**BUTTONWOOD FARM** '99, Santa Ynez Vly. $22
			Σ		S				**CLINE CELLARS** '00, Los Carneros $28
B			B						**CLOS DU BOIS** '98, Alexander Vly. Rsv. $16
					Σ	S			**FORESTVILLE VINEYARD** '00, California $6
	S					B			**FRESNO STATE VINEYARDS** '99, John Diener Vnyd., 14.25% Alc. $13
					S	S			**FRESNO STATE VINEYARDS** '00, California $10
	G					B			**GRANITE SPRINGS** '99, El Dorado $16
		G					S		**HAGAFEN CELLARS** '99, Napa Vly. $27
	G	B							**JANKRIS VINEYARD** '00, Paso Robles Sojourn $14.50
						G	B		**JORY** '00, Central Coast $19
S					S				**JORY** '00, Paso Robles, Lock Vnyd.
						S	B		**JUSTIN** '99, Paso Robles, Halter Vyd. $22.50
					S	S			**LAVA CAP** '99, El Dorado Rsv. $20
S			S						**LINCOURT** '00, Santa Barbara Co. $20
		B				B			**LOCKWOOD VINEYARD** '99, Monterey Co. Estate $16
S		S							**MC MANIS FAMILY VINEYARDS** '00, California $9

Syrah

2 AWARDS

Wine	L.A.	Orange	Riverside	San Fran	West Coast	State Fair	New World	Pacific Rim	San Diego
ROBERT MONDAVI COASTAL '00, Central Coast $11				S			B		
ORFILA VINEYARDS '98, San Pasqual Vly., Val De La Mer $24						B			B
PARADISE RIDGE '00, Sonoma Co., Ladi's Vnyd. $24				B		Σ			
MICHAEL POZZAN WINERY '98, Napa Vly., Special Rsv. $15							B	S	
RENWOOD WINES '99, Amador Co. $25					S	B			
ROSENBLUM CELLARS '00, Solano, England-Shaw Vyd. $37				B				S	
JEFF RUNQUIST WINES '00, Paso Robles, Hilltop Vnyd. $24	Σ			Σ					
SEVEN PEAKS '00, Paso Robles $14	B			G					
SIERRA VISTA '99, El Dorado Red Rock Ridge $25		B	B						
SILKWOOD WINES '00, Stanislaus Co. $22				S		G			
SILVER RIDGE VINEYARDS '99, California Barrel Fermented $10			B					B	
SUNSTONE VINEYARDS & WINERY '99, Santa Ynez Vly. Estate $40				B		B			
VOSS VINEYARDS '99, Napa Vly. $24				S				B	
WINDMILL ESTATES '00, Lodi $10		B				B			
WOODBRIDGE WINERY '99, California $9				B			S		
ZACA MESA '99, Santa Barbara Co. Zaca Vnyd. $20			B				S		

Healdsburg, California

DEMPEL
SANTA ROSA - HOPLAND
98

Viognier

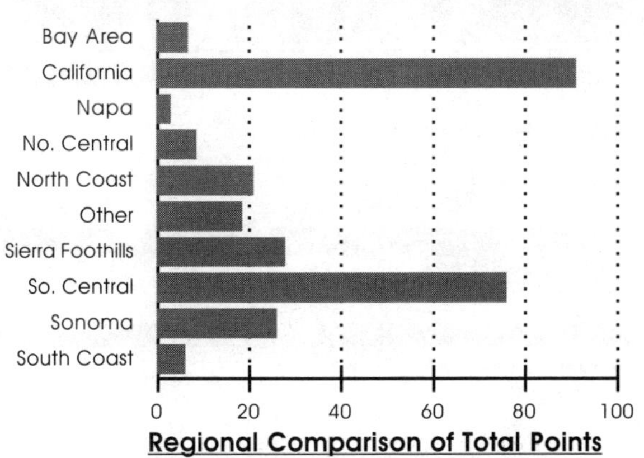

Regional Comparison of Total Points

(Gold-plus=7 Gold=5 Silver=3 Bronze=1)

Highest Individual Wine Totals

Points	Wine
21	**EBERLE** '01, Paso Robles, Mill Road Vyd., $18.00
19	**CILURZO VINEYARD & WINERY** '01, California, $17.00
16	**LIONS PEAK** '01, California, $14.00
15	**EBERLE** '01, Paso Robles, Glenrose Vnyd., $22.00
11	**THOMAS COYNE** '01, California, $16.00
11	**MONTPELLIER VINEYARDS** '00, California, $7.00
11	**R. H. PHILLIPS** '00, EXP, Dunnigan Hills, $14.00
10	**CHANGALA WINERY** '00, Santa Barbara Co., $16.00
10	**CHRISTOPHER CREEK** '00, Russian River, Catie Corner Vnyd., $24.00
9	**BONTERRA** '00, Mendocino Co., $19.00
9	**CECCHETTI SEBASTIANI CELLAR** '00, North Coast, $13.00

Viognier

Wine	L.A.	Orange	Riverside	San Fran	West Coast	State Fair	New World	Pacific Rim	San Diego
7 AWARDS									
EBERLE '01, Paso Robles, Glenrose Vnyd. $22	S	B	S	S	S			B	B
EBERLE '01, Paso Robles, Mill Road Vyd. $18	S	B	G	S		B		Σ	B
6 AWARDS									
CHRISTOPHER CREEK '00, Russian River, Catie Corner Vnyd. $24	S		B		S	B	B		B
5 AWARDS									
CILURZO VINEYARD & WINERY '01, California $17	S	S	S		Σ	S			
ECHELON '00, Clarksburg, Esperanza Vyd. $14			B	B	B			B	S
MONTPELLIER VINEYARDS '00, California $7					B	S	S	B	S
R. H. PHILLIPS '00, EXP, Dunnigan Hills $14	B	B					B	S	G
4 AWARDS									
CHANGALA WINERY '00, Santa Barbara Co. $16					S	B	S		S
KENDALL-JACKSON WINERY '00, Grand Rsv., California $20	S		B		S				B
LIONS PEAK '01, California $14	S				S	S	Σ		
PEPPERWOOD GROVE '00, California $7			B				B	S	B
ROSENBLUM CELLARS '01, Lodi, Ripkin Vnyd. $19		S	S	B		B			
THORNTON '00, South Coast $13		B	B		S			B	
WATTLE CREEK '00, Alexander Vly. $24.75	B		S		B			B	
3 AWARDS									
BONTERRA '00, Mendocino Co. $19			S	B			G		
CECCHETTI SEBASTIANI CELLAR '00, North Coast $13					S		S	S	

Viognier

L.A.	Orange	Riverside	San Fran	West Coast	State Fair	New World	Pacific Rim	San Diego	Wine
3 AWARDS									
		B					S	B	**CONCANNON VINEYARD** '99, Rhone Style, Central Coast $15
		G		S	S				**THOMAS COYNE** '01, California $16
	G	B			B				**CURTIS** '00, Santa Barbara Co. $18
		B				S	B		**GEYSER PEAK** '00, Alexander Vly., Sonoma Moment Vnyd. Block Collection $19
	S	S						B	**HAWLEY WINES** '01, Placer Co. $20.50
B				S		B			**KENDALL-JACKSON WINERY** '00, Vintner's Rsv., California $14
B					B	B			**ZACA MESA** '00, Santa Barbara Co. $16.50
2 AWARDS									
	B				B				**INCOGNITO** '01, California $22
					B	B			**PEIRANO ESTATE VINEYARDS** '99, Lodi Estate $11
G		B							**PERRY CREEK VINEYARDS** '00, El Dorado Estate $16

White Dessert

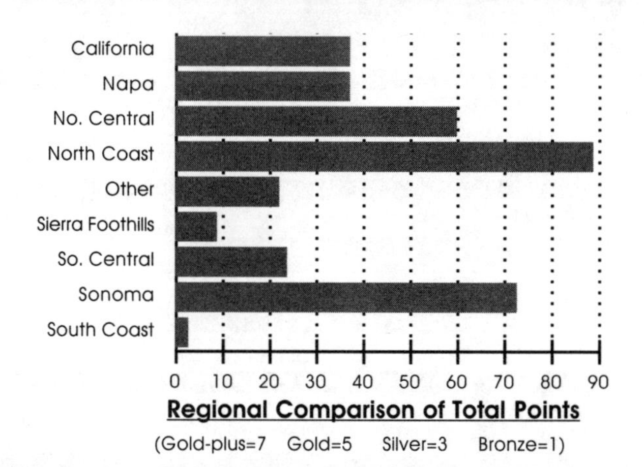

Highest Individual Wine Totals

46 **JEKEL VINEYARDS**
'00, Riesling, Monterey Co., Late Harvest, $22.00

22 **BAYWOOD**
'00, Symphony, Lodi, Late Harvest, $18.00

21 **GREENWOOD RIDGE VINEYARDS**
'01, Riesling, Late Harvest, Estate, $24.00

19 **GEYSER PEAK**
'00, Riesling, Dry Creek Vly., LH Rsv., $19.00

17 **NEWLAN VINEYARDS & WINERY**
'00, White Riesling, Napa Vly., $25.00

16 **EOS**
'00, Moscato Tears of Dew, Paso Robles, Estate, $24.00

15 **GEYSER PEAK**
'00, Riesling, Mendocino Co., LH Rsv., $19.00

15 **NAVARRO VINEYARDS**
'00, Riesling, SLH, Anderson Vly. Vnyd. Select, $25.00

15 **WINDSOR VINEYARDS**
'01, Muscat Canelli, Alexander Vly., Murphy Ranch, $15.25

14 **QUADY**
'01, Electra Orange Muscat, California, $8.00

13 **NAVARRO VINEYARDS**
'00, Gewurztraminer, Anderson Vly., Vyd. Select, $25.00

White Dessert

Winery / Wine	L.A.	Orange	Riverside	San Fran	West Coast	State Fair	New World	Pacific Rim	San Diego
8 AWARDS									
JEKEL VINEYARDS '00, Riesling, Monterey Co., Late Harvest, R.S. 16 $22	Σ	Σ	G	S	G		G	Σ	Σ
7 AWARDS									
GEYSER PEAK '00, Riesling, Dry Creek Vly., LH Rsv., R.S. 15.50 $19	B	B	S			S	S	G	S
GEYSER PEAK '00, Riesling, Mendocino Co., LH Rsv., R.S. 16 $19	S		S	B	B		S	S	B
6 AWARDS									
GAN EDEN '00, Gewurztraminer, Monterey Co., Zabala Vnyd., R.S. 9 $14	B	S	B	S		B		B	
QUADY '01, Electra Orange Muscat, California, R.S. 15.70 $8	B	B	B	G				G	B
5 AWARDS									
GREENWOOD RIDGE VINEYARDS '01, Riesling, Late Harvest, Estate $24	S	G		S	S	Σ			
WINDSOR VINEYARDS '01, Muscat Canelli, Alexander Vly., Murphy Ranch $15.25	B	G			G	S			B
4 AWARDS									
BAYWOOD '00, Symphony, Lodi, Late Harvest $18		G				Σ	Σ	S	
EOS '00, Moscato Tears of Dew, Paso Robles, Estate, R.S. 18.10 $24		S	Σ	S	S				
MARTIN & WEYRICH WINERY '01, Moscato Allegro, California $12	S	S		B		S			
WINDSOR VINEYARDS '00, Muscat Canelli, Alexander Vly., Murphy Ranch, R.S. 6.60 $15.25	S				B		B		S
3 AWARDS									
DRY CREEK VINEYARD '00, Sauvignon Blanc, Sonoma Co. Soleil $20			B			B	S		

White Dessert

3 AWARDS

L.A.	Orange	Riverside	San Fran	West Coast	State Fair	New World	Pacific Rim	San Diego	Wine
	S		B		S				**FOLIE A'DEUX** '99, Gewürtzraminer Icewine Frost Mendocino, R.S. 21.40 $31
S	G			S					**GRGICH HILLS** '00, Violetta, Napa Vly., Late Harvest $40
	S		S		S				**NAVARRO VINEYARDS** '01, White Riesling, Anderson Vly., Cluster Select, R.S. 24.20 $49
		Σ				S	S		**NAVARRO VINEYARDS** '00, Gewurztraminer, Anderson Vly., Vyd. Select $25
		G				Σ	S		**NAVARRO VINEYARDS** '00, Riesling, SLH, Anderson Vly. Vnyd. Select $25
	S		Σ		Σ				**NEWLAN VINEYARDS & WINERY** '00, White Riesling, Napa Vly., R.S. 13.80 $25

2 AWARDS

L.A.	Orange	Riverside	San Fran	West Coast	State Fair	New World	Pacific Rim	San Diego	Wine
B					S				**MAURICE CAR'RIE WINERY** '01, Summer's End
		S				B			**CONCANNON VINEYARD** '98, Riesling, Monterey, SLH $20
	B	B							**COSENTINO WINERY** '00, Vin Doux Viognier Kay, Late Harvest, R.S. 8.20 $30
	G					Σ			**MC ILROY WINES** '00, Gewurztraminer, Russian River Vly., Aquarius Ranch, R.S. 8 $15
	G				S				**NAVARRO VINEYARDS** '01, Gewurztraminer, Anderson Vly., Cluster Select, R.S. 21.40 $49

White Meritage

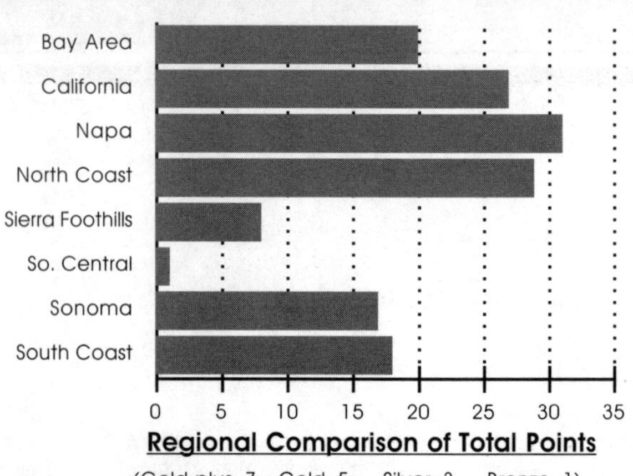

Regional Comparison of Total Points

(Gold-plus=7 Gold=5 Silver=3 Bronze=1)

Highest Individual Wine Totals

31 **ST. SUPÉRY**
'00, Napa Vly., $22.00

27 **KENDALL-JACKSON WINERY**
'00, Grand Rsv., California, $13.00

18 **CONCANNON VINEYARD**
'00, White Assemblage, Rsv., $15.00

17 **BAILY VINEYARD & WINERY**
'01, Montage, Temecula, $18.00

15 **GUENOC**
'00, Langtry, Guenoc Vly., $21.00

14 **YORKVILLE CELLARS**
'00, Eleanor of Aquitaine, Yorkville Highlands, $17.00

11 **DE LORIMIER WINERY**
'99, Spectrum, Alexander Vly. Estate, $16.00

7 **SONORA WINERY & PORT WORKS**
'01, Sauvignon Blanc, Amador Co.,

4 **BERINGER**
'00, Alluvium Blanc, Knights Vly., $16.00

2 **MURRIETA'S WELL**
'99, White Vendimia, Livermore Vly., $22.00

White Meritage Type

L.A.	Orange	Riverside	San Fran	West Coast	State Fair	New World	Pacific Rim	San Diego	White Meritage Type
									7 AWARDS
Σ		S	S		Σ	S	B	S	**KENDALL-JACKSON WINERY** '00, Grand Rsv., California $13
S	G	G		Σ		B	G	G	**ST. SUPÉRY** '00, Napa Vly. $22
									6 AWARDS
S		S	B	S	S		B		**YORKVILLE CELLARS** '00, Eleanor of Aquitaine, Yorkville Highlands $17
									5 AWARDS
B	B	Σ	S		G				**BAILY VINEYARD & WINERY** '01, Montage, Temecula $18
S		B	B		S			S	**DE LORIMIER WINERY** '99, Spectrum, Alexander Vly. Estate $16
B		S		S		Σ		B	**GUENOC** '00, Langtry, Guenoc Vly. $21
									4 AWARDS
	G			S	S	Σ			**CONCANNON VINEYARD** '00, White Assemblage, Rsv. $15
									2 AWARDS
				B	S				**BERINGER** '00, Alluvium Blanc, Knights Vly. $16
B						B			**MURRIETA'S WELL** '99, White Vendimia, Livermore Vly. $22

F9

White Zinfandel

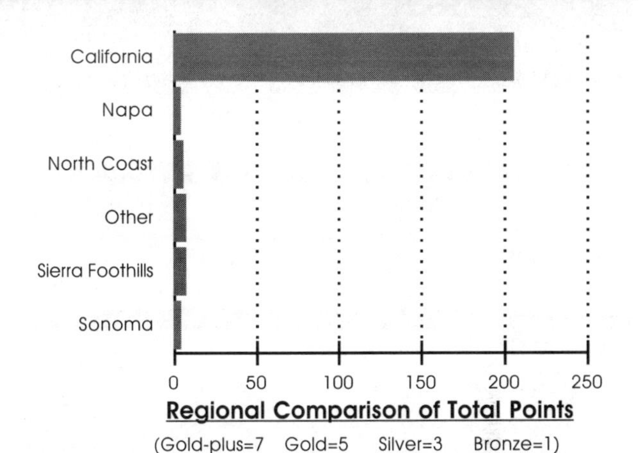

Regional Comparison of Total Points

(Gold-plus=7 Gold=5 Silver=3 Bronze=1)

Highest Individual Wine Totals

30 **FETZER**
'01, Echo Ridge, California, $8.00

24 **BERINGER**
'01, California, $6.00

16 **MONTPELLIER VINEYARDS**
'00, California, $6.00

14 **HACIENDA WINERY**
'00, California Clair de Lune, $6.00

14 **SALMON CREEK CELLARS**
'01, California, $7.00

13 **BAREFOOT CELLARS**
'NV, California, $4.00

13 **BEL ARBOR**
'00, California, $5.00

11 **V. SATTUI WINERY**
'00, California, $9.00

10 **BARON HERZOG WINE CELLARS**
'01, California, $7.00

10 **SUTTER HOME**
'00, California, $5.00

White Zinfandel

Wine	L.A.	Orange	Riverside	San Fran	West Coast	State Fair	New World	Pacific Rim	San Diego
8 AWARDS									
FETZER '01, Echo Ridge, California $8	B	B	S	B	Σ	Σ		Σ	S
6 AWARDS									
BERINGER '01, California $6	Σ		G	S	B		Σ		B
SALMON CREEK CELLARS '01, California $7	B		G	B	S	S			B
5 AWARDS									
BAREFOOT CELLARS 'NV, California $4	S		B		S	S	S		
BEL ARBOR '00, California $5	B		S		S		S		S
BERINGER '00, North Coast, Vineyard Select $8	S		B	B	B			B	
MONTEVINA '01, Amador Co. $7	B	B		B		B			B
V. SATTUI WINERY '00, California $9	B		G		B			B	S
4 AWARDS									
BARON HERZOG WINE CELLARS '01, California $7	S			B			S		S
BUEHLER VINEYARDS '01, Napa Vly. $7	B		B	B	B				
HACIENDA WINERY '00, California Clair de Lune $6	S		Σ				S		B
MONTPELLIER VINEYARDS '00, California $6	G		G				S	S	
SUTTER HOME '00, California $5	S		B		S		S		
3 AWARDS									
BAREFOOT CELLARS 'NV, Barefoot On The Beach $4	B	B	B						
CORBETT CANYON VINEYARDS '01, California Select $6			G			B			B
DE LOACH VINEYARDS '01, California $8		S	S					B	

White Zinfandel

2 AWARDS

L.A.	Orange	Riverside	San Fran	West Coast	State Fair	New World	Pacific Rim	San Diego	Wine
	S				G				**BEL ARBOR** '01, California $6
					S	B			**ESTRELLA RIVER** '01, California $5
B						S			**FRESNO STATE VINEYARDS** '01, Fresno State Vnyd, California $6
			S		S				**GLEN ELLEN WINERY** '00, California $7
				B		B			**MONTEVINA** '00, Amador Co. $6.50
	S						B		**J. PEDRONCELLI** '01, Zinfandel Rose, Vintage Selection $8.50
		G				S			**RUTHERFORD VINTNERS** '00, Lodi, Barrel Select $8

GREENWOOD
RIDGE
VINEYARDS
SONOMA COUNTY
ZINFANDEL
Carol Shelton
OLD VINES ZINFANDEL

Zinfandel

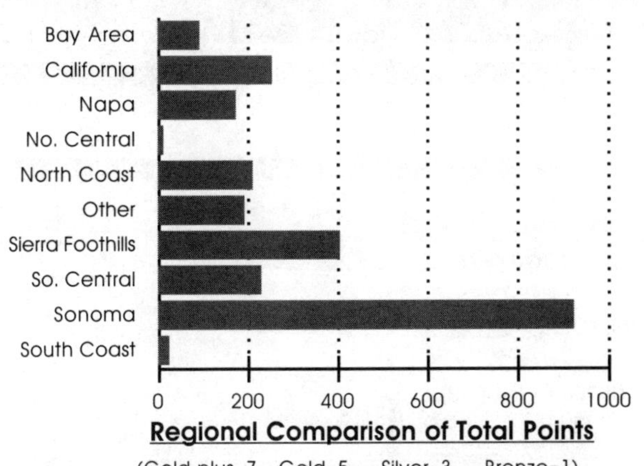

Regional Comparison of Total Points

(Gold-plus=7 Gold=5 Silver=3 Bronze=1)

Highest Individual Wine Totals

28 **FANUCCHI VINEYARDS**
'98, Russian River Vly., Fanucchi Wood Rd. Vnyd., Old Vine, $49.00

27 **PERRY CREEK VINEYARDS**
'00, Sierra Foothills, Zin Man, $12.00

27 **TRENTADUE**
'00, La Storia, Dry Creek Vly., $30.00

25 **JESSIE'S GROVE WINERY**
'00, Lodi, Westwind Vyd., Old Vine, $22.00

24 **KENWOOD VINEYARDS**
'99, Sonoma Co., $16.00

24 **TRENTADUE**
'00, Alexander Vly. Geyserville Ranch, $20.00

23 **GEYSER PEAK**
'00, Sonoma Co., $17.00

23 **JESSIE'S GROVE WINERY**
'00, Lodi, Old Vine, Vintners Choice, $15.00

23 **MURPHY-GOODE**
'00, Liar's Dice, Sonoma Co., $20.00

23 **JEFF RUNQUIST WINES**
'00, Amador Co., Massoni Ranch, $22.00

Zinfandel

Wine	L.A.	Orange	Riverside	San Fran	West Coast	State Fair	New World	Pacific Rim	San Diego
9 AWARDS									
TRENTADUE '00, La Storia, Dry Creek Vly. $30	B	Σ	S	B	S	S	Σ	B	B
8 AWARDS									
BOGLE '00, Old Vine, California $11	S	S		B	S	B	S	B	S
CHATEAU SOUVERAIN '99, Dry Creek Vly. $13	B	S	B	B	B	Σ	S	B	
CHRISTOPHER CREEK '00, Dry Creek Vly. $26	S		B	B	S	B	S	B	S
FANUCCHI VINEYARDS '99, Russian River Vly., Fanucchi Wood Rd. Vnyd., Old Vine $49	B		S	S	B	B	S	B	B
FANUCCHI VINEYARDS '98, Russian River Vly., Fanucchi Wood Rd. Vnyd., Old Vine $49	S		S	B	B	Σ	G	G	S
GREENWOOD RIDGE VINEYARDS '00, Scherrer Vnyds., Sonoma Co. $24	B	S	S		G	B	S	S	B
KENWOOD VINEYARDS '99, Sonoma Co. $16	S	S	G	B	G	B	B		G
RANCHO ZABACO '99, Dry Creek Vly. $18	B	S	B	B	S	B	S	S	
RANCHO ZABACO '00, Dancing Bull, California $12	S	B	S		S	B	Σ	B	B
TRENTADUE '00, Alexander Vly. Geyserville Ranch $20	S	S	B	B	G	S	G		S
7 AWARDS									
FETZER '99, Barrel Select, Mendocino Co. $14	S	G	B	B		G	S		S
GEYSER PEAK '00, Sonoma Co. $17	S		B	S	S	S	G	G	
JESSIE'S GROVE WINERY '00, Lodi, Old Vine, Vintners Choice $15	Σ	B	B	G		S	S	S	
JESSIE'S GROVE WINERY '00, Lodi, Westwind Vyd., Old Vine $22	G	G	B			S	G	G	B
KENDALL-JACKSON WINERY '98, Grand Rsv., California $17	B		B	B	B	S	B	S	

L.A.	Orange	Riverside	San Fran	West Coast	State Fair	New World	Pacific Rim	San Diego	Zinfandel
									7 AWARDS
B	S	B	S	S		B		S	**LAKE SONOMA WINERY** '99, Dry Creek Vly., Saini Farms Old Vine $20
S	S	S	S		B		S	Σ	**MURPHY-GOODE** '00, Liar's Dice, Sonoma Co. $20
G	G	G		S	S		S	S	**PERRY CREEK VINEYARDS** '00, Sierra Foothills, Zin Man $12
G	B	B		S		S	S	G	**ROSENBLUM CELLARS** '00, Dry Creek Vly. Rockpile Road Vnyd. $25
G		B	G	S	B	G		S	**JEFF RUNQUIST WINES** '00, Amador Co., Massoni Ranch $22
									6 AWARDS
		G	S	S	B	S	B		**BRUTOCAO** '99, Mendocino Co., Brutocao Vnyd. $16
S		B	B			B	B	S	**CONCANNON VINEYARD** '99, San Francisco Bay, Livermore Vly. $15
	S	G	B	S		B		G	**FENESTRA** '99, Livermore Vly. $18
	S	B	B	S		B		Σ	**VICTOR HUGO** '99, Paso Robles $17
B		B	B	B		S		Σ	**LA CREMA** '98, Sonoma Co. $22
	S	B		B		B	Σ	G	**J. LOHR ESTATE** '99, Lodi, Bramblewood $20
G	S	G	S	S	B				**MONTEVINA** '99, Terra d'Oro, Amador Co., Home Vnyd. $24
S	S	B	B	S		Σ			**JEFF RUNQUIST WINES** '00, Amador Co., Nostro Vino Vnyd. Primitivo $24
S	B		B	B	B			S	**SAUCELITO CANYON** '00, Arroyo Grande Vly. $23
B	G	S		S	B	S			**CAROL SHELTON** '00, Dry Creek Vly., Rocky Rsv. $32
	S	B	B	S		B	B		**RODNEY STRONG** '99, Northern Sonoma, Knotty Vines $18
S	S		B	S	B	S			**VAN RUITEN-TAYLOR WINERY** '00, Lodi Rsv., Old Vine $15

Zinfandel

Wine	L.A.	Orange	Riverside	San Fran	West Coast	State Fair	New World	Pacific Rim	San Diego
6 AWARDS									
WHITE OAK VINEYARDS '00, Alexander Vly. Estate $33		B	G	B	G	G			B
WINDSOR VINEYARDS '99, North Coast $12	B		S	B	S		B	B	
5 AWARDS									
ARMIDA WINERY '00, Dry Creek Vly., Maple Vnyd. $30	B	B			B	S			S
DE ROSE '99, Cienega Vly. Cedolini Vnyd. $19			B	G	B		S		S
DOCE ROBLES WINERY '99, Paso Robles, Estate $18		S		S		S	B		G
EDMEADES '98, Mendocino Co. $16	B		B	B		B	B		
EOS '00, Paso Robles, Estate $16	S		S	B	B			B	
FOLIE A'DEUX '99, Amador Co. $18	B	B	B	S			S		
FOLIE A'DEUX '99, Amador Co., The Wild Bunch Vnyd, $22	S	B	S			S	S		
FOPPIANO VINEYARDS '00, Dry Creek Vly. $15	S		B		S		B		B
GALLO OF SONOMA '98, Dry Creek Vly., Frei Vnyd. $20				B	S		B	B	B
GUENOC '99, California $11.50	S	S	B				S	S	
HIDDEN MOUNTAIN RANCH '99, Paso Robles Dante Dusi Vnyd. $22			B	B	B	S			S
HOP KILN WINERY '99, Russian River Vly. Old Windmill Vnyd. $20		B	B	S	S		S		
HOP KILN WINERY '99, Russian River Vly. Primitivo Vnyd, $18			B	S	S		G	B	
IRONSTONE VINEYARDS '00, California $10	G	S			B	S	B		
JESSIE'S GROVE WINERY '00, Lodi Royal-tee Vnyd. $25	S	S	B				G	B	
KEMPTON CLARK '99, Mad Zin, California $10	G		S	S			S	B	

L.A.	Orange	Riverside	San Fran	West Coast	State Fair	New World	Pacific Rim	San Diego	Zinfandel
									5 AWARDS
	B			S	B		B	B	**KENDALL-JACKSON WINERY** '00, Vintner's Rsv., California $12
G	S	B			G	S			**MICHAEL-DAVID PHILLIPS** '00, Lodi, Maley Vnyd. $24
B	B		Σ			G	G		**MONTEVINA** '99, Terra d'Oro, Amador Co., SHR $24
S	S	S			B	G			**PEPPERWOOD GROVE** '99, California $7
		G	B	S		S		G	**RAYMOND** '99, Napa Vly. Rsv. $22
Σ	B		G		B			S	**RENWOOD WINES** '99, Amador Co., Old Vine $20
	B	G	S	B				S	**V. SATTUI WINERY** '99, Napa Vly. Suzanne's Vnyd. $20
Σ	S	B			G	G			**CAROL SHELTON** '00, Mendocino, Cox Vnyd., Wild Thing $28
B		B	B	S		G			**SONORA WINERY & PORT WORKS** '99, Amador Co. TC Vnyd. $24
B		G		G	B			B	**SONORA WINERY & PORT WORKS** '00, Amador Co. Linsteadt Vnyd. $22
S		B	S		S	B			**TOPOLOS AT RUSSIAN RIVER** '99, Sonoma Co. Old Vine $20
S		B	S	S		Σ			**VILLA MT. EDEN** '99, California, Old Vines $10
									4 AWARDS
S	B			G				B	**ABUNDANCE WINERY** '00, Lodi, Mencarini Vnyds. Old Vine $14
		B		G		Σ	B		**ALDERBROOK WINERY** '99, Sonoma Co. $19
		B			S	B	B		**BAILEYANA VINEYARD** '99, Paso Robles $18
S				G	S	G			**BEAULIEU** '00, Napa Vly. $14
S	S	S	B						**BERINGER** '99, Founders Estate, California $12
	G		Σ		G	B			**BRADFORD MOUNTAIN WINERY** '99, Dry Creek Vly., Grist Vnyd. $30

Zinfandel

4 AWARDS

Winery	L.A.	Orange	Riverside	San Fran	West Coast	State Fair	New World	Pacific Rim	San Diego
DAVID BRUCE WINERY '00, Paso Robles $17	S	B					S	G	
CASTORO CELLARS '99, Paso Robles $14				B	B		S		G
CHUMEIA VINEYARDS '00, Paso Robles $22		B	B			S			G
DK CELLARS '99, Sierra Foothills $20		S	S		B				S
DOMAINE ST. GEORGE WINERY '98, Dry Creek Vly., Wells Vnyd. $16			B	S	B				S
DRY CREEK VINEYARD '98, Dry Creek Vly. Rsv. $30	B			S			B	B	
EBERLE '00, Paso Robles, Sauret Vnyd. $20			B	B	B			B	
EDGEWOOD '99, Napa Vly. $22		Σ				B	S		G
FETZER '99, Valley Oaks, California $10	B	S	B				S		
FOLIE A'DEUX '99, Amador Co., DeMille Vnyd. $24	S		G	B		B			
GRGICH HILLS '99, Napa and Sonoma Countries $25		B	S		S		S		
GUNDLACH-BUNDSCHU WINERY '00, Sonoma Vly., Rhinefarm Vnyd. $26	S	B		B		B			
MARIAH '99, Mendocino Ridge $31			G	B			B	S	
MC ILROY WINES '99, Russian River Vly., Porter Bass Vyds. $24			G	B				B	S
MICHAEL-DAVID PHILLIPS '00, Lodi, Seven Deadly Zins $17	B	G	Σ			B			
MONTEVINA '99, Terra d'Oro, Amador Co. $18		S	B		S			S	
MONTEVINA '98, Terra D'oro Estate, Amador Co. $18					B		B	B	B
RANCHO ZABACO '99, Dry Creek Vly. Stefani Vnyd. $25			B		S			B	B

Zinfandel

L.A.	Orange	Riverside	San Fran	West Coast	State Fair	New World	Pacific Rim	San Diego	Zinfandel
									4 AWARDS
	S		S	B	S				**RENWOOD WINES** '99, Amador Co., Grandpere $35
		B			B	S	B		**ROSENBLUM CELLARS** '00, Paso Robles Sauret Vnyd. $19
			B	S		B	S		**ROSENBLUM CELLARS** '00, Russian River Vly., Old Vines $23
	S			S	S	B			**ROSENBLUM CELLARS** '00, San Francisco Bay, Planchon Vnyd. $19
Σ	G		B		S				**SANTA BARBARA WINERY** '00, Santa Ynez Vly., Lafond Vnyd. LH $30
	G	B	B	B					**V. SATTUI WINERY** '00, Contra Costa Co. Duarte Vnyd. $35
		B	B	B				S	**SAUSAL WINERY** '99, Alexander Vly. Private Rsv. $20
	Σ	B		S		B			**CAROL SHELTON** '00, Cucamonga Vly., Lopez Vnyd. $24
		S			B		B	G	**SINGLE LEAF** '99, El Dorado Rsv. $16
	B			B		S	B		**TALUS** '99, California $9
S		S		S	S				**VILLA MT. EDEN** '00, Sonoma Vly., Monte Rosso Vnyd. Rsv. $23
B		G		S		S			**WINDSOR VINEYARDS** '99, Mendocino Co., Signature Series $17.75
									3 AWARDS
B			B	S					**ALBERTONI VINEYARDS** '00, California Primitivo $13
B				B				S	**ARMIDA WINERY** '00, Dry Creek Vly. $20
B	B	S							**BANDIERA WINERY** '00, California Vnyd. Rsv. $8
S				B		B			**BAREFOOT CELLARS** '98, Sonoma Co. Rsv. $15
					B	S	B		**BAYWOOD** '99, Paso Robles, Vyd., Select $14

Zinfandel

3 AWARDS

Wine	L.A.	Orange	Riverside	San Fran	West Coast	State Fair	New World	Pacific Rim	San Diego
BEAULIEU '00, Signet Collection, Napa Vly. $30	B					B			B
BELLA VINEYARDS '00, Alexander Vly., Big River Ranch $28	S	B		Σ					
BELVEDERE '99, Dry Creek Vly. $20		B	S				S		
BENZIGER '99, Dry Creek Vly. $19		B		B		S			
CASTORO CELLARS '00, Paso Robles, Vnyd. Tribute $18	S	S			S				
CATACULA LAKE WINERY '99, Napa Vly. $27	B	Σ	B						
CHANGALA WINERY '99, Paso Robles, Dante Dusi Vnyd. $18		B		B			S		
CHATOM VINEYARDS '99, Sierra Foothills $16				S			B	B	
CHILES LAKE WINERY '00, Napa Vly., Rancho Catacula $29	B	S				S			
CLOS DU BOIS '99, Dry Creek Vly. Rsv. $21		B		B		S			
CLOS DU BOIS '99, Sonoma Co. $14	Σ	B		S					
COSENTINO WINERY '00, Lodi, The Zin $30	B		S		B				
CYPRESS VINEYARD '00, California $10					B		S	B	
DARK STAR CELLARS '99, Paso Robles $18		B		B					S
DE LOACH VINEYARDS '00, Russian River Vly. Estate $20		B	B				S		
DOMAINE ST. GEORGE WINERY '99, Chalk Hill, Old Vines $16			S			B		B	
DRY CREEK VINEYARD '99, Dry Creek Vly., Late Harvest $13		S					S	B	
DRY CREEK VINEYARD '00, Heritage Clone, Sonoma Co. $15					S	S			S

Zinfandel

3 AWARDS

L.A.	Orange	Riverside	San Fran	West Coast	State Fair	New World	Pacific Rim	San Diego	Zinfandel
B							B	B	**EBERLE** '00, Paso Robles, Steinbeck Vyd. $16
		B				G	B		**EDMEADES** '99, Mendocino Ridge Ciapusci Vnyd. $25
S		S		G					**EVERETT RIDGE VINEYARDS & WINERY** '99, Dry Creek Vly. Estate $26
S	S				G				**GARY FARRELL** '00, Dry Creek Vly. $24
		B	B		B				**FOLIE A'DEUX** '99, Amador Co., Harvey Vnyd. $28
		B			B		S		**GEYSER PEAK** '00, Cucamonga Vly., DeAmbrogio Vnyd. Block Collection $30
		Σ	B	B					**HIDDEN MOUNTAIN RANCH** '99, Paso Robles Wine Bush Vnyd. East $16
			B	S	G				**IMAGERY SERIES** '99, Taylor Vnyd., Dry Creek Vly. $35
S		S			G				**MADRONA** '00, El Dorado Estate $14
B		B			B				**MICHAEL-DAVID PHILLIPS** '00, Lodi, Old Vine $20
		B				B	S		**MILL CREEK VINEYARDS** '99, Russian River, Matteucci Vyds. $26
					G	S	S		**NAVARRO VINEYARDS** '00, Mendocino Co. $19
				S	Σ	G			**NEESE VINEYARDS** '00, Redwood Vly. $17
					G	S	B		**NEVADA CITY WINERY** '99, Sierra Foothills $15
B							B	B	**NORMAN VINEYARDS** '00, Paso Robles, The Monster $18
G				B		B			**PERRY CREEK VINEYARDS** '99, Sierra Foothills, Potter Vnyd. $24
	Σ				G			S	**QUAIL RIDGE** '00, Old Vines, Napa Vly. $25
Σ	S	B							**QUIVIRA** '99, Dry Creek Vly., Dieden Vnyd. $35

Zinfandel

	L.A.	Orange	Riverside	San Fran	West Coast	State Fair	New World	Pacific Rim	San Diego
3 AWARDS									
RENWOOD WINES '00, California, Sierra Series $11		S				S			B
ROSENBLUM CELLARS 'NV, California Cuvee XXIV $9.50	S		S		G				
JEFF RUNQUIST WINES '00, Amador Co., Nostro Vino Vnyd,. $24		B	B		S				
V. SATTUI WINERY '00, Napa Vly., Howell Mtn. $27	B						B		B
SEVEN LIONS WINERY '00, Sonoma Co., Three Amigo's Vnyds. $28	B	S			B				
SINGLE LEAF '99, El Dorado $13			B					B	B
STARRY NIGHT WINERY '00, Russian River, Tom Feeney Ranch $24		B				S			B
STEVENOT '00, Sierra Foothills, Costello Vnyd. $30	B	B		S					
STONEHEDGE '99, Napa Vly. $20		B		B			B		
STORRS '99, Santa Clara Co., Rusty Ridge $25		B		Σ		S			
TRINITY OAKS '99, California $10			B		G		S		
TURNING LEAF '98, Coastal Rsv., North Coast $10	S			B		B			
VILLA MT. EDEN '00, Napa Vly., Mead Ranch Rsv. $22	B			B		S			
VILLA MT. EDEN '00, Sierra Foothills, Fox Creek Vnyd. $23	G					S	B		
VISTA DEL REY VINEYARDS '99, Paso Robles, Puno Hierro Estet $20				S	S				S
WILSON WINERY '00, Dry Creek Vly. Carl's Vnyd. $25		B	S			B			
ZINGARO '99, Mendocino Co., Rsv. $18		S				S			S
2 AWARDS									
AMADOR FOOTHILL WINERY '99, Shenandoah Vly., Ferrero Vnyd. $15			B			B			

Zinfandel

2 AWARDS

L.A.	Orange	Riverside	San Fran	West Coast	State Fair	New World	Pacific Rim	San Diego	Wine
	B				G				**BARGETTO** '00, Lodi, Rauser Vnyd. $12
S			S						**BARON HERZOG WINE CELLARS** '00, Old Vine Lodi $13
	G				B				**BATTAGLINI ESTATE WINERY** '00, Russian River Vly. Rsv. $33
	S				G				**BATTAGLINI ESTATE WINERY** '00, Russian River Vly., Twin Pines $25
B			B						**BEAR CREEK** '00, Old Vine Zinfandel Lodi $18
	B				B				**BENESSERE VINEYARDS** '00, Napa Vly., BK Collins $28
S			S						**BENESSERE VINEYARDS** '00, Napa Vly., Black Glass Vnyd. $35
B			B						**BLACK SHEEP** '99, Calaveras Co., Beckman Vnyd. $15
B			S						**BOEGER** '99, El Dorado, Walker Vnyd. $15
S		S							**BUEHLER VINEYARDS** '99, Napa Vly. $12
	G	B							**BUEHLER VINEYARDS** '99, Napa Vly. Estate $25
B	B								**CAMELLIA CELLARS** '00, Dry Creek Vly., Lencioni Vnyd. $22
B			B						**CASTLE VINEYARDS** '99, Sonoma Vly. $19
		B				B			**CLAUDIA SPRINGS** '99, Redwood Vly., Vassar Vnyd. $20
	S		B						**CLINE CELLARS** '00, Contra Costa, Live Oak $28
	S				B				**COULSON EL DORADO** '00, El Dorado Safari Vnyd. $18
						G	B		**DE LOACH VINEYARDS** '99, California $11
	S	Σ							**DEUX AMIS** '99, Sonoma Co. $19

Zinfandel	L.A.	Orange	Riverside	San Fran	West Coast	State Fair	New World	Pacific Rim	San Diego
2 AWARDS									
DOMAINE DANICA '00, Russian River Vly., Salzgaber Vnyd. $30		S				S			
DRY CREEK VINEYARD '00, Sonoma Co. Old Vines $21					S				S
EDMEADES '99, Mendocino Ridge $25			B		B				
EDMEADES '99, Mendocino Ridge Zeni Vnyd. $25			S				B		
GARY FARRELL '00, Dry Creek Vly., Bradford Mtn. $36	B	S							
FORESTVILLE VINEYARD '00, California $6						S	B		
FRESNO STATE VINEYARDS '00, California, Duarte Linden Hills Vnyd., Primitivo Rsv. $15	Σ						S		
FREY VINEYARDS '00, Mendocino Co., Organic $10.50	S				Σ				
GALLO OF SONOMA '98, Alexander Vly., Barelli Creek Vnyd. $20	B				B				
GRANITE SPRINGS '99, Sierra Foothills, La Falda de la Sierra $13		B				S			
EMILIO GUGLIELMO WINERY '99, Santa Clara Vly., Rsv. $13		B		B					
HIDDEN CELLARS '98, Old Vines, Mendocino Co. $13		B							B
HUNT CELLARS '00, Paso Robles, Outlaw Ridge $35	G	B							
HUNT CELLARS '00, Paso Robles, Zinphony 2 $30		S			G				
KENDALL-JACKSON WINERY '00, Great Estates, Mendocino Co. $30		G				S			
KENWOOD VINEYARDS '99, Sonoma Vly., Nun's Canyon Vnyd. $20				Σ			G		
LATCHAM VINEYARDS '99, El Dorado $16							S	B	
LEDSON WINERY & VINEYARDS '99, Russian River Vly. Old Vine $36		B					B		

Zinfandel

2 AWARDS

L.A.	Orange	Riverside	San Fran	West Coast	State Fair	New World	Pacific Rim	San Diego	Wine
B								S	**J. LOHR ESTATE** '00, Cypress, California $10
	B		S						**LOLONIS** '99, Redwood Vly. Estate, Organic $18
	B				S				**MADRONA** '99, El Dorado Rsv. Estate $20
B								S	**MARTIN & WEYRICH WINERY** '99, Paso Robles, Dante Dusi Rsv. $24
			B				G		**LOUIS M. MARTINI** '99, Sonoma Vly., Monte Rosso Vnyd. $35
	S		S						**MILLIAIRE** '98, Sierra Foothills, Ghirardelli $18
		S		S					**MONTEVINA** '99, Amador Co. $12
		B		B					**MONTEVINA** '98, Amador Co., Deaver Vnyd. $29
						S		B	**MONTHAVEN** '99, Coastal, California $10
B						B			**MOSS CREEK** '98, Napa Vly. $34
		S					B		**NAPA RIDGE** '97, North Coast $9
S					B				**J. PEDRONCELLI** '01, Sonoma Co., Vintage Select
		G					B		**PEIRANO ESTATE VINEYARDS** '97, Old Vine, Lodi Estate $11
		S				S			**PERRY CREEK VINEYARDS** '99, Sierra Foothills, Zin Man $12
			S	S					**QUIVIRA** '99, Dry Creek Vly. $20
G	Σ								**QUIVIRA** '99, Dry Creek Vly., Wine Creek Ranch $35
					B			S	**RANCHO ZABACO** '00, Dry Creek Vly., Chiotti Vnyds. $25
		B			B				**RANCHO ZABACO** '00, Sonoma Co. Heritage Vines $15

Zinfandel	L.A.	Orange	Riverside	San Fran	West Coast	State Fair	New World	Pacific Rim	San Diego
2 AWARDS									
RAVENSWOOD '99, Lodi $13				B		G			
RAVENSWOOD '99, Mendocino Co. $14				S		S			
RED ROCK '98, California $10		B	B						
ROSENBLUM CELLARS '00, Alexander Vly., Harris Kratka Vyd. $28							B	Σ	
ROSENBLUM CELLARS '00, Russian River Vly., Alegria $34	S			B					
ROSENBLUM CELLARS '00, San Francisco Bay, Carla's Vnyd. $23		Σ				G			
ROSENBLUM CELLARS '00, San Francisco Bay, Continente Vnyd. $16	Σ						B		
ROSENBLUM CELLARS '00, Sonoma Vly., Samsel Vnyd., Maggie's Rsv. $40		Σ						B	
ERIC ROSS '99, Russian River Vly., Feeney Ranch $27		G		B					
ERIC ROSS '99, Russian River Vly., Occidental Vnyd. $30		S		S					
SANTA BARBARA WINERY '01, Beaujour, California $10	G	G							
V. SATTUI WINERY '99, Napa Vly. Quaglia Vnyd. $22			B		S				
SAUSAL WINERY '99, Alexander Vly. $15			B		S				
SAUSAL WINERY '99, Century Vines, Estate $24	G		B						
SEVEN LIONS WINERY '00, Russian River, Joe & Emily's Vnyd. $60	S	B							
SEVEN LIONS WINERY '00, Russian River, Poor Man's Flat Vnyd. $35		S			S				
SONORA WINERY & PORT WORKS '00, Amador Co. $22		B						G	

L.A.	Orange	Riverside	San Fran	West Coast	State Fair	New World	Pacific Rim	San Diego	Zinfandel
									2 AWARDS
B		G							**SONORA WINERY & PORT WORKS** '00, Amador Co. TC Vnyd. $26
					B			B	**STARRY NIGHT WINERY** '00, Lodi $16
						S	B		**STONEHEDGE** '00, California $10
				G		S			**STRYKER SONOMA WINERY &** '99, Dry Creek Vly., Sommer Vnyd. $22
				S		G			**STRYKER SONOMA WINERY &** '99, Old Vine, Alexander Vly. $25
		Σ			B				**SUNSET CELLARS** '99, Dry Creek Vly. $23
	S			S					**TOPOLOS AT RUSSIAN RIVER** '99, Sonoma Vly., Rossi Ranch $27.50
				B		B			**VALLEY OF THE MOON** '99, Sonoma Co. $15
		S		S					**VAN ASPEREN** '99, Napa Vly. $18
B					S				**WILD HORSE** '99, The Slacker, Paso Robles
			S	G					**ZAHTILA VINEYARDS** '99, Napa Vly. Estate $30

Bordeaux

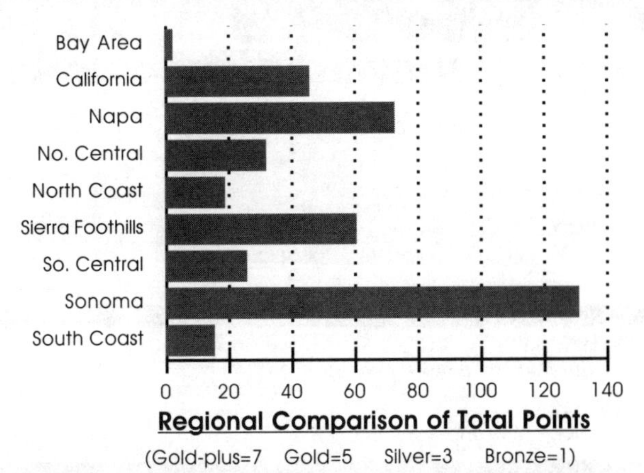

Regional Comparison of Total Points

(Gold-plus=7 Gold=5 Silver=3 Bronze=1)

Highest Individual Wine Totals

35 — **GEYSER PEAK**
'99, Petite Verdot, Sonoma Co., $20.00

26 — **GEYSER PEAK**
'99, Cabernet Franc, Alexander Vly., $20.00

25 — **ST. SUPÉRY**
'99, Cabernet Franc, Napa Vly., Dollarhide Ranch, $35.00

24 — **RAYMOND BURR VINEYARDS**
'99, Cabernet Franc, Dry Creek Vly., $36.00

21 — **PEPPERWOOD GROVE**
'99, Cabernet Franc, California, $9.00

20 — **GEYSER PEAK**
'99, Malbec, Alexander Vly., $20.00

19 — **KENDALL-JACKSON WINERY**
'99, Cabernet Franc, Vintner's Rsv., California, $15.00

17 — **CONN CREEK**
'99, Cabernet Franc, Napa Vly. Rsv., $25.00

16 — **INDIAN SPRINGS VINEYARDS**
'99, Cabernet Franc, Nevada Co., $16.00

16 — **STUART CELLARS**
'00, Cabernet Franc, South Coast, $25.00

15 — **LATCHAM VINEYARDS**
'99, Cabernet Franc, Fair Play Estate, $15.00

Other Bordeaux Varietals

Wine	L.A.	Orange	Riverside	San Fran	West Coast	State Fair	New World	Pacific Rim	San Diego
9 AWARDS									
GEYSER PEAK '99, Petite Verdot, Sonoma Co. $20	G	S	Σ	B	B	G	G	Σ	B
PEPPERWOOD GROVE '99, Cabernet Franc, California $9	B	G	B	B	B	S	S	B	G
ST. SUPÉRY '99, Cabernet Franc, Napa Vly., Dollarhide Ranch $35	S	B	B	S	S	S	Σ	S	B
8 AWARDS									
GEYSER PEAK '99, Cabernet Franc, Alexander Vly. $20	S	G	S	B	B	G	B	Σ	
GEYSER PEAK '99, Malbec, Alexander Vly. $20	B	S	S		S	S	S	S	B
7 AWARDS									
KENDALL-JACKSON WINERY '99, Cabernet Franc, Vintner's Rsv., California $15	Σ	S		B	B	S		S	B
6 AWARDS									
RAYMOND BURR VINEYARDS '99, Cabernet Franc, Dry Creek Vly. $36	S	G	Σ	B		G			S
DE ROSE '99, Cabernet Franc, Cienega, Cardillo Vnyd. $20			B	B	B	Σ	S		B
INDIAN SPRINGS VINEYARDS '99, Cabernet Franc, Nevada Co. $16		B	S	B		S	Σ	B	
5 AWARDS									
CONN CREEK '99, Cabernet Franc, Napa Vly. Rsv. $25	S		S		B	G		G	
IMAGERY SERIES '99, Malbec, Alexander Vly. $33	S			B	S	G		B	
LATCHAM VINEYARDS '99, Cabernet Franc, Fair Play Estate $15		G	S	S		S		B	
4 AWARDS									
LEANING OAK '98, Cabernet Franc, Napa Vly. $28			S	B	B	B			
R. H. PHILLIPS '99, Malbec, Toasted Head, Dunnigan Hills $17	B	S		B			B		

Other Bordeaux Varietals

4 AWARDS

L.A.	Orange	Riverside	San Fran	West Coast	State Fair	New World	Pacific Rim	San Diego	Wine
	S	G			S			G	**STUART CELLARS** '00, Cabernet Franc, South Coast $25
B		B			B	B			**YORKVILLE CELLARS** '99, Malbec, Rennie Vnyd. $17
		B	S			B		S	**YORKVILLE CELLARS** '99, Petite Verdot, Rennie Vnyd. $17

3 AWARDS

L.A.	Orange	Riverside	San Fran	West Coast	State Fair	New World	Pacific Rim	San Diego	Wine
			B			B	B		**BUTTONWOOD FARM** '98, Cabernet Franc, Santa Ynez Vly. $18
	S				S	S			**EDGEWOOD** '98, Malbec, Napa Vly. $22
B			B		S				**IRONSTONE VINEYARDS** '99, Cabernet Franc, Sierra Foothills Rsv. $18
	G		S		S				**RANCHO SISQUOC** '99, Malbec, Santa Barbara, Flood Vnyd. $30

2 AWARDS

L.A.	Orange	Riverside	San Fran	West Coast	State Fair	New World	Pacific Rim	San Diego	Wine
		S	B						**COSENTINO WINERY** '99, Cabernet Franc, Napa Vly. $34
	B					G			**IRONSTONE VINEYARDS** '99, Cabernet Franc, California $9
	B				B				**MADRONA** '00, Cabernet Franc, El Dorado Est. $15
		B				S			**MC ILROY WINES** '99, Cabernet Franc, RRV, Salzgeber Vnyd. $24
B					S				**NEVADA CITY WINERY** '00, Cabernet Franc, Sierra Foothills
B	S								**RIO SECO VINEYARD** '99, Cabernet Franc, Paso Robles $24
	S						B		**SINGLE LEAF** '00, Cabernet Franc, Fair Play $16
	S				G				**STONY RIDGE WINERY** '99, Cabernet Franc, Cienega Vly. Rsv. $20
			S			S			**YORKVILLE CELLARS** '99, Cabernet Franc, Rennie Vnyd., Organic $17

Red Italian

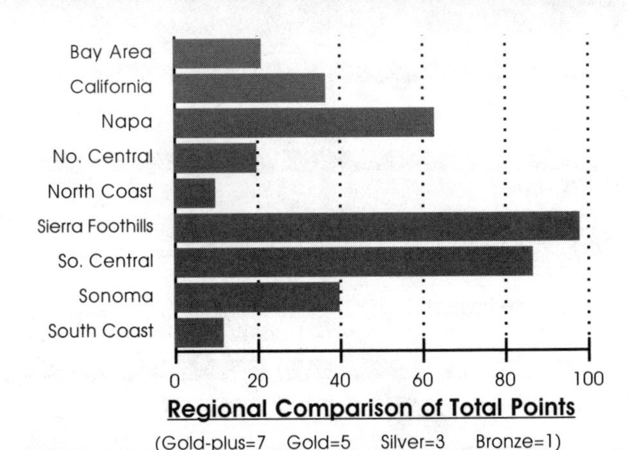

Regional Comparison of Total Points

(Gold-plus=7 Gold=5 Silver=3 Bronze=1)

Highest Individual Wine Totals

21 **JEFF RUNQUIST WINES**
'00, Barbera, Amador, Cooper Vnyd., $18.00

18 **FLORA SPRINGS**
'99, Poggio Del Papa, Cypress Ranch, $35.00

17 **EQUUS WINERY**
'99, Grenache, James Berry Vnyd., $18.00

17 **ROBERT PEPI WINERY**
'00, Barbera, California, $16.00

16 **DOCE ROBLES WINERY**
'99, Barbera, Paso Robles, $28.00

16 **MONTEVINA**
'98, Barbera, Terra D'Oro, Amador Co., $18.00

14 **BARGETTO**
'98, La Vita, Santa Cruz, Regan Vnyd., $50.00

13 **MONTEVINA**
'99, Barbera, Amador Co., $12.00

12 **MOSBY**
'00, Teroldego, Santa Barbara Co., $28.00

12 **SUNSET CELLARS**
'00, Barbera, Napa, Twin Creeks Vnyd., $18.00

Other Red Italian Varietals

Wine	L.A.	Orange	Riverside	San Fran	West Coast	State Fair	New World	Pacific Rim	San Diego
8 AWARDS									
FLORA SPRINGS '99, Poggio Del Papa, Cypress Ranch $35	B	B		B	G	B	Σ	B	B
7 AWARDS									
MONTEVINA '99, Barbera, Amador Co. $12	S	B	B	B	B	S		S	
ROBERT PEPI WINERY '00, Barbera, California $16	S		B	B		G	B	S	S
JEFF RUNQUIST WINES '00, Barbera, Amador, Cooper Vnyd. $18	B	B	B	S	Σ	B			Σ
6 AWARDS									
MONTEVINA '98, Barbera, Terra D'Oro, Amador Co. $18	S	S	B	B			S	G	
5 AWARDS									
EBERLE '00, Barbera, Sauret & Steinbeck Vnyds. $18	B	B	B	B					S
GALLO OF SONOMA '99, Barbera, AV, Barrelli Creek Vnyd. $22		B	B	B	B	B			
4 AWARDS									
BARGETTO '98, La Vita, Santa Cruz, Regan Vnyd. $50	B	S		Σ		S			
DOCE ROBLES WINERY '99, Barbera, Paso Robles $28	Σ		B				Σ		B
MARTIN & WEYRICH WINERY '99, Nebbiolo Il Vecchio, Paso Robles $24	S	S		S		B			
MOSBY '00, Teroldego, Santa Barbara Co. $28	S	B				G			S
MOUNT PALOMAR WINERY '99, Castelletto, Trovato, Temecula Vly. $18	B	S		B				B	
ROBERT PEPI WINERY '98, Colline Di Sassi, Napa Vly. $25	G		B	B	B				
3 AWARDS									
ALLORA VINEYARDS '99, Cielo, Stag's Leap/Howell Mtn. $45	S			B			S		
BOEGER '99, Charbono, Arrastra, El Dorado $25	S			S		S			
CAMELLIA CELLARS '99, Diamo Grazie, Dry Creek Vly. $42	B					S			B

Other Red Italian Varietals

L.A.	Orange	Riverside	San Fran	West Coast	State Fair	New World	Pacific Rim	San Diego	Winery / Wine
									3 AWARDS
	G		S		B				**CASA NUESTRA** '00, Tinto Classico, Oakville Estate $30
			S		G	B			**DE ROSE** '99, Negrette, Cienega, Miller Vnyd. $20
	S		Σ		Σ				**EQUUS WINERY** '99, Grenache, James Berry Vnyd. $18
S	B		B						**LOUIS M. MARTINI** '98, Barbera, Lake Co. $12
	B					S	B		**CHARLES B. MITCHELL VINEYARDS** 'NV, Bella Rossa, California $15
		B			S			S	**PIETRA SANTA** '99, Dolcetto, Cienega Vly. $20
	B	B		B					**RIOS-LOVELL WINERY** '01, Barbera, Livermore Vly. Estate $19
S	S			S					**TRENTADUE** '99, La Storia, Sonoma Co. $32
									2 AWARDS
B	B								**BOEGER** '00, Barbera, El Dorado Estate $15
	S			S					**LUCAS & LEWELLEN** '00, Barbera, Santa Barbara Co. $14
			S			B			**LA FAMIGLIA DI ROBERT MONDAVI** '99, Barbera, California $20
S						S			**MONTPELLIER VINEYARDS** '99, Tuscan Blend, California $7
	S				Σ				**MOSBY** '00, Dolcetto, Santa Barbara Co. $14
		B		S					**RIOS-LOVELL WINERY** '00, Barbera, Livermore Vly. Estate $17.50
Σ			B						**SHYPOKE WINERY** '99, Charbono, Napa Vly. $18
S	G								**ST. AMANT WINERY** '00, Barbera, Lodi $14
			Σ		G				**SUNSET CELLARS** '00, Barbera, Napa, Twin Creeks Vnyd. $18
S	S								**WILD HORSE** '99, Negrette, Calleri Vnyd. $18

Red Rhone

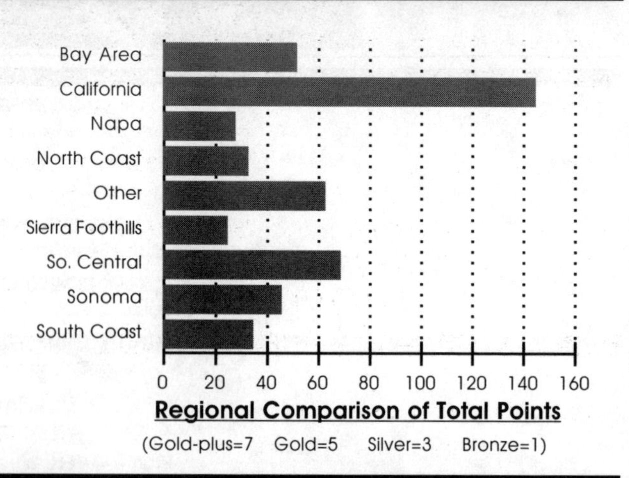

Regional Comparison of Total Points

(Gold-plus=7 Gold=5 Silver=3 Bronze=1)

Highest Individual Wine Totals

30 **VAN RUITEN-TAYLOR WINERY**
'00, Shiraz/Cab, Lodi Rsv., $12.00

24 **JADE MOUNTAIN**
'99, La Provencale, California, $17.50

24 **JESSIE'S GROVE WINERY**
'00, Carignane, Lodi, $15.00

23 **WINDSOR VINEYARDS**
'99, Carignane, Alexander Vly., Oat Vly. Vyds., $16.75

19 **STONE CELLARS**
'00, Syrah/Cab, California, $8.00

18 **WINDSOR VINEYARDS**
'98, Carignane, Mendocino Co., $11.50

17 **ZACA MESA**
'00, Santa Barbara Co. Z Cuvee, $16.00

16 **EBERLE**
'00, Syrah/Cab, Paso Robles, $24.00

16 **KENDALL-JACKSON WINERY**
'00, Collage, Shiraz/Cabernet, $10.00

16 **SWANSON**
'99, Alexis, Napa Vly., $50.00

Other Red Rhone Varietals & Blends

L.A.	Orange	Riverside	San Fran	West Coast	State Fair	New World	Pacific Rim	San Diego	Winery / Wine
8 AWARDS									
Σ	S	G	S	B		S	B	B	**JADE MOUNTAIN** '99, La Provencale, California $17.50
S	B	S	B		G	S	S	G	**JESSIE'S GROVE WINERY** '00, Carignane, Lodi $15
B		S	S	S	B	B	S	B	**KENDALL-JACKSON WINERY** '00, Collage, Shiraz/Cabernet $10
S	S	S	G	G	S	S		G	**VAN RUITEN-TAYLOR WINERY** '00, Shiraz/Cab, Lodi Rsv. $12
7 AWARDS									
B	S	S	G		B	S		S	**STONE CELLARS** '00, Syrah/Cab, California $8
B	G	B	B	S		B	B		**THORNTON** '99, Cote Red, South Coast $14
S	S	G	B	G	S		S		**WINDSOR VINEYARDS** '99, Carignane, Alexander Vly., Oat Vly. Vyds. $16.75
6 AWARDS									
S	S	B		S	G		B		**EBERLE** '00, Syrah/Cab, Paso Robles $24
B	S	G	B			B	B		**R. H. PHILLIPS** '99, Syrah/Cab, Toasted Head $17
	B	B		S	B		B	B	**WINDSOR VINEYARDS** '99, Carignane, Mendocino Co. $11.50
S	S	S			S	S	S		**WINDSOR VINEYARDS** '98, Carignane, Mendocino Co. $11.50
5 AWARDS									
S	S				B	B		Σ	**BEAULIEU** '99, Ensemble, Signet, California $25
B			B	S			Σ	B	**PERRY CREEK VINEYARDS** '00, Coteau De Michel, California $16
S	G	B	B	S					**QUIVIRA** '00, Dry Creek Cuvee $19
B		G			S		S	S	**SIERRA VISTA** '00, Fleur De Montagne, El Dorado $21
B	B	B			B		G		**STELTZNER VINEYARDS** '99, Pinotage, Napa Vly. Stags Leap $26

Other Red Rhone Varietals & Blends

Winery / Wine	L.A.	Orange	Riverside	San Fran	West Coast	State Fair	New World	Pacific Rim	San Diego
5 AWARDS									
ZACA MESA '00, Santa Barbara Co. Z Cuvee $16	B	S	Σ	S		S			
4 AWARDS									
CONCANNON VINEYARD '99, Rhone Blend, San Francisco Bay $18	S	B		B	S				
KENDALL-JACKSON WINERY '99, Collage, Shiraz/Zinfandel $10	B				B		B		B
NEVADA CITY WINERY '99, Solaire, California $16	B		B			S		S	
SEVEN PEAKS '99, Cab/Syrah, Paso Robles $20	S	G	S						B
SWANSON '99, Alexis, Napa Vly. $50	Σ	G		B					S
3 AWARDS									
BONNY DOON VINEYARD '00, Le Cigare Volant, California $32	S	G		G					
EQUUS WINERY '99, Mourvedre, Paso Robles $18	S	S				S			
HART WINERY '99, Grenache-Syrah, South Coast $14	B						S		B
2 AWARDS									
CLINE CELLARS '00, Mourvèdre, Contra Costa $32		Σ		S					
THOMAS COYNE '00, Mourvedre, Contra Costa Co. $14		G				S			
THOMAS COYNE '00, Quest, California $11		G				B			
CURTIS '99, Heritage Cuvee, Central Coast $12	G						B		
GALLEANO '99, Ramon's Red, Cucamonga Vly. $9	B	S							
INCOGNITO 'NV, Rhone Blends, Lodi $22		G				B			
J. LOHR ESTATE '00, Painter Bridge, Syrah/Zinfandel $7				B		S			
NAVARRO VINEYARDS '99, Mourvedre, Mendocino $20							B	S	

Other Red Rhone Varietals & Blends

2 AWARDS

L.A.	Orange	Riverside	San Fran	West Coast	State Fair	New World	Pacific Rim	San Diego	Wine
	S		Σ						**RAVENSWOOD** '99, Icon, Sonoma Co. $20
	G	B							**RENAISSANCE** '00, Sierra Foothills Mediterranean Red $19
	B		B						**TULIP HILL WINERY** '00, Shiraz/Cab, San Joaquin $38
G		G							**WILSON CREEK WINERY & VINEYARD** '00, Mourvedre, Temecula $23

White Varietals

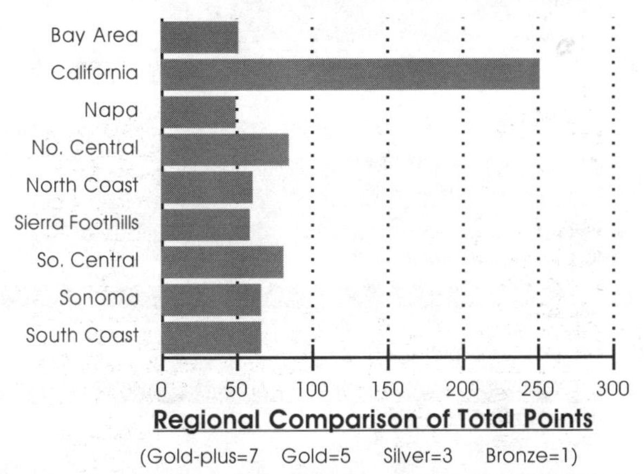

Regional Comparison of Total Points

(Gold-plus=7 Gold=5 Silver=3 Bronze=1)

Highest Individual Wine Totals

27	**CURTIS** '00, Heritage Blanc, Santa Barbara Co., $12.00
25	**ST. SUPÉRY** '01, Moscato, California, $15.00
23	**KENDALL-JACKSON WINERY** '00, Marsanne, Vintner's Rsv., $16.00
20	**KENDALL-JACKSON WINERY** '00, Semillon, Vintner's Rsv., $10.00
20	**NAVARRO VINEYARDS** '01, Chenin Blanc, Old Vine Cuveé, $9.75
19	**FANUCCHI VINEYARDS** '01, Trousseau Gris, Russian River Vly., Fanucchi Wood Road Vnyd., $13.00
19	**IRONSTONE VINEYARDS** '01, Obsession Symphony, $8.00
19	**MIRASSOU** '00, Pinot Blanc, Coastal Selection, $9.00
16	**MAURICE CAR'RIE WINERY** '01, Muscat Canelli, Temecula, $11.00
16	**PERRY CREEK VINEYARDS** '01, Muscat, El Dorado Estate, $9.00
15	**GNEKOW FAMILY WINERY** '00, YN, Blended Vnyd., California, $4.00

Other White Varietals & Blends

Wine	L.A.	Orange	Riverside	San Fran	West Coast	State Fair	New World	Pacific Rim	San Diego
9 AWARDS									
CURTIS '00, Heritage Blanc, Santa Barbara Co. $12	B	G	Σ	B	B	S	Σ	B	B
KENDALL-JACKSON WINERY '00, Marsanne, Vintner's Rsv. $16	S	G	Σ	B	B	B	B	B	S
ST. SUPÉRY '01, Moscato, California, R.S. 6.82 $15	B	G	S	S	S	S	B	S	S
7 AWARDS									
MIRASSOU '00, Pinot Blanc, Coastal Selection $9	B		B		Σ	S	S	S	B
6 AWARDS									
MAURICE CAR'RIE WINERY '01, Muscat Canelli, Temecula $11	S	G	B			S	S		B
EBERLE '01, Muscat Canelli, Paso Robles $12	S		B	G		S	B	B	
KENDALL-JACKSON WINERY '00, Semillon, Vintner's Rsv. $10	S	B		G		S	Σ		B
ORFILA VINEYARDS 'NV, Lotus, San Pasqual Vly. $28		S		S		B	B	B	B
PERRY CREEK VINEYARDS '01, Muscat, El Dorado Estate $9	S	S		B	B		Σ	B	
ST. SUPÉRY '00, Semillon, Napa Vly., Dollarhide $21	B	G	B		B	G		B	
WINDSOR VINEYARDS '01, French Colombard, California $7.25	B	S	B	B	S	B			
5 AWARDS									
ABUNDANCE WINERY '00, Pinot Blanc, Napa, Yount Mill Vnyds. $18	B	S			S	S			S
FANUCCHI VINEYARDS '01, Trousseau Gris, Russian River Vly., Fanucchi Wood Road Vnyd. $13	B	Σ	G	B	G				
FANUCCHI VINEYARDS '00, Trousseau Gris, Russian River Vly., Fanucchi Wood Road Vnyd. $13	B		S	B			S		B
GNEKOW FAMILY WINERY '00, YN, Blended Vnyd., California $4	B	S	G	B		G			
IRONSTONE VINEYARDS '01, Obsession Symphony $8	S	S			S	S	Σ		

Other White Varietals & Blends

5 AWARDS

L.A.	Orange	Riverside	San Fran	West Coast	State Fair	New World	Pacific Rim	San Diego	Wine
S	G	B	B	B					**MEADOR ESTATE** '00, Chenin Blanc, Arroyo Seco $18
B	B	B			S			B	**MOUNT PALOMAR WINERY** '00, Cortese - Castelletto, Temecula $18
S			S			S	B	B	**SUTTER HOME** '00, Chenin Blanc, Signature, California $6

4 AWARDS

L.A.	Orange	Riverside	San Fran	West Coast	State Fair	New World	Pacific Rim	San Diego	Wine
	G	B	S		S				**BAILY VINEYARD & WINERY** '01, Muscat, Temecula $15
B	S		S		G				**BLACK SHEEP** '01, Semillon, Calaveras Co. $12
B				S	G		B		**CONCANNON VINEYARD** '01, Orange Muscat, Livermore Vly. $11
		S	B	S				S	**DK CELLARS** '00, Semillon, Sierra Foothills $15
S	G		B		B				**EQUUS WINERY** '00, Roussanne Paso Robles $16
		S	B		S	B			**FOLIE A'DEUX** '00, Petite Folie, Menage a Trois California $12
S		B		S			B		**KENDALL-JACKSON WINERY** '00, Pinot Blanc, Vintner's Rsv. $13
	G	Σ		Σ			B		**NAVARRO VINEYARDS** '01, Chenin Blanc, Old Vine Cuveé $9.75
S				S	G			S	**SONORA WINERY & PORT WORKS** '01, Verdelho, California $13
B		B		S			S		**VENTANA VINEYARDS** '99, Pinot Blanc, Monterey, Arroyo Seco $14
		B		S	B		B		**VENTANA VINEYARDS** '00, Chenin Blanc, Monterey $10
B	B			B		B			**WEIBEL** 'NV, Green Hungarian, California $6

3 AWARDS

L.A.	Orange	Riverside	San Fran	West Coast	State Fair	New World	Pacific Rim	San Diego	Wine
					S	B	B		**BAYWOOD** '00, Symphony, California Vyd. Select $8
Σ	B		B						**BONNY DOON VINEYARD** '01, Malvasia Bianca, Ca'del Solo $12

Other White Varietals & Blends

3 AWARDS

Winery / Wine	L.A.	Orange	Riverside	San Fran	West Coast	State Fair	New World	Pacific Rim	San Diego
CONCANNON VINEYARD '00, Rhone Blend, San Francisco Bay $16		G		B	B				
THOMAS COYNE '01, Pinot Blanc, Detjens Farms $16		S			S	G			
DRY CREEK VINEYARD '01, Chenin Blanc, Clarksburg $9	S	S							B
KENDALL-JACKSON WINERY '01, Muscat Canelli, Vintner's Rsv. $10			S		B				B
MIRASSOU '00, Pinot Blanc, Mission Vnyd. $24		B	G		B				
ROSENBLUM CELLARS '00, Marsanne, Dry Creek Vly. $28		S		S	Σ				
ROSENBLUM CELLARS '00, Muscat De Glacier, California $17		B			B		G		
V. SATTUI WINERY '01, Muscat, California $16				S		Σ			S
SUTTER HOME '00, Moscato California, R.S. 8 $8		Σ		B		B			
THORNTON '00, Moscato, South Coast $10	B		B						B
THORNTON '00, Pinot Blanc, So. Coast, Miramonte $10	B	S							S
VENTANA VINEYARDS '00, Pinot Blanc, Monterey, Arroyo Seco $14	S	B				S			
WILD HORSE '01, Malvasia Bianca, Monterey $13	B	S		B					
YORKVILLE CELLARS '00, Semillon, Randle Hill Vnyd. $13	S		B				B		

2 AWARDS

Winery / Wine	L.A.	Orange	Riverside	San Fran	West Coast	State Fair	New World	Pacific Rim	San Diego
BAREFOOT CELLARS 'NV, Barefoot On The Beach White $4								B	S
BARON HERZOG WINE CELLARS '01, Chenin Blanc, Clarksburg $7	S		Σ						
BUTTONWOOD FARM '00, Marsanne, Santa Ynez Vly. $12			S				B		
MAURICE CAR'RIE WINERY '01, Chenin Blanc, Temecula $7			S			S			

Other White Varietals & Blends

2 AWARDS

L.A.	Orange	Riverside	San Fran	West Coast	State Fair	New World	Pacific Rim	San Diego	Winery / Wine
		G						B	**CHUMEIA VINEYARDS** '00, Pinot Blanc, Monterey Co. $14
	B	B							**COSENTINO WINERY** '00, Semillon Dry, Napa Vly. The Sem $22
		B					S		**HANDLEY** '01, Brightlighter White, Anderson Vly. $11
			B	B					**IMAGERY SERIES** '99, Pinot Blanc, Santa Maria $21
				B			G		**IMAGERY SERIES** '99, White Burgundy, Napa Vly. $25
B							S		**IMAGERY SERIES** '00, White Burgundy, Napa Vly.
							S	S	**LAETITIA** '00, Pinot Blanc, Arroyo Grande $25
	B	Σ							**LOUIS M. MARTINI** '00, Folle Blanc, Sonoma, Monte Rosso $15
			B			G			**LA FAMIGLIA DI ROBERT MONDAVI** '00, Moscato Bianco California $16
				S		S			**MONTPELLIER VINEYARDS** '99, Semillion/Chardonnay, California $7
		S		S					**NAPA RIDGE** '98, Semillon, Napa Vly. $9
			B		S				**NAVARRO VINEYARDS** '01, Edelzwicker Mendocino $10
	S			S					**RIDEAU VINEYARD** '01, Chenin Blanc, Santa Barbara $15
B						B			**V. SATTUI WINERY** '00, Muscat, California $15.75
	B				S				**ST. AMANT WINERY** '01, Le Mystere, Amador Co. $18
							B	B	**VENTANA VINEYARDS** '99, Muscat D'orange, Monterey Co. $12
B	B								**WILD HORSE** '01, Arneis, San Benito $16
S								S	**WINDSOR VINEYARDS** '01, Chenin Blanc, California $8.25

Other White Varietals & Blends

2 AWARDS

	L.A.	Orange	Riverside	San Fran	West Coast	State Fair	New World	Pacific Rim	San Diego
WINDSOR VINEYARDS '00, Chenin Blanc, California $8.25			B					B	
WINDSOR VINEYARDS '00, French Colombard, North Coast $7.25							S	B	
WINDSOR VINEYARDS '00, Semillon, Mendocino Co. Rsv. $15.75							B		S
YORK MOUNTAIN '01, Roussane Paso Robles $20				S		S			

Hop Kiln Winery, Russian River Valley, Sonoma County

ALL VARIETALS

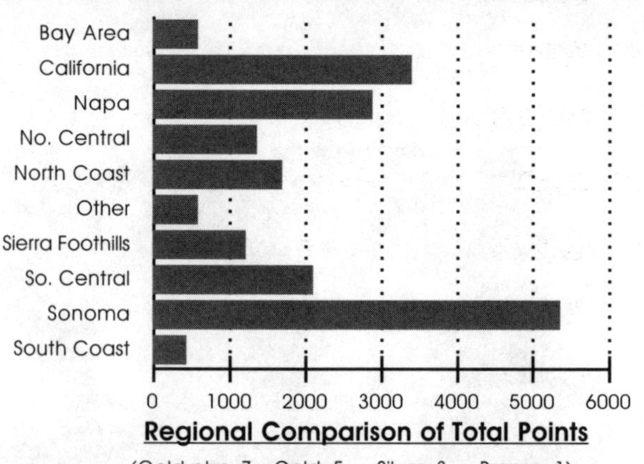

Regional Comparison of Total Points

(Gold-plus=7 Gold=5 Silver=3 Bronze=1)

Highest Individual Wine Totals

(Number of wines)	Total	Average	Winery
(53)	**679**	*12.8*	**KENDALL-JACKSON WINERY** Santa Rosa CA
(34)	**515**	*15.1*	**GEYSER PEAK** Geyserville CA
(47)	**409**	*8.7*	**WINDSOR VINEYARDS** Windsor CA
(24)	**319**	*13.3*	**FETZER** Hopland CA
(30)	**287**	*9.6*	**GALLO OF SONOMA** Healdsburg CA
(15)	**281**	*18.7*	**ST. SUPÉRY** Rutherford CA
(37)	**228**	*6.2*	**BERINGER** St Helena CA
(31)	**210**	*6.8*	**ROSENBLUM CELLARS** Alameda CA
(21)	**209**	*10.0*	**NAVARRO VINEYARDS** Philo CA
(20)	**188**	*9.4*	**GUENOC** Middletown CA
(16)	**188**	*11.8*	**MERIDIAN VINEYARDS** Paso Robles CA
(15)	**180**	*12.0*	**JEKEL VINEYARDS** Greenfield CA

(23)	**170**	*7.4*	**V. SATTUI WINERY** St Helena CA
(27)	**162**	*6.0*	**CONCANNON VINEYARD** Livermore CA
(15)	**161**	*10.7*	**RODNEY STRONG** Windsor CA
(10)	**150**	*15.0*	**JEFF RUNQUIST WINES** X CA
(13)	**147**	*11.3*	**LA CREMA** Windsor CA
(15)	**147**	*9.8*	**PERRY CREEK VINEYARDS** Somerset CA
(17)	**141**	*8.3*	**EBERLE** Paso Robles CA
(16)	**139**	*8.7*	**MONTEVINA** Plymouth CA
(29)	**138**	*4.8*	**BEAULIEU** Rutherford CA
(18)	**136**	*7.6*	**J. LOHR ESTATE** San Jose CA
(14)	**133**	*9.5*	**MIRASSOU** San Jose CA
(8)	**131**	*16.4*	**TRENTADUE** Geyserville CA
(15)	**129**	*8.6*	**KENWOOD VINEYARDS** Kenwood CA
(10)	**127**	*12.7*	**RAYMOND** St Helena CA
(7)	**124**	*17.7*	**GLORIA FERRER** Sonoma CA
(19)	**117**	*6.2*	**DRY CREEK VINEYARD** Healdsburg CA
(9)	**115**	*12.8*	**GREENWOOD RIDGE** Philo CA
(11)	**114**	*10.4*	**STERLING VINEYARDS** Calistoga CA
(9)	**113**	*12.6*	**DOMAINE CHANDON** Yountville CA
(17)	**111**	*6.5*	**IMAGERY SERIES** Glen Ellen CA
(9)	**110**	*12.2*	**WATTLE CREEK** Healdsburg CA

ABUNDANCE WINERY

6194 Lockwood Dr., Windsor 95492

Chardonnay, '00, Clarksburg, Clos d'Abundance $21.00 (2)
Chardonnay, '00, Santa Maria, Bien Nacido Vnyd. $21.00 (3)
Pinot Noir, '99, Sonoma Coast, Brick Hill Block $28.00 (B-San Diego)
Syrah, '99, Paso Robles, French Camp Vnyd. $18.00 (2)
Viognier, '00, Talmage Block (B-L.A.)
White Varietals, '00, Pinot Blanc, Napa, Yount Mill Vnyds. $18.00 (5)
Zinfandel, '00, Lodi, Mencarini Vnyds. Old Vine $14.00 (4)

ACACIA WINERY

2750 Las Amigas Road, Napa 94558
www.chalonewinegroup.com

Chardonnay, '00, Carneros $21.75 (S-Riverside)
Pinot Noir, '00, Carneros, Napa Vly. $27.00 (5)

ADLER FELS

5325 Corrick Lane, Santa Rosa 95405
www.adlerfels.com

Gewurztraminer, '01, Russian River Vly. $12.00 (4)
Sauvignon Blanc, '00, Russian River Fume Blanc $14.00 (2)
White Dessert, '00, Gewurztraminer, RRV $14.00 (S-New World)

AHLGREN VINEYARD

20320 Hwy. 9, Boulder Creek 95006
www.ahlgrenvineyard.com

Bordeaux, '99, Cabernet Franc, Bates Ranch $26.00 (B-San Fran)
Cabernet Sauvignon, '99, SCM, Bates Ranch $28.00 (B-San Fran)
Syrah, '99, Monterey Co., Ventana Vnyds. $24.00 (2)

ALBERTONI VINEYARDS

Address Not Available

Cabernet Sauvignon, '99, California $13.00 (2)
Merlot, '00, California $13.00 (2)
Pinot Gris, '00, California Pinot Grigio $13.00 (5)
Sangiovese, '01, California $13.00 (4)
Sangiovese, '99, California $13.00 (2)
Zinfandel, '00, California Primitivo $13.00 (3)
Zinfandel, '98, California Primitivo $13.00 (B-Riverside)

ALDERBROOK WINERY

2306 Magnolia Drive, Healdsburg 95448
www.alderbrook.com

Zinfandel, '99, Sonoma Co. $19.00 (4)

ALEXANDER VALLEY VINEYARDS

8644 Highway 128, Healdsburg 95448
www.avvwine.com

Bordeaux, '00, Cabernet Franc, Alexander Vly. $20.00 (B-San Fran)
Cabernet Sauvignon, '00, Alexander Vly. Estate $20.00 (S-San Fran)
Cabernet Sauvignon, '99, Alexander Vly. Estate $20.00 (2)
Chardonnay, '00, Alexander Vly. Estate $15.25 (3)
Chardonnay, '00, Alexander Vly. Rsv. $20.00 (S-W. Coast)
Gewurztraminer, '01, North Coast, Mendocino Co. $9.00 (4)
Merlot, '00, Alexander Vly. Estate $20.00 (2)
Merlot, '99, Alexander Vly. Estate $20.00 (S-New World)
Pinot Noir, '00, Alexander Vly. Estate $20.00 (4)
Red Meritage, '98, Cyrus, Alexander Vly. $50.00 (4)

Sangiovese, '00, Alexander Vly. Estate $20.00 (3)
Syrah, '00, Alexander Vly. Estate $20.00 (5)
Syrah, '99, Alexander Vly. Estate $20.00 (G-New World)
Viognier, '00, Alexander Vly. Estate $25.00 (S-San Fran)

ALLORA VINEYARDS

Address Not Available
www.alloravineyards.com

Red Italian, '99, Cielo, Stag's Leap/Howell Mtn. $45.00 (3)
Red Meritage, '99, Tresca, Napa Vly., Allora Vnyd. $60.00 (4)

ALPEN CELLARS

P.O. Box 3966, Trinity Center 96091

Dry Riesling, '01, Trinity Co. (B-L.A.)
Gewurztraminer, '01, Trinity Co. $7.50 (2)

ALTERRA

Address Not Available

Sangiovese, '97, Sonoma Co. $18.00 (S-New World)
Sangiovese, '98, Sonoma Co. $18.00 (3)
Syrah, '98, Russian River Vly. $18.00 (G-New World)
Syrah, '99, Russian River Vly. $18.00 (3)

ALZANTE

Address Not Available

Red Italian, '99, Sierra Foothills (G-State Fair)
Sangiovese, '99, Sierra Foothills (S-State Fair)

AMADOR FOOTHILL WINERY

12500 Steiner Road, Plymouth 95669

Sauvignon Blanc, '00, Shenandoah Vly. $10.00 (2)
Syrah, '00, Sierra Foothills, Hollander Vnyd. $20.00 (2)
Zinfandel, '99, Shenandoah Vly., Ferrero Vnyd. $15.00 (2)

AMBERHILL

849 Zinfandel Lane, Saint Helena 94574
www.raymondwine.com

Cabernet Sauvignon, '99, California $12.00 (5)
Chardonnay, '00, California $10.00 (2)
Merlot, '99, California $12.00 (6)
Sauvignon Blanc, '00, California $6.00 (5)

ANAPAMU

3387 Dry Creek Rd., Healdsburg 95448
www.gallosonoma.com

Chardonnay, '00, Monterey Co. $16.00 (4)
Dry Riesling, '00, Monterey Co. $16.00 (5)
Syrah, '99, Paso Robles/Central Coast $20.00 (2)

ANTERRA

Address Not Available

Cabernet Sauvignon, '98, Napa Vly. Rsv. $37.00 (4)
Merlot, '98, Napa Vly. Rsv. $30.00 (5)

ARBIOS CELLARS

Address Not Available

Cabernet Sauvignon, '99, Alexander Vly. $30.00 (2)

ARMIDA WINERY

2201 Westside Road, Healdsburg 95448

Cabernet Sauvignon, '99, Dry Creek Vly., Scharf Vnyd. $30.00 (4)
Chardonnay, '00, Alexander Vly., Stuhlmuller Vnyd. $25.00 (2)

Chardonnay, '00, Russian River Vly. $19.00 (B-San Diego)
Chardonnay, '99, Russian River Vly. $19.00 (2)
Chardonnay, '99, Russian River Vly. Rsv. (2)
Merlot, '99, Russian River Vly. $24.00 (3)
Pinot Noir, '99, Russian River Vly. $22.00 (2)
Zinfandel, '00, Dry Creek Vly. $20.00 (3)
Zinfandel, '00, Dry Creek Vly., Maple Vnyd. $30.00 (5)

ARROW CREEK WINERY

Address Not Available

Cabernet Sauvignon, '99, California $10.00 (2)
Chardonnay, '00, California $10.00 (2)
Merlot, '99, California $10.00 (2)

ARROWOOD

14347 Sonoma Hwy., Glen Ellen 95442

Cabernet Sauvignon, '99, Sonoma Co. $22.00 (B-San Fran)
Chardonnay, '00, Sonoma Co., Grand Archer (S-State Fair)
Merlot, '99, Sonoma Co., Grand Archer $20.00 (B-San Fran)

ATLAS PEAK VINEYARD

3700 Soda Canyon Rd., Napa 95448
www.atlaspeak.com

Cabernet Sauvignon, '96, Napa Vly., Consenso Vnyd. $30.00 (3)
Chardonnay, '00, Napa Vly. $16.00 (S-San Fran)
Sangiovese, '99, Napa Vly. $16.00 (4)
Sangiovese, '99, Napa Vly., Atlas Peak Rsv. $30.00 (4)

B

BAILEYANA VINEYARD

5880 Edna Rd., San Luis Obispo 93401

Chardonnay, '00, Edna Vly., Firepeak Vnyd. $30.00 (4)
Chardonnay, '00, San Luis Obispo-Monterey $18.00 (4)
Chardonnay, '99, Edna Vly., Firepeak Vnyd. $30.00 (2)
Pinot Noir, '00, Edna Vly. $23.00 (3)
Pinot Noir, '00, Edna Vly., Firepeak Vnyd. (Σ-State Fair)
Pinot Noir, '99, Edna Vly. $23.00 (3)
Pinot Noir, '99, Edna Vly., Firepeak Vnyd. $38.00 (4)
Sauvignon Blanc, '00, Edna Vly. $13.00 (2)
Sauvignon Blanc, '01, Edna Vly., Paragon Vnyd. $13.00 (3)
Syrah, '00, Paso Robles (G-State Fair)
Syrah, '99, Edna Vly., Firepeak Vnyd. $38.00 (5)
Syrah, '99, Paso Robles $18.00 (2)
Zinfandel, '99, Paso Robles $18.00 (4)

BAILY VINEYARD & WINERY

36150 Pauba Road, Temecula 92390

Cabernet Sauvignon, '01, Temecula (G-L.A.)
Cabernet Sauvignon, '99, Temecula (Σ-L.A.)
Chardonnay, '01, Temecula, Los Amantes Vnyd. (B-L.A.)
Dry Riesling, '01, Dry, Temecula $15.00 (B-Orange)
Dry Riesling, '01, Temecula $15.00 (2)
Merlot, '99, Temecula $21.00 (2)
Red Meritage, '98, Temecula $35.00 (3)
White Dessert, '00, Chardonnay, Serenity $20.00 (S-Orange)
White Meritage, '00, Montage, Temecula $17.00 (B-New World)
White Meritage, '01, Montage, Temecula $18.00 (5)
White Varietals, '01, Muscat, Temecula $15.00 (4)

BALLATORE CHAMPAGNE CELLARS

P.O. Box 1130, Modesto 95353

Sparkling Wine, 'NV, Gran Spumante, California $6.00 (7)
Sparkling Wine, 'NV, Rosso Red Spumante, California $6.00 (4)

BANDIERA WINERY

155 Cherry Creek Rd., Cloverdale 95425

Cabernet Sauvignon, '00, California Vnyd. Rsv. (G-L.A.)
Merlot, '00, California Vnyd. Rsv. $8.00 (B-Orange)
Zinfandel, '00, California Vnyd. Rsv. $8.00 (3)

BANNISTER

Address Not Available

Pinot Noir, '99, Anderson Vly., Floodgate Vnyd. $30.00 (2)

BAREFOOT CELLARS

420 Aviation Blvd., Ste.106, Santa Rosa 95403
www.barefootwine.com

Cabernet Sauvignon, '99, Knights Vly. Rsv. $15.00 (6)
Cabernet Sauvignon, 'NV, California $6.00 (4)
Chardonnay, '00, Sonoma Co. Rsv. $10.00 (3)
Chardonnay, 'NV, California $6.00 (7)
Merlot, '99, Knights Vly. Rsv. $15.00 (5)
Merlot, 'NV, California (B-L.A.)
Pinot Noir, '00, Sonoma Co. Rsv. $13.00 (4)
Sauvignon Blanc, 'NV, California $6.00 (B-San Fran)
Sparkling Wine, 'NV, Barefoot Bubbly Brut, California (2)
Sparkling Wine, 'NV, Barefoot Bubbly, Extra Dry, CA (S-State Fair)
White Varietals, 'NV, Barefoot On The Beach White $4.00 (2)
White Zinfandel, 'NV, Barefoot On The Beach $4.00 (3)
White Zinfandel, 'NV, California $4.00 (5)
Zinfandel, '98, Sonoma Co. Rsv. $15.00 (3)
Zinfandel, 'NV, California (B-L.A.)

BARGETTO

3535 N. Main Street, Soquel 95073
www.webwinery.com/bargetto

Chardonnay, '00, Santa Cruz Mtns, Regan Vnyd. $20.00 (5)
Gewurztraminer, '00, Santa Cruz Mtns., Dry $12.00 (B-Orange)
Merlot, '99, Santa Cruz Mtns. $20.00 (2)
Pinot Gris, '01, Pinot Grigio $16.00 (3)
Pinot Noir, '00, Santa Cruz Mtns, Regan Vnyd. $30.00 (6)
Red Italian, '00, Dolcetto, California (S-State Fair)
Red Italian, '98, La Vita, Santa Cruz, Regan Vnyd. $50.00 (4)
Zinfandel, '00, Lodi, Rauser Vnyd. $12.00 (2)

BARON HERZOG WINE CELLARS

5965 Almaden Expwy, Suite M, San Jose 95120

Cabernet Sauvignon, '00, California (B-L.A.)
Cabernet Sauvignon, '00, Paso Robles $13.00 (B-San Fran)
Chardonnay, '00, California $13.00 (2)
Merlot, '00, Paso Robles $13.00 (3)
Sauvignon Blanc, '01, California $9.00 (3)
White Varietals, '01, Chenin Blanc, Clarksburg $7.00 (2)
White Zinfandel, '01, California $7.00 (4)
Zinfandel, '00, Old Vine Lodi $13.00 (2)

BARTHOLOMEW PARK

1000 Vineyard Lane, Sonoma 95476
www.bartholomewparkwinery.com

Cabernet Sauvignon, '99, Sonoma Vly., Desnudos V. $40.00 (5)
Cabernet Sauvignon, '99, Sonoma Vly., Kasper Vnyd. $40.00 (6)
Chardonnay, '99, Sonoma Vly., Estate Vnyd. $29.00 (B-W. Coast)
Merlot, '99, Sonoma Vly., Desnudos Vnyd. $33.00 (4)
Merlot, '99, Sonoma Vly., Frank's Vnyd. $27.00 (5)
Pinot Noir, '99, Sonoma Vly., Frank's Vnyd. $26.00 (3)
Red Meritage, '99, Sonoma Vly., Mayacamas Cuvee $21.00 (3)

BATTAGLINI ESTATE WINERY

Address Not Available

Zinfandel, '00, Russian River Vly. Rsv. $33.00 (2)
Zinfandel, '00, Russian River Vly., Rsv. Select (Σ-State Fair)
Zinfandel, '00, Russian River Vly., Twin Pines $25.00 (2)

BAYSTONE

2078 Firwood Ave., Santa Rosa 95403
www.baystonewines.com

Chardonnay, '00, Russian River Vly., Saralee's Vnyd. $20.00 (6)
Syrah, '00, Dry Creek Vly. $24.00 (5)

BAYWOOD

5573 Woodbridge Rd., Lodi 95242
www.baywood-cellars.com

Cabernet Sauvignon, '00, Paso Robles Rsv. (G-State Fair)
Chardonnay, '98, Monterey Vyd., Select (B-Pac. Rim)
Gewurztraminer, '00, Monterey Vyd., Select $15.00 (2)
Sangiovese, '99, Alexander Vly., Rsv. $45.00 (3)
Syrah, '99, Monterey Co. Rsv. (B-State Fair)
White Dessert, '00, Symphony, Lodi, Late Harvest $18.00 (4)
White Varietals, '00, Symphony, California Vyd. Select $8.00 (3)
Zinfandel, '99, Paso Robles, Vyd., Select $14.00 (3)

BEAR CREEK

11900 N. Furry Rd., Lodi 95240

Petite Sirah, '00, Lodi $18.00 (G-San Fran)
Zinfandel, '00, Old Vine Zinfandel Lodi $18.00 (2)

BEAULIEU

1960 St. Helena Highway, Rutherford 94573
www.beaulieuvineyard.com

Cabernet Sauvignon, '98, George de Latour, Napa $100.00 (4)
Cabernet Sauvignon, '98, Napa Vly., Clone 4 $130.00 (S-Orange)
Cabernet Sauvignon, '99, California, Coastal (B-Pac. Rim)
Cabernet Sauvignon, '99, Napa Vly. $17.00 (3)
Cabernet Sauvignon, '99, Rutherford $25.00 (3)
Chardonnay, '00, California Coastal (S-L.A.)
Chardonnay, '00, Carneros $18.00 (4)
Chardonnay, '00, Carneros Rsv. $28.00 (3)
Chardonnay, '00, Napa Vly. Rsv. $28.00 (S-San Diego)
Chardonnay, '00, Sonoma (B-Pac. Rim)
Chardonnay, '99, Carneros Rsv. (B-San Diego)
Merlot, '00, California Coastal (2)
Merlot, '99, California Coastal $12.00 (S-W. Coast)
Merlot, '99, Napa Vly. (S-Pac. Rim)
Pinot Gris, '99, California Winemaker's Collection $14.00 (2)
Pinot Noir, '00, California Coastal $11.00 (3)

Pinot Noir, '00, Carneros $18.00 (2)
Pinot Noir, '99, Carneros Rsv. (B-Pac. Rim)
Red Meritage, '98, Tapestry Rsv., Napa Vly. $45.00 (5)
Red Rhone, '99, Ensemble, Signet, California $25.00 (5)
Sangiovese, '99, Signet Collection, N. Coast $18.00 (S-New World)
Sauvignon Blanc, '00, California, Coastal (B-Pac. Rim)
Sauvignon Blanc, '00, Napa Vly. $13.00 (2)
Syrah, '00, California (B-L.A.)
Syrah, '99, Signet Collection, Napa Vly. $25.00 (B-New World)
Viognier, '00, Signet Collection, Napa Vly. $17.00 (S-San Diego)
Zinfandel, '00, Coastal, California $10.00 (S-Orange)
Zinfandel, '00, Napa Vly. $14.00 (4)
Zinfandel, '00, Signet Collection, Napa Vly. $30.00 (3)

BECKMEN VINEYARDS

2670 Ontiveros Rd., Los Olivos 93441
www.beckmenvineyards.com
Cabernet Sauvignon, '99, Santa Barbara Co. $22.00 (S-Orange)
Sauvignon Blanc, '01, Santa Ynez Vly. Estate $12.00 (B-San Fran)
Sparkling Wine, '00, Cuvée Le Bec $14.00 (S-San Fran)
Syrah, '00, Santa Ynez Vly. Estate $22.00 (G-San Fran)

BEL ARBOR

P.O. Box 611, Hopland 95449
Cabernet Sauvignon, '00, California $7.00 (3)
Chardonnay, '00, California $6.00 (2)
Merlot, '00, California $6.00 (2)
White Zinfandel, '00, California $5.00 (5)
White Zinfandel, '01, California $6.00 (2)

BELL WINE CELLARS

P.O. Box 460, Rutherford 94573
Cabernet Sauvignon, '98, Napa Vly., Baritelle Vnyd. $55.00 (5)
Syrah, '99, Sierra Foothills, Canterbury Vnyd. $28.00 (3)

BELLA VINEYARDS

Address Not Available
White Dessert, '01, Late Harvest, Alexander Vly. (S-L.A.)
Zinfandel, '00, Alexander Vly., Big River Ranch $28.00 (3)
Zinfandel, '00, Dry Creek, Lily Hill Bella Vnyds. $28.00 (G-San Fran)

BELO

Address Not Available
White Dessert, '99, Muscat, California $18.00 (G-Orange)

BELVEDERE

4035 Westside Road, Healdsburg 95448
www.belvederewinery.com
Cabernet Sauvignon, '98, Sonoma, Healdsburg Rnchs. $22.00 (4)
Chardonnay, '00, Russian River Vly. $20.00 (3)
Chardonnay, '00, Sonoma, Healdsburg Rnchs. $14.00 (S-Riverside)
Pinot Noir, '00, Russian River Vly. $30.00 (3)
Zinfandel, '00, Sonoma Co., Healdsburg Ranches (B-State Fair)
Zinfandel, '99, Dry Creek Vly. $20.00 (3)

BENESSERE VINEYARDS

1010 Big Tree Rd., Saint Helena 94574
www.benesserevineyards.com
Pinot Gris, '01, Napa-Carneros Pinot Grigio (B-L.A.)
Sangiovese, '99, Napa Vly. $29.00 (4)

Zinfandel, '00, Napa Vly., BK Collins $28.00 (2)
Zinfandel, '00, Napa Vly., Black Glass Vnyd. $35.00 (2)

BENZIGER

1883 London Ranch Rd., Glen Ellen 95442
www.benziger.com

Cabernet Sauvignon, '98, Sonoma Co. Rsv. (B-State Fair)
Cabernet Sauvignon, '99, Sonoma $19.00 (2)
Chardonnay, '00, Carneros $16.00 (2)
Chardonnay, '99, Carneros Rsv. $27.00 (S-Orange)
Merlot, '98, Sonoma / Mendocino Rsv. $42.00 (B-San Fran)
Merlot, '98, Sonoma Co. Rsv. (G-L.A.)
Pinot Noir, '99, Sonoma Co. $22.00 (4)
Sauvignon Blanc, '00, Sonoma Co. $13.00 (B-Orange)
Syrah, '99, Sonoma Co. $22.00 (4)
Zinfandel, '99, Dry Creek Vly. $19.00 (3)

BERINGER

2000 Main Street, St Helena 94574

Bordeaux, '96, Cabernet Franc, Napa Vly. $80.00 (G-San Fran)
Cabernet Sauvignon, '90, Napa Vly. Priv. Rsv. $100.00 (S-San Fran)
Cabernet Sauvignon, '95, Napa Vly. Priv. Rsv. $100.00 (B-San Fran)
Cabernet Sauvignon, '96, Napa Vly. Priv. Rsv. $100.00 (B-San Fran)
Cabernet Sauvignon, '97, Bancroft Vnyd. $100.00 (S-San Fran)
Cabernet Sauvignon, '97, Tre Colline Vnyd. $100.00 (B-San Fran)
Cabernet Sauvignon, '97, Chabot Vnyd. $100.00 (G-San Fran)
Cabernet Sauvignon, '97, Marston Vnyd. $100.00 (S-San Fran)
Cabernet Sauvignon, '97, Napa Vly. Priv. Rsv. $100.00 (B-San Fran)
Cabernet Sauvignon, '97, Quarry Vnyd. $100.00 (B-San Fran)
Cabernet Sauvignon, '98, Knights Vly. $26.00 (4)
Cabernet Sauvignon, '99, Founders Estate, California $12.00 (6)
Chardonnay, '00, Founders Estate, California $12.00 (3)
Chardonnay, '00, Napa Vly. $16.00 (B-W. Coast)
Chardonnay, '00, Napa Vly., Sbragia $40.00 (S-San Fran)
Chardonnay, '99, Napa Vly., Private Rsv. $35.00 (3)
Chardonnay, '99, Napa Vly., Sbragia $40.00 (B-San Fran)
Dry Riesling, '00, California $7.00 (7)
Merlot, '90, Howell Mtn., Bancroft Vnyd. $75.00 (S-San Fran)
Merlot, '91, Howell Mtn., Bancroft Vnyd. $75.00 (Σ-San Fran)
Merlot, '95, Howell Mtn., Bancroft Vnyd. $75.00 (B-San Fran)
Merlot, '96, Howell Mtn., Bancroft Vnyd. $100.00 (G-San Fran)
Merlot, '97, Howell Mtn., Bancroft Vnyd. $100.00 (S-San Fran)
Merlot, '99, Founders Estate, California $12.00 (4)
Merlot, '99, Napa Vly. $26.00 (2)
Pinot Noir, '00, Founders Estate, California $12.00 (6)
Pinot Noir, '99, Appellation Collection, North Coast $16.00 (7)
Red Meritage, '98, Alluvium, Knights Vly. $30.00 (6)
Sauvignon Blanc, '00, Founders Estate, California $11.00 (3)
Sauvignon Blanc, '00, Napa Vly. $12.00 (2)
Syrah, '99, Founders Estate, California $12.00 (6)
White Meritage, '00, Alluvium Blanc, Knights Vly. $16.00 (2)
White Meritage, '99, Alluvium Blanc Knight's Vly. $16.00 (B-San Fran)
White Zinfandel, '00, North Coast, Vineyard Select $8.00 (5)
White Zinfandel, '01, California $6.00 (6)
Zinfandel, '98, Founders Estate, California $12.00 (G-New World)
Zinfandel, '99, Founders Estate, California $12.00 (4)

BIANCHI VINEYARDS

5806 N. Modoc Ave., Kerman 93630
www.bianchiwine.com

Cabernet Sauvignon, '99, Barrel Select, California $9.00 (4)
Merlot, '99, Madera Co. (B-Pac. Rim)
Pinot Noir, '99, Anderson Vly. (B-L.A.)
Syrah, '98, Paso Robles $14.00 (3)

BIG HORN CELLARS

1085 Atlas Peak Rd., Napa 94558

Cabernet Sauvignon, '98, Napa, Soda Canyon Vnyd. $19.50 (2)
Cabernet Sauvignon, '98, Napa, Coombsville Vnyd. $40.00 (4)
Chardonnay, '99, Carneros, Camelback Vnyd. $16.00 (4)
Chardonnay, '99, Napa-Carneros Grand Rsv. $24.00 (3)

BLACK SHEEP

P.O. Box 1851, Murphys 95247
www.blacksheepwinery.com

Merlot, '00, Calaveras Co., Broll Mtn. Vnyds. $15.00 (B-San Fran)
White Varietals, '01, Semillon, Calaveras Co. $12.00 (4)
Zinfandel, '99, Calaveras Co., Beckman Vnyd. $15.00 (2)
Zinfandel, '99, Sierra Foothills, Amador Co. $15.00 (S-San Fran)

BLACKSTONE WINERY

P.O. Box 43, Graton 95444
www.blackstone-winery.com

Merlot, '00, California $11.00 (S-San Fran)
Merlot, '00, Napa $18.00 (2)

BOEGER

1709 Carson Road, Placerville 95667
www.boegerwinery.com

Bordeaux, '98, Cabernet Franc, El Dorado $15.00 (G-Orange)
Cabernet Sauvignon, '99, El Dorado Estate $15.00 (3)
Chardonnay, '00, El Dorado Estate $12.00 (S-Orange)
Pinot Gris, '01, El Dorado, Johnson Vnyd. Pinot Grigio $12.00 (3)
Pinot Noir, '99, El Dorado Rsv. $25.00 (2)
Red Italian, '00, Barbera, El Dorado Estate $15.00 (2)
Red Italian, '99, Charbono, Arrastra, El Dorado $25.00 (3)
Red Meritage, '99, Rsv. Meritage El Dorado $23.00 (2)
White Dessert, '01, Muscat Canelli, El Dorado $12.00 (B-Orange)
Zinfandel, '99, El Dorado $15.00 (B-San Fran)
Zinfandel, '99, El Dorado, Walker Vnyd. $15.00 (2)

BOGLE

Rt. 1, Box 276, Clarksburg 95612
www.boglewinery.com

Cabernet Sauvignon, '00, California (S-State Fair)
Chardonnay, '00, California $9.00 (5)
Chardonnay, '01, California (S-State Fair)
Merlot, '00, California $9.00 (4)
Petite Sirah, '00, California $10.00 (8)
Sauvignon Blanc, '01, California $8.00 (5)
Zinfandel, '00, Old Vine, California $11.00 (8)

BOISSET WINES

650 Fifth St., #403, San Francisco 94107

Pinot Noir, '99, Bouchard Aine & Fils, Bourgogne (B-L.A.)

BONNY DOON VINEYARD

10 Pine Flat Road, Santa Cruz 95061
www.bonnydoonvineyard.com

Generic Red, '00, Ca'del Solo, Big House Red $9.00 (B-Orange)
Red Rhone, '00, Le Cigare Volant, California $32.00 (3)
Sangiovese, '00, Ca'del Solo, Monterey Co. (B-L.A.)
Sangiovese, '99, Ca'del Solo, Monterey Co. (B-L.A.)
Sparkling Wine, '00, Muscat, Ca' del Solo $15.00 (G-San Fran)
Sparkling Wine, '01, Spumante, Ca' del Solo $20.00 (S-San Fran)
White Dessert, '00, Muscat Vin de Glaciere (S-L.A.)
White Varietals, '00, Muscat Vin de Glaciere $17.00 (B-San Fran)
White Varietals, '01, Malvasia Bianca, Ca'del Solo $12.00 (3)
Zinfandel, '00, Cardinal Zin $20.00 (G-Orange)

BONTERRA

13325 So. Highway 101, Hopland 95449
www.bonterra.com

Cabernet Sauvignon, '99, North Coast $17.00 (3)
Chardonnay, '00, Mendocino Co. $15.00 (7)
Merlot, '99, Mendocino Co. $16.00 (6)
Syrah, '99, Mendocino Co. $19.00 (7)
Viognier, '00, Mendocino Co. $19.00 (3)
Viognier, '01, Mendocino Co. $19.00 (S-Orange)

BOUCHAINE

1075 Buchli Station Rd., Napa 94559
www.bouchaine.com

Pinot Noir, '99, Carneros $34.00 (6)

BRADFORD MOUNTAIN WINERY

Address Not Available
www.bradfordmountain.com

Cabernet Sauvignon, '98, Dry Creek, Headwater Vnyd. $40.00 (2)
Zinfandel, '99, Dry Creek Vly., Grist Vnyd. $30.00 (4)

BRIDLEWOOD

355 Roblar Ave., Santa Ynez 93460
www.bridlewoodwinery.com

Red Rhone, '99, Arabesque, California $14.00 (Σ-New World)

BROPHY CLARK

Address Not Available

Pinot Noir, '00, Santa Maria Vly. $22.00 (2)
Syrah, '00, Edna Vly. $20.00 (B-Orange)
Syrah, '00, Santa Ynez Vly., Rodney's Vnyd. $20.00 (G-Orange)
Zinfandel, '00, Paso Robles, Lone Oak Vnyd. $16.50 (Σ-Orange)

DAVID BRUCE WINERY

21439 Bear Creek Rd., Los Gatos 95030

Petite Sirah, '00, Central Coast $16.00 (4)
Petite Sirah, '00, Paso Robles, Shell Creek Vnyd. $25.00 (2)
Pinot Noir, '00, Carneros, Truchard Vnyd. $35.00 (2)
Pinot Noir, '00, Central Coast $20.00 (4)
Pinot Noir, '00, Russian River Vly. $35.00 (4)
Pinot Noir, '00, Santa Cruz Mtns. $35.00 (3)
Pinot Noir, '00, Sonoma Co. $25.00 (4)
Pinot Noir, '99, Santa Cruz Mtns. $30.00 (S-New World)
Pinot Noir, '99, Sonoma Co. $25.00 (B-Pac. Rim)
Zinfandel, '00, Paso Robles $17.00 (4)

BRUTOCAO

1400 Hwy. 175, Hopland 95449
www.brutocaocellars.com

Cabernet Sauvignon, '99, Mendocino, Brutocao Vnyd. $20.00 (6)
Chardonnay, '00, Mendocino Co., Bliss Vnyd. (B-L.A.)
Merlot, '98, Riserva D' Argento (B-L.A.)
Merlot, '99, Mendocino Co., Brutocao Vnyd. $20.00 (4)
Zinfandel, '99, Mendocino Co., Brutocao Vnyd. $16.00 (6)

BUEHLER VINEYARDS

820 Greenfield Rd., St Helena 94574
www.buehlervineyards.com

Cabernet Sauvignon, '98, Napa Vly. Estate $40.00 (4)
Cabernet Sauvignon, '99, Napa Vly. $22.00 (6)
Chardonnay, '00, Russian River Vly. $15.00 (3)
Chardonnay, '00, Russian River Vly. Rsv. $30.00 (4)
White Zinfandel, '01, Napa Vly. $7.00 (4)
Zinfandel, '99, Napa Vly. $12.00 (2)
Zinfandel, '99, Napa Vly. Estate $25.00 (2)

BUENA VISTA

27000 Ramal Road, Sonoma 95476
www.buenavistawinery.com

Cabernet Sauvignon, '98, Carneros Estate $22.00 (2)
Chardonnay, '99, Carneros Estate $18.00 (3)
Merlot, '99, Carneros Estate $22.00 (3)
Pinot Noir, '99, Carneros Estate Sonoma $22.00 (3)
Sauvignon Blanc, '00, California $10.00 (2)

RAYMOND BURR VINEYARDS

Address Not Available

Bordeaux, '99, Cabernet Franc, Dry Creek Vly. $36.00 (6)
Cabernet Sauvignon, '98, Dry Creek Vly. $38.00 (3)
Chardonnay, '00, Dry Creek Vly. $28.00 (2)

BUTTERFIELD STATION

Address Not Available

Cabernet Sauvignon, '00, California $8.00 (2)
Chardonnay, '01, California $8.00 (2)
Merlot, '00, California $8.00 (2)

BUTTONWOOD FARM

1500 Alamo Pintado Rd., Solvang 93463
www.buttonwoodwinery.com

Bordeaux, '98, Cabernet Franc, Santa Ynez Vly. $18.00 (3)
Merlot, '99, Santa Ynez Vly. $18.00 (B-Riverside)
Red Meritage, '97, Trevin, Santa Ynez Vly. $30.00 (5)
Red Meritage, '99, Devin Santa Ynez Vly. $16.00 (B-San Fran)
Sauvignon Blanc, '00, Santa Ynez Vly. $12.00 (2)
Syrah, '99, Santa Ynez Vly. $22.00 (2)
White Varietals, '00, Marsanne, Santa Ynez Vly. $12.00 (2)

BYINGTON

21850 Bear Creek Rd., Los Gatos 95030
www.byington.com

Red Meritage, '99, Alliage, Sonoma Co. $21.00 (Σ-New World)

BYRON

5230 Tepusquet Rd., Santa Maria 93454
www.robertmondavi.com

Chardonnay, '00, Santa Maria Vly. $24.00 (S-San Fran)
Pinot Noir, '00, Santa Maria Vly. $28.00 (3)

C

CALISTOGA CELLARS

Address Not Available

Merlot, '00, Blossom Creek, Napa Vly. (G-L.A.)
Sauvignon Blanc, '01, Blossom Creek, Napa Vly. (B-L.A.)

CALLAWAY COASTAL

32720 Rancho California, Temecula 92589
www.callawaycoastal.com

Cabernet Sauvignon, '99, California $11.00 (B-Orange)
Chardonnay, '99, Rsv., California $14.00 (3)
Merlot, '99, California $11.00 (2)
Sauvignon Blanc, '00, California (S-State Fair)
Syrah, '99, Rsv. San Luis Obispo $16.00 (B-San Fran)

CAMELLIA CELLARS

Address Not Available
www.camelliacellars.com

Cabernet Sauvignon, '98, Dry Creek, Lencioni Vnyd. $45.00 (3)
Cabernet Sauvignon, '99, Dry Creek, Lencioni Vnyd. (Σ-State Fair)
Red Italian, '00, Diamo Grazie, Dry Creek Vly. $42.00 (S-Orange)
Red Italian, '99, Diamo Grazie, Dry Creek Vly. $42.00 (3)
Sangiovese, '00, Dry Creek Vly., Merlo Vnyds. $28.00 (3)
Sangiovese, '99, Dry Creek Vly., Merlo Vnyds. $28.00 (2)
Zinfandel, '00, Dry Creek Vly., Lencioni Vnyd. $22.00 (2)

CAMELOT WINERY

5680 Tepusquet Canyon Rd., Santa Maria 93454
www.camelotwine.com

Cabernet Sauvignon, '99, California $9.00 (3)
Chardonnay, '00, California $9.00 (2)
Merlot, '98, California $9.00 (G-Pac. Rim)
Merlot, '99, California $9.00 (3)
Pinot Noir, '00, California $9.00 (4)
Pinot Noir, '01, California $9.00 (2)
Sauvignon Blanc, '00, California $9.00 (4)
Syrah, '99, California $9.00 (5)

CANYON ROAD WINERY

22281 Chianti Rd., Geyserville 95441
www.canyonroadwinery.com

Cabernet Sauvignon, '00, California $10.00 (5)
Chardonnay, '00, California $9.00 (6)
Merlot, '00, California $10.00 (4)
Sauvignon Blanc, '01, California $9.00 (6)
Syrah, '00, California Shiraz $10.00 (5)

CAPELLO WINERY

Address Not Available
capellowinery.com

Chardonnay, '99, California $9.00 (B-San Fran)
Merlot, '99, California $9.00 (2)

MAURICE CAR'RIE WINERY

34225 Rancho Calif. Rd., Temecula 92390

Chardonnay, '00, Temecula $9.00 (2)
Merlot, '00, Temecula $10.00 (B-Riverside)
Petite Sirah, '98, Temecula (B-L.A.)
Sauvignon Blanc, '00, Temecula $8.00 (5)
White Dessert, '01, Summer's End (2)
White Varietals, '01, Chenin Blanc, Temecula $7.00 (2)
White Varietals, '01, Muscat Canelli, Temecula $11.00 (6)

CARMENET VINEYARD

1700 Moon Mountain Rd, Sonoma 95476
www.carmenetwinery.com

Cabernet Sauvignon, '00, Dynamite, North Coast $17.25 (S-L.A.)
Cabernet Sauvignon, '99, Dynamite, North Coast $17.25 (5)
Merlot, '00, Dynamite, North Coast $17.25 (7)
Merlot, '99, Dynamite, North Coast $17.25 (G-New World)

CARMODY MCKNIGHT

11240 Chimney Rock Rd., Paso Robles 93446
www.carmodymckight.com

Bordeaux, '99, Cabernet Franc, Paso Robles $22.50 (G-Orange)
Merlot, '99, Paso Robles, Estate $20.00 (4)
Red Meritage, '99, Cadenza, Conway Vnyd. $25.00 (5)

CARTLIDGE & BROWN

3222 Ehlers Lane, Saint Helena 94574

Cabernet Sauvignon, '00, California $10.00 (B-Orange)
Merlot, '00, California $9.00 (S-Orange)
Syrah, '00, California $9.00 (B-Orange)

CASA DE CABALLOS

2225 Raymond Ave., Templeton 93465
www.casdecaballos.com

Dry Riesling, '00, Paso Robles $15.00 (3)
Dry Riesling, '01, Paso Robles $15.00 (S-Orange)
Pinot Noir, '00, Paso Robles Periwinkle $17.00 (B-Riverside)
Red Meritage, '99, Forgetmenot Paso Robles $24.00 (2)

CASA NUESTRA

Address Not Available
www.casanuestra.com

Merlot, '99, Napa Vly., Estate $38.00 (4)
Red Italian, '00, Tinto Classico, Oakville Estate $30.00 (3)
Red Meritage, '99, Napa Vly. $45.00 (4)
White Varietals, '00, Chenin Blanc, Napa Vly., Rsv. (B-Pac. Rim)

CASTLE VINEYARDS

1105 Castle Rd., Sonoma 95476
www.castlevineyards.com

Cabernet Sauvignon, '98, Sonoma Vly. $21.00 (G-Orange)
Merlot, '98, Los Carneros, Sangiacomo-Durell Vnyds. $25.00 (3)
Pinot Noir, '99, Los Carneros $25.00 (2)
Pinot Noir, '99, Los Carneros, Durell Vnyd. $35.00 (3)
Pinot Noir, '99, Carneros, Sangiacomo Vnyd. $30.00 (B-Orange)
Syrah, '00, Sonoma Vly. $25.00 (S-San Fran)
Viognier, '01, California $19.00 (G-San Fran)
White Dessert, '00, Viogner Ripkin California $15.00 (B-San Fran)
Zinfandel, '99, Sonoma Vly. $19.00 (2)

CASTORO CELLARS

1480 No. Bethel Road, Templeton 93465
www.castorocellars.com

Cabernet Sauvignon, '99, Paso Robles $14.00 (5)
Chardonnay, '00, Central Coast $12.00 (3)
Merlot, '99, Paso Robles $13.00 (2)
Pinot Noir, '00, Central Coast Rsv. $18.00 (4)
Sauvignon Blanc, '00, Paso Robles Fume Blanc $8.50 (B-Riverside)
White Varietals, '01, Muscat Canelli, Paso Robles $8.00 (B-Orange)
Zinfandel, '00, Paso Robles, Late Harvest $17.00 (S-W. Coast)
Zinfandel, '00, Paso Robles, Vnyd. Tribute $18.00 (3)
Zinfandel, '99, Paso Robles $14.00 (4)

CATACULA LAKE WINERY

Address Not Available

Red Meritage, '99, Napa Vly. Rancho Cuvee $35.00 (3)
Sauvignon Blanc, '00, Napa Vly. $15.00 (B-Riverside)
Zinfandel, '99, Napa Vly. $27.00 (3)

CE2V

7415 St. Helena Hwy., Yountville 94599

Red Meritage, '99, Napa Vly. Estate $75.00 (6)
Sangiovese, '00, Napa Vly., Pope Vly. Vnyd. $30.00 (4)

CECCHETTI SEBASTIANI CELLAR

8440 St. Helena Hwy., Rutherford 94573

Cabernet Sauvignon, '97, Napa Vly. $50.00 (4)
Cabernet Sauvignon, '99, Central Coast $13.00 (5)
Chardonnay, '00, Central Coast $13.00 (4)
Merlot, '99, North Coast $13.00 (8)
Pinot Noir, '00, Central Coast $13.00 (2)
Pinot Noir, '99, Central Coast $12.00 (3)
Pinot Noir, '99, North Coast (S-Pac. Rim)
Syrah, '00, North Coast $13.00 (8)
Viognier, '00, North Coast $13.00 (3)

CEDAR MOUNTAIN WINERY

7000 Tesla Road, Livermore 94550
www.wines.com/cedarmountain

Cabernet Sauvignon, '98, Livermore, Blanches Rsv. $22.00 (2)
Merlot, '98, Livermore Vly. $22.00 (2)
Red Meritage, '98, Duet, Livermore Vly. $22.00 (S-W. Coast)

CHALONE VINEYARD

P.O. Box 855, Soledad 93960
www.chalonegroup.com

White Varietals, '00, Pinot Blanc, Estate $21.00 (G-Orange)

CHAMELEON CELLARS

1330 Sylvaner Ave., St Helena 94574
www.chameleoncellars.com

Syrah, '00, California $14.00 (4)
Syrah, '00, Napa Vly. $29.00 (6)

CHAMPAGNE LANSON

Address Not Available

Sparkling Wine, 'NV, Black Label Brut, Champagne (Σ-L.A.)

CHANDELLE OF SONOMA

14301 Arnold Drive, Glen Ellen 95442

Cabernet Sauvignon, '00, Sonoma Co. $15.00 (2)
Chardonnay, '00, Sonoma Co. $13.50 (2)

CHANGALA WINERY

Address Not Available
www.changalawinery.com

Viognier, '00, Santa Barbara Co. $16.00 (4)
Zinfandel, '99, Paso Robles $16.00 (G-Orange)
Zinfandel, '99, Paso Robles, Dante Dusi Vnyd. $18.00 (3)

CHAPPELLET

1581 Sage Canyon Rd, St Helena 94574
www.chappellet.com

Cabernet Sauvignon, '99, Signature, Napa Vly. $44.00 (2)
Sangiovese, '99, Napa Vly. $24.00 (B-San Diego)
White Varietals, '00, Chenin Blanc, Napa Vly. (B-Pac. Rim)

CHARLES CREEK VINEYARDS

Address Not Available

Merlot, '00, Miradero, Sonoma Co. $18.00 (3)

CHATEAU LASGOITY

Address Not Available

White Varietals, '01, Blanc du Val, Madera $10.00 (G-W. Coast)

CHATEAU MARGENE

Address Not Available

Cabernet Sauvignon, '99, San Luis Obispo $30.00 (3)

CHATEAU SOUVERAIN

400 Souverain Road, Geyserville 95441
www.chateausouverain.com

Cabernet Sauvignon, '98, Alexander Vly. (B-Pac. Rim)
Chardonnay, '00, Sonoma Co. $14.00 (2)
Chardonnay, '99, Russian River, Winemakers Rsv. $25.00 (5)
Merlot, '99, Alexander Vly. $17.00 (5)
Sauvignon Blanc, '00, Alexander Vly. $12.00 (5)
Zinfandel, '99, Dry Creek Vly. $13.00 (8)

CHATEAU ST. JEAN

8555 Sonoma Hwy., Kenwood 95452
www.chateaustjean.com

Bordeaux, '98, Cabernet Franc, Napa Vly. (S-L.A.)
Chardonnay, '00, Sonoma Co. $15.00 (5)
Chardonnay, '99, Alexander Vly., Robert Young Vnyd. $25.00 (4)
Dry Riesling, '01, Sonoma Co. $15.00 (4)
Gewurztraminer, '01, Sonoma Co. $15.00 (5)
Merlot, '99, Sonoma Co. $25.00 (6)
Pinot Noir, '00, Sonoma Co. $19.00 (7)
Sauvignon Blanc, '00, Fume Blanc, Sonoma Co. $13.00 (3)
Zinfandel, '00, Lodi, Late Harvest (B-L.A.)

CHATOM VINEYARDS

7449 Esmeralda Rd, San Andreas 95249
www.chatomvineyards.com

Cabernet Sauvignon, '99, Calaveras Co. $18.00 (B-San Diego)
Sangiovese, '99, Calavares Co., Gitano $12.00 (2)
Sauvignon Blanc, '00, Calaveras Co. $10.00 (4)
Zinfandel, '99, Sierra Foothills $16.00 (3)

CHILES LAKE WINERY

Address Not Available

Zinfandel, '00, Napa Vly., Rancho Catacula $29.00 (3)

CHIMNEY ROCK

5320 Silverado Trail, Napa 94558

Cabernet Sauvignon, '99, Napa Vly., Stags Leap $45.00 (2)

CHOUINARD VINEYARDS

33853 Palomares Rd., Castro Valley 94552

Gewurztraminer, '01, Monterey $10.00 (B-San Fran)
Petite Sirah, '00, California (S-State Fair)
White Varietals, '01, Orange Muscat, Joan's Vnyd. (B-L.A.)

CHRISTOPHER CREEK

641 Limerick Lane, Healdsburg 95448
www.christophercreek.com

Chardonnay, '00, Russian River Vly. (B-Pac. Rim)
Petite Sirah, '00, Russian River Vly. Estate $28.00 (5)
Syrah, '00, Russian River Vly. Estate $22.00 (4)
Syrah, '99, Russian River Vly. Estate $22.00 (3)
Viognier, '00, Russian River, Catie Corner Vnyd. $24.00 (6)
Zinfandel, '00, Dry Creek Vly. $26.00 (8)

CHUMEIA VINEYARDS

Address Not Available

Chardonnay, '00, Central Coast $16.00 (B-Orange)
Pinot Noir, '00, Edna Vly. $16.00 (S-Riverside)
Pinot Noir, '00, Santa Lucia Highlands $28.00 (2)
Viognier, '00, California $12.00 (B-Riverside)
White Varietals, '00, Pinot Blanc, Monterey Co. $14.00 (2)
Zinfandel, '00, Paso Robles $22.00 (4)

CILURZO VINEYARD & WINERY

41220 Calle Contento, Temecula 92390
www.cilurzowine.com

Chardonnay, '01, Temecula (S-L.A.)
Merlot, '99, Temecula, April's Vnyd. $15.00 (S-San Fran)
Petite Sirah, '00, Temecula Rsv. Late Harvest $11.00 (2)
Petite Sirah, '01, Temecula Rsv. Late Harvest (G-State Fair)
Petite Sirah, '99, Temecula Estate $25.00 (3)
Viognier, '01, California $17.00 (5)

CINNABAR

2300 Congress Springs Rd., Saratoga 95071
www.cinnabarwine.com

Chardonnay, '99, Santa Cruz Mtns. Estate $25.00 (3)
Merlot, '00, Paso Robles $20.00 (3)
Pinot Noir, '99, Santa Cruz Mtns. $38.00 (3)
Red Meritage, '99, Mercury Rising, California (B-L.A.)

CLAUDIA SPRINGS

P.O. Box 4350, Napa 94558

Petite Sirah, '99, Redwood Vly., Rhodes Vnyd. $28.00 (B-Riverside)
Pinot Gris, '00, Anderson Vly. $15.00 (B-New World)
Pinot Noir, '99, Anderson Vly. $25.00 (3)
Pinot Noir, '99, Mendocino Co. $20.00 (2)
Red Rhone, '98, Grenache, Mendocino $15.00 (B-Riverside)
Zinfandel, '99, Mendocino, Eaglepoint Rnch. $22.00 (B-New World)
Zinfandel, '99, Redwood Vly., Rhodes Vnyd. $26.00 (G-New World)

Zinfandel, '99, Redwood Vly., Vassar Vnyd. $20.00 (2)

CLINE CELLARS

24737 Arnold Drive, Sonoma 95476
www.clinecellars.com

Red Rhone, '00, Mourvèdre, Contra Costa $32.00 (2)
Red Rhone, '99, Carignane, Contra Costa $15.00 (S-Orange)
Red Rhone, '99, Mourvèdre, Big Break Vnyd. $25.00 (G-Orange)
Syrah, '00, Los Carneros $28.00 (2)
Syrah, '00, Sonoma $16.00 (3)
Viognier, '01, Sonoma $16.00 (B-San Fran)
Zinfandel, '00, Contra Costa, Big Break $28.00 (S-San Fran)
Zinfandel, '00, Contra Costa, Live Oak $28.00 (2)

CLONINGER CELLARS

1645 River Rd., Salinas 93902
www.cloningerwine.com

Cabernet Sauvignon, '99, Carmel Vly., Quinn Vyd. $19.00 (2)
Chardonnay, '00, Santa Lucia Highlands Estate $17.00 (4)
Pinot Noir, '00, Monterey, Santa Lucia Highlands $23.00 (3)

CLOS DU BOIS

19410 Geyserville, Geyserville 95441
www.closdubois.com

Cabernet Sauvignon, '98, Alexander Vly., Briarcrest $43.00 (2)
Cabernet Sauvignon, '99, Alexander Vly. Rsv. $21.00 (3)
Cabernet Sauvignon, '99, Sonoma Co. $17.00 (3)
Chardonnay, '00, Alexander Vly. Rsv. $16.00 (2)
Chardonnay, '01, Sonoma Co. (S-State Fair)
Chardonnay, '98, Dry Creek Vly., Flintwood Vnyd. (B-L.A.)
Chardonnay, '99, Alexander Vly., Calcaire $22.00 (B-Orange)
Merlot, '99, Alexander Vly. Rsv. $22.00 (S-San Fran)
Merlot, '99, Sonoma Co. $18.00 (3)
Pinot Noir, '00, Sonoma Co. $17.00 (2)
Red Meritage, '98, Marlstone Vnyd, Alexander Vly. $39.00 (3)
Sauvignon Blanc, '00, North Coast $10.00 (2)
Sauvignon Blanc, '01, North Coast (B-State Fair)
Syrah, '98, Alexander Vly. Rsv. $16.00 (2)
Zinfandel, '99, Dry Creek Vly. Rsv. $21.00 (3)
Zinfandel, '99, Sonoma Co. $14.00 (3)

COASTAL RIDGE WINERY

Address Not Available

Cabernet Sauvignon, '99, California $7.00 (8)
Chardonnay, '00, California $7.00 (2)
Chardonnay, '99, California $7.00 (3)
Merlot, '99, California $7.00 (5)
Sauvignon Blanc, '99, California $7.00 (2)
Syrah, '00, Shiraz, California $7.00 (4)

CONCANNON VINEYARD

4590 Tesla Road, Livermore 94550
www.concannonvineyard.com

Cabernet Sauvignon, '97, Livermore Vly. Rsv. $25.00 (4)
Cabernet Sauvignon, '98, Central Coast Select Vnyd. $11.50 (3)
Chardonnay, '99, Central Coast, Rsv. $20.00 (2)
Chardonnay, '99, Central Coast, Selected Vyd. (B-Pac. Rim)
Dry Riesling, '01, Monterey Johannisberg Limited Bottling $10.00 (3)
Merlot, '98, Central Coast $18.00 (B-New World)

Merlot, '99, Central Coast $18.00 (3)
Petite Sirah, '98, Central Coast Selected Vnyd. $11.50 (3)
Petite Sirah, '98, Rsv., San Francisco Bay $25.00 (4)
Petite Sirah, '99, San Francisco Bay Rsv. $25.00 (B-San Fran)
Red Meritage, '00, Assemblage, Rsv., San Francisco $19.00 (B-L.A.)
Red Meritage, '98, Central Coast, Rsv. $19.00 (2)
Red Meritage, '99, Assemblage, Rsv., San Francisco $19.00 (4)
Red Rhone, '01, San Francisco Bay (S-L.A.)
Red Rhone, '98, Rhone Blend, Contra Costa $17.00 (S-New World)
Red Rhone, '99, Rhone Blend, San Francisco Bay $18.00 (4)
Sauvignon Blanc, '99, S. F. Bay, Selected Vnyd. $9.00 (S-San Diego)
Syrah, '98, Rhone Style, San Francisco Bay $19.00 (3)
Syrah, '99, Rhone Style, San Francisco Bay $19.00 (4)
Viognier, '99, Rhone Style, Central Coast $15.00 (3)
White Dessert, '98, Riesling, Monterey, SLH $20.00 (2)
White Meritage, '00, White Assemblage, Rsv. $15.00 (4)
White Varietals, '00, Rhone Blend, San Francisco Bay $16.00 (3)
White Varietals, '01, Orange Muscat, Livermore Vly. $11.00 (4)
White Varietals, '99, Muscat, Yolo Co. $11.00 (B-Orange)
White Varietals, '99, Rhone Blend, S. F. Bay $16.00 (S-New World)
Zinfandel, '99, San Francisco Bay, Livermore Vly. $15.00 (6)

CONN CREEK

8711 Silverado Trail, St Helena 94574

Bordeaux, '99, Cabernet Franc, Napa Vly. Rsv. $25.00 (5)
Cabernet Sauvignon, '98, Napa Vly., Limited Release $26.00 (3)
Merlot, '99, Napa Vly., Limited Release $25.00 (3)
Red Meritage, '98, Anthology, Napa Vly. $54.00 (3)

COOK'S CHAMPAGNE CELLARS

One Winemaster Way, Lodi 95240

Sparkling Wine, 'NV, Brut, California Grand Rsv. $4.50 (B-Riverside)
Sparkling Wine, 'NV, California Brut $4.50 (2)
Sparkling Wine, 'NV, California Spumante $5.00 (2)
Sparkling Wine, 'NV, Sparkling White Zinfandel $4.50 (B-Riverside)

COOPER-GARROD

22600 Mt. Eden Rd., Saratoga 95070
www.cgv.com

Bordeaux, '98, Cabernet Franc, Santa Cruz $24.00 (B-W. Coast)
Cabernet Sauvignon, '97, Santa Cruz Mtns. George's Vnyd. $35.00
Cabernet Sauvignon, '98, Santa Cruz Mtns. Estate $28.00 (3)
Chardonnay, '99, Santa Cruz Mtns. Estate (S-Pac. Rim)

CORBETT CANYON VINEYARDS

P.O. Box 3159, San Luis Obispo 93403

Cabernet Sauvignon, '00, California Rsv. $7.00 (2)
Cabernet Sauvignon, '99, California Rsv. $7.00 (G-New World)
Chardonnay, '00, California Rsv. $7.00 (4)
Merlot, '99, California Rsv. $7.00 (2)
Sauvignon Blanc, '01, California Select (B-Pac. Rim)
Syrah, '99, California Rsv. $7.00 (B-New World)
White Zinfandel, '01, California Select $6.00 (3)

CORLEY FAMILY NAPA VALLEY

Address Not Available

Cabernet Sauvignon, '99, Napa Vly. Rsv. (S-State Fair)
Chardonnay, '00, Napa Vly., Home Ranch Vnyd. (G-State Fair)
Red Meritage, '99, Napa Vly. $45.00 (2)

COSENTINO WINERY

7415 St. Helena Hwy., Yountville 94599

Bordeaux, '99, Cabernet Franc, Napa Vly. $34.00 (2)
Cabernet Sauvignon, '99, Napa Vly. Rsv. $80.00 (2)
Cabernet Sauvignon, '99, Napa, Punched Cap $34.00 (B-Orange)
Chardonnay, '00, Napa Vly. $22.00 (B-Orange)
Gewurztraminer, '00, Napa Vly., Yountville $22.00 (S-Orange)
Pinot Noir, '00, Carneros, Punched Cap Ferm. $30.00 (4)
Pinot Noir, '99, Napa Vly., Yountville $34.00 (S-Orange)
Red Meritage, '99, M. Coz, Napa Vly. $100.00 (4)
Red Meritage, '99, The Novelist, California (S-L.A.)
Red Meritage, '99, The Poet, Napa Vly. $65.00 (3)
Sangiovese, '00, Napa Vly. Estate $30.00 (S-W. Coast)
White Dessert, '00, Vin Doux Viognier Kay, Late Harvest $30.00 (2)
White Varietals, '00, Semillon Dry, Napa Vly. The Sem $22.00 (2)
Zinfandel, '00, Lodi, The Zin $30.00 (3)

COULSON EL DORADO

3550 Carson Rd., Camino 95709

Bordeaux, '98, Cabernet Franc, Clos du Lac Vnyd. (B-Pac. Rim)
Pinot Gris, '01, El Dorado, Von Huene, Vnyd. $16.00 (B-Orange)
Red Meritage, '98, El Dorado, Von Huene Vyd. (2)
Red Rhone, '00, El Dorado Vintner's Select $16.00 (S-Riverside)
Red Rhone, '00, Mourvedre, Stone Vnyd. $15.00 (B-Riverside)
Zinfandel, '00, El Dorado Clarke Vnyd. $22.00 (B-Riverside)
Zinfandel, '00, El Dorado Safari Vnyd. $18.00 (2)

THOMAS COYNE

2162 Broadmoor St., Livermore 94550

Merlot, '99, El Dorado Quartz Hill Vnyd. $16.00 (3)
Merlot, '99, Livermore Vly., Detjens Farms $20.00 (3)
Red Meritage, '99, Confluence, California $20.00 (3)
Red Rhone, '00, Mourvedre, Contra Costa Co. $14.00 (2)
Red Rhone, '00, Quest, California $11.00 (2)
Syrah, '99, Livermore Vly., Detjens Farms $16.00 (B-W. Coast)
Viognier, '01, California $16.00 (3)
White Varietals, '01, Pinot Blanc, Detjens Farms $16.00 (3)

CRANE LAKE WINERY

Address Not Available

Chardonnay, '00, California (S-State Fair)
Merlot, '00, California (S-State Fair)
Sangiovese, '00, California (B-State Fair)
White Zinfandel, '01, California (S-State Fair)

CROZE

Address Not Available
www.croze-cab.com

Cabernet Sauvignon, '98, Napa Vly. (B-State Fair)
Cabernet Sauvignon, '99, Napa Vly. $38.00 (3)

CRYSTAL VALLEY CELLARS

7415 St. Helena Hwy., Yountville 94599

Merlot, '00, California $18.00 (B-Orange)
Pinot Noir, '00, California $16.00 (B-Riverside)
Syrah, '00, California $18.00 (3)

CURTIS

5249 Foxen Canyon Rd., Los Olivos 93441
www.curtiswine.com

Red Meritage, '99, Cuvee, Central Coast $12.00 (G-W. Coast)
Red Rhone, '99, Heritage Cuvee, Central Coast $12.00 (2)
Sparkling Wine, '99, Cuvee, Central Coast $12.00 (B-San Fran)
Viognier, '00, Santa Barbara Co. $18.00 (3)
White Varietals, '00, Heritage Blanc, Santa Barbara Co. $12.00 (9)

CUVAISON

P.O. Box 2230, Napa 94559
www.cuvaison.com

Chardonnay, '00, Napa Carneros $24.00 (2)
Chardonnay, '00, Napa Vly. $22.00 (2)

CYPRESS VINEYARD

1000 Lenzen Ave., San Jose 95126
www.jlohr.com

Cabernet Sauvignon, '99, California $10.00 (2)
Merlot, '99, California $10.00 (2)
White Zinfandel, '01, California $6.00 (B-New World)
Zinfandel, '00, California $10.00 (3)

CYRUS

Address Not Available

Red Meritage, '98, Alexander Vly. Estate $50.00 (G-Orange)

D

DARK STAR CELLARS

2985 Anderson Dr., Paso Robles 93446

Cabernet Sauvignon, '99, Paso Robles $20.00 (4)
Merlot, '99, Paso Robles (B-L.A.)
Red Meritage, '99, Ricordati, Paso Robles $24.00 (5)
Zinfandel, '99, Paso Robles $18.00 (3)

DE LOACH VINEYARDS

1791 Olivet Rd., Santa Rosa 95401
www.deloachvineyards.com

Cabernet Sauvignon, '98, Los Amigos Ranch $28.00 (S-Riverside)
Chardonnay, '00, California $11.00 (2)
Chardonnay, '00, Russian River Vly. $18.00 (2)
Chardonnay, '99, Russian River Vly., Olivet Ranch (B-Pac. Rim)
Gewurztraminer, '00, Russian River Vly. Early Harvest $12.00 (3)
Gewurztraminer, '01, Russian River Vly. EH $12.00 (S-New World)
Merlot, '99, Russian River Vly. Estate $20.00 (2)
Pinot Noir, '00, OFS, Russian River Vly., Estate $40.00 (5)
Pinot Noir, '00, Russian River Vly. Estate $20.00 (S-Riverside)
Sauvignon Blanc, '00, Fume Blanc, Russian River Vly. $14.00 (4)
White Zinfandel, '01, California $8.00 (3)
Zinfandel, '00, California $11.00 (B-Riverside)
Zinfandel, '00, Russian River Vly. Estate $20.00 (3)
Zinfandel, '99, California $11.00 (2)

DE LORIMIER WINERY

2001 Hwy. 128, Geyserville 95441
www.delorimierwinery.com

Chardonnay, '00, Alexander Vly., Estate $16.00 (S-State Fair)
Chardonnay, '99, Alexander Vly., Clonal Select $24.00 (4)
Chardonnay, '99, Alexander Vly., Estate $16.00 (2)

Merlot, '99, Alexander Vly. $20.00 (2)
Red Meritage, '99, Mosaic, Alexander Vly. $30.00 (6)
Sauvignon Blanc, '99, Alexander Vly. Estate $10.00 (4)
White Meritage, '99, Spectrum, Alexander Vly. Estate $16.00 (5)

DE ROSE

1183 Nikulina Court, San Jose 95120
www.derosewine.com

Bordeaux, '99, Cabernet Franc, Cienega, Cardillo $20.00 (6)
Merlot, '98, Napa Vly., Rsv. $23.00 (B-New World)
Red Italian, '99, Negrette, Cienega, Miller Vnyd. $20.00 (3)
Zinfandel, '99, Cienega Vly. Cedolini Vnyd. $19.00 (5)

DEERFIELD RANCH

Address Not Available

Merlot, '99, Russian River Vly. $35.00 (3)
Sangiovese, '00, Windsor Oaks Vnyd, Chalk Hill $28.00 (2)
Sauvignon Blanc, '00, Peterson Vnyd. $18.00 (G-New World)
Syrah, '00, Sonoma Co., Lodi's Vnyd. $40.00 (B-New World)
White Dessert, '99, Riesling, Gold Orion Vyd. $100.00 (S-New World)

DELICATO

12001 S. Hwy. 99, Manteca 95336
www.delicato.com

Cabernet Sauvignon, '00, California $8.00 (4)
Chardonnay, '00, California $8.00 (S-Riverside)
Merlot, '00, California $8.00 (3)
Syrah, '01, Shiraz, California $8.00 (4)
Viognier, '01, Lodi, Clay Station (Σ-State Fair)

DEUX AMIS

78670 Welter Lane, Sebastopol 95472

Zinfandel, '99, Sonoma Co. $19.00 (2)

DIABLO CREEK

Address Not Available

Cabernet Sauvignon, '00, California (S-State Fair)
Chardonnay, '01, California $8.00 (2)
Merlot, '00, California $8.00 (B-Orange)

DIABLO GRANDE

Address Not Available

Cabernet Sauvignon, '00, Desire $26.00 (S-San Fran)
Chardonnay, '01, Fruit of the Vine Diablo Grande $18.00 (2)
Red Italian, '00, Barbera, Diablo Grande $19.00 (B-San Fran)

DIAMONDBACK VINEYARDS

Address Not Available

Cabernet Sauvignon, '99, Mendocino Co. Estate $28.00 (3)
Red Rhone, '99, Syrah/Cabernet, Mendocino Co. (B-State Fair)

DK CELLARS

4054 Sayoma Lane, Placerville 95667
www.dkcellars.com

White Varietals, '00, Semillon, Sierra Foothills $15.00 (4)
Zinfandel, '99, Sierra Foothills $20.00 (4)

DOCE ROBLES WINERY

Address Not Available

Merlot, '99, Paso Robles $17.00 (4)
Red Italian, '99, Barbera, Paso Robles $28.00 (4)

Syrah, '99, Paso Robles, Estate $20.00 (5)
Zinfandel, '99, Paso Robles, Estate $18.00 (5)

DOLCE

P.O. Box 327, Oakville 94562

White Dessert, '98, Semillon, Napa Vly. LH $75.00 (G-Orange)

DOMAINE ALFRED

7525 Orcutt Rd., San Luis Obispo 93401
www.domainealfred.com

Chardonnay, '00, Califa Chamisal Vnyd., Edna Vly. $32.00 (3)
Pinot Noir, '99, Califa Chamisal Vnyd., Edna Vly. $42.00 (5)

DOMAINE CARNEROS

1240 Duhig Road, Napa 94558

Pinot Noir, '99, Napa (S-L.A.)
Sparkling Wine, '95, Brut, Le Reve By Taittinger, Carneros (B-L.A.)
Sparkling Wine, '98, Brut, Carneros Sparkling Wine (B-L.A.)

DOMAINE CHANDON

California Drive, Yountville 94599

Chardonnay, '00, Carneros (G-L.A.)
Pinot Noir, '00, Carneros $29.00 (4)
Sparkling Wine, '95, Brut, Sonoma-Napa Counties $50.00 (5)
Sparkling Wine, 'NV, Blanc De Noir, Carneros $17.00 (5)
Sparkling Wine, 'NV, Brut, Classic, California $17.00 (3)
Sparkling Wine, 'NV, Brut, Etoile, Napa & Sonoma $35.00 (6)
Sparkling Wine, 'NV, Brut, Rsv., Sonoma & Napa $24.00 (5)
Sparkling Wine, 'NV, Etoile Rose, Napa & Sonoma $40.00 (4)
Sparkling Wine, 'NV, Extra Dry, Chandon Riche, California $17.00

DOMAINE DANICA

Address Not Available
www.domainedanica.com

Pinot Noir, '99, Carneros $35.00 (3)
Zinfandel, '00, Russian River Vly., Salzgaber Vnyd. $30.00 (2)
Zinfandel, '99, Sonoma Co. $32.00 (G-Orange)

DOMAINE SONOMA WINERY

Address Not Available

Cabernet Sauvignon, '99, Russian River Vly. (G-L.A.)
Chardonnay, '99, Sonoma Co., Chalk Hill $14.00 (2)

DOMAINE ST. GEORGE WINERY

1141 Grant Ave., Healdsburg 95448

Cabernet Sauvignon, '00, Dry Creek Vly., Wells Vnyd. $15.00 (5)
Cabernet Sauvignon, '98, Russian River, STG Rsv. $17.00 (B-Orange)
Cabernet Sauvignon, '99, California Barrel Rsv. $10.00 (4)
Chardonnay, '00, California Barrel Rsv. $10.00 (3)
Chardonnay, '99, California Barrel Rsv. $10.00 (2)
Chardonnay, '99, Chalk Hill, Blasi Vnyd. $14.00 (2)
Merlot, '00, California Barrel Rsv. $8.00 (4)
Merlot, '99, California Barrel Rsv. $10.00 (B-San Fran)
Merlot, '99, Russian River Vly., Rsv. Estate $17.00 (B-San Fran)
Sauvignon Blanc, '01, St. George, California (B-L.A.)
Zinfandel, '98, Dry Creek Vly., Wells Vnyd. $16.00 (4)
Zinfandel, '99, Chalk Hill, Old Vines $16.00 (3)

DOUBLE OAK

Address Not Available

Cabernet Sauvignon, '99, Sierra Foothills (G-State Fair)

DRY CREEK VINEYARD

3770 Lambert Bridge, Healdsburg 95448
www.drycreekvineyard.com

Cabernet Sauvignon, '98, Dry Creek Vly. Rsv. $35.00 (3)
Cabernet Sauvignon, '99, Sonoma Co. $21.00 (4)
Chardonnay, '00, Sonoma Co. $16.00 (3)
Chardonnay, '99, Dry Creek Vly. Rsv. (2)
Merlot, '98, Dry Creek Vly. Rsv. $35.00 (3)
Merlot, '99, Sonoma Co. $21.00 (B-Riverside)
Red Meritage, '99, Dry Creek Vly. $28.00 (4)
Sauvignon Blanc, '00, Dry Creek Vly. Rsv. Fume $18.00 (6)
Sauvignon Blanc, '01, Dry Creek Vly., DCV3 Estate $16.00 (4)
Sauvignon Blanc, '01, Fume Blanc, Sonoma Co. $12.75 (4)
Sauvignon Blanc, '99, Fume, Dry Creek Rsv. $18.00 (B-New World)
White Dessert, '00, Sauvignon Blanc, Sonoma Co. Soleil $20.00 (3)
White Varietals, '00, Chenin Blanc, Clarksburg $9.00 (B-New World)
White Varietals, '01, Chenin Blanc, Clarksburg $9.00 (3)
Zinfandel, '00, Heritage Clone, Sonoma Co. $15.00 (3)
Zinfandel, '00, Sonoma Co. Old Vines $21.00 (2)
Zinfandel, '98, Dry Creek Vly. Rsv. $30.00 (4)
Zinfandel, '99, Dry Creek Vly., Late Harvest $13.00 (3)
Zinfandel, '99, Sonoma Co. Old Vines $21.00 (S-New World)

DUNNEWOOD

P.O. Box 268, Ukiah 95482
www.cwine.com

Cabernet Sauvignon, '97, Clara's Vnyd. $15.00 (S-W. Coast)
Cabernet Sauvignon, '99, North Coast $15.00 (2)
Pinot Noir, '99, North Coast $9.00 (S-New World)
Sauvignon Blanc, '00, Mendocino Co. $9.00 (S-New World)
Zinfandel, '98, Mendocino Co. $9.00 (B-New World)

DUTCH HENRY

4300 Silverado Trail, Calistoga 94515
www.dutchhenry.com

Cabernet Sauvignon, '99, Napa Vly. $58.00 (S-New World)
Cabernet Sauvignon, '99, Napa, Chafen Rsv. $78.00 (S-San Fran)
Merlot, '00, Napa Vly. $28.00 (B-San Fran)
Merlot, '99, Napa Vly. $28.00 (S-New World)
Red Meritage, '00, Argos, Napa Vly. $37.00 (S-San Fran)
Red Meritage, '99, Argos, Napa Vly. $35.00 (S-New World)
Zinfandel, '99, Napa Vly. $27.00 (S-New World)

E

EAGLE CASTLE WINERY

Address Not Available

Chardonnay, '00, Paso Robles $16.00 (4)

EBERLE

P.O. Box 2459, Paso Robles 93447
www.eberlewinery.com

Cabernet Sauvignon, '00, Paso Robles $24.00 (B-San Fran)
Cabernet Sauvignon, '99, Paso Robles Estate $28.00 (6)
Chardonnay, '01, Paso Robles (S-Pac. Rim)

Red Italian, '00, Barbera, Sauret & Steinbeck Vnyds. $18.00 (5)
Red Rhone, '00, Syrah/Cab, Paso Robles $24.00 (6)
Red Rhone, '01, Paso Robles (G-L.A.)
Sangiovese, '00, Paso Robles, Filipponi & Thompson $16.00 (5)
Syrah, '00, Paso Robles, Reid Vnyd. $20.00 (3)
Syrah, '00, Paso Robles, Steinbeck Vnyd. $20.00 (5)
Viognier, '00, Paso Robles, Glenrose Vnyd. $22.00 (Σ-New World)
Viognier, '00, Paso Robles, Mill Road Vyd. $18.00 (B-New World)
Viognier, '01, Paso Robles, Glenrose Vnyd. $22.00 (7)
Viognier, '01, Paso Robles, Mill Road Vyd. $18.00 (7)
White Varietals, '01, Muscat Canelli, Paso Robles $12.00 (6)
Zinfandel, '00, Paso Robles, Sauret Vnyd. $20.00 (4)
Zinfandel, '00, Paso Robles, Steinbeck Vyd. $16.00 (3)
Zinfandel, '99, Paso Robles, Sauret Vnyd. $20.00 (B-New World)

ECHELON

621 Airpak Dr., Napa 94558
www.chalonewinegroup.com

Cabernet Sauvignon, '00, California $15.00 (6)
Chardonnay, '00, Central Coast $12.50 (4)
Merlot, '00, Central Coast $13.50 (6)
Pinot Gris, '01, Central Coast Pinot Grigio $11.00 (3)
Pinot Noir, '00, Central Coast $14.00 (7)
Syrah, '00, Clarksburg, Esperanza Vyd. $13.50 (5)
Viognier, '00, Clarksburg, Esperanza Vyd. $14.00 (5)

ECKERT ESTATE WINERY

Address Not Available

Petite Sirah, '00, Lodi (G-State Fair)
Viognier, '00, Lodi (B-State Fair)
Zinfandel, '00, Contra Costa Co. (B-State Fair)

EDGEWOOD

401 S. St. Helena Hwy, Saint Helena 94574

Bordeaux, '98, Malbec, Napa Vly. $22.00 (3)
Cabernet Sauvignon, '98, Napa Vly. $22.00 (S-San Diego)
Chardonnay, '00, Napa Vly. $22.00 (2)
Zinfandel, '99, Napa Vly. $22.00 (4)

EDMEADES

5500 Hwy. 128, Philo 95466

Chardonnay, '00, Anderson Vly. $18.00 (4)
Gewurztraminer, '99, Anderson Vly. $16.00 (B-Pac. Rim)
Petite Sirah, '99, Mendocino Co., Eaglepoint Ranch $25.00 (6)
Pinot Noir, '99, Anderson Vly. $20.00 (7)
Syrah, '99, Mendocino Co., Eaglepoint Ranch $23.00 (3)
Zinfandel, '98, Mendocino Co. $16.00 (5)
Zinfandel, '99, Mendocino Ridge $25.00 (2)
Zinfandel, '99, Mendocino Ridge Ciapusci Vnyd. $25.00 (3)
Zinfandel, '99, Mendocino Ridge Zeni Vnyd. $25.00 (2)

EDNA VALLEY VINEYARD

2585 Biddle Ranch Rd., San Luis Obispo 93401
www.ednavalley.com

Chardonnay, '00, Edna Vly., Paragon Vyd. $16.50 (4)
Pinot Noir, '00, Edna Vly., Paragon Vyd. $20.00 (7)

ELKHORN PEAK

200 Polson Rd., Napa 94558

Chardonnay, '99, Napa Vly. Rsv. (S-State Fair)
Pinot Noir, '99, Napa Vly. (S-W. Coast)
Pinot Noir, '99, Napa Vly., Fagan Creek Vyd. $30.00 (4)

ENGELMANN CELLARS

Address Not Available

Red Rhone, '00, Shiraz/Cabernet, Fresno Co. Rsv. (B-State Fair)
Sangiovese, '00, California (B-L.A.)
White Varietals, '01, Summer Quartet, Fresno Co. (S-State Fair)
Zinfandel, '00, Frseno Co. Old Vine (B-State Fair)

EOS

P.O. Box 1287, Paso Robles 93447

Cabernet Sauvignon, '00, Paso Robles, Estate $18.00 (5)
Cabernet Sauvignon, '99, Paso Robles, Est. $15.00 (S-New World)
Merlot, '00, Paso Robles (B-State Fair)
Sauvignon Blanc, '00, Paso Robles, Estate $13.00 (B-San Fran)
White Dessert, '00, Moscato Tears of Dew, Paso Robles $24.00 (4)
Zinfandel, '00, Paso Robles, Estate $16.00 (5)
Zinfandel, '99, Paso Robles, Estate $15.00 (B-New World)

EQUUS WINERY

Address Not Available
www.wildhorsewinery.com

Red Italian, '99, Grenache, James Berry Vnyd. $18.00 (3)
Red Rhone, '99, Mourvedre, Paso Robles $18.00 (3)
Syrah, '98, Paso Robles (S-State Fair)
Syrah, '99, Paso Robles $18.00 (S-San Fran)
Viognier, '00, Central Coast (B-L.A.)
White Varietals, '00, Roussanne Paso Robles $16.00 (4)
White Varietals, '99, Roussanne, Paso Robles (G-L.A.)

ESTRELLA RIVER

Shandon Star Rte., Paso Robles 93446

Cabernet Sauvignon, '99, California $6.00 (G-New World)
Chardonnay, '00, California $6.00 (B-New World)
Merlot, '00, California Rsv. (B-State Fair)
Sauvignon Blanc, '99, California $6.00 (G-New World)
White Varietals, 'NV, White Table Wine, California (B-State Fair)
White Zinfandel, '01, California $5.00 (2)

ETOILE

Address Not Available

Sparkling Wine, 'NV, Napa / Sonoma $35.00 (G-Orange)
Sparkling Wine, 'NV, Rosé, Napa / Sonoma $40.00 (B-Orange)

EVERETT RIDGE VINEYARDS & WINERY

435 W. Dry Creek Rd., Healdsburg 95448
www.everettridge.com

Cabernet Sauvignon, '98, Dry Creek Vly. $24.00 (S-Riverside)
Sauvignon Blanc, '00, Powerhouse Vnyd. $14.00 (B-Riverside)
Syrah, '99, Sonoma Vly. Nuns Canyon Vnyd. $26.00 (3)
Zinfandel, '00, Dry Creek Vly., Pena Creek Vnyd. (S-State Fair)
Zinfandel, '99, Dry Creek Vly. Estate $26.00 (3)

FALKNER WINERY

Address Not Available

Chardonnay, '00, South Coast $10.00 (B-Riverside)
Dry Riesling, '00, South Coast $11.00 (S-Orange)
Sauvignon Blanc, '00, South Coast $10.00 (2)

FANUCCHI VINEYARDS

P.O. Box 290, Fulton 95439
fanucchivineyards.com

White Varietals, '00, Trousseau Gris, Russian River Vly. $13.00 (5)
White Varietals, '01, Trousseau Gris, Russian River Vly. $13.00 (5)
Zinfandel, '98, Russian River Vly., $49.00 (8)
Zinfandel, '99, Russian River Vly., $49.00 (8)

GARY FARRELL

P.O. Box 342, Forestville 95436
www.garyfarrellwines.com

Chardonnay, '00, Russian River Vly., Westside Farms $34.00 (2)
Merlot, '99, Sonoma Co., Hillside Vnyds. (G-State Fair)
Pinot Noir, '00, Russian River Vly. (S-State Fair)
Pinot Noir, '00, Russian River Vly., Olivet Lane $38.00 (2)
Pinot Noir, '00, Russian River Vly., Starr Ridge Vnyd. (B-State Fair)
Sauvignon Blanc, '01, Sonoma Co., Redwood Ranch $20.00 (2)
Zinfandel, '00, Dry Creek Vly. $24.00 (3)
Zinfandel, '00, Dry Creek Vly., Bradford Mtn. $36.00 (2)

FENESTRA

83 Vallecitos Rd., Livermore 94550
www.fenestrawinery.com

Bordeaux, '99, Cabernet Franc, Livermore Vly. $14.00 (B-Riverside)
Cabernet Sauvignon, '96, Smith & Hook Vnyd. $19.00 (S-Riverside)
Chardonnay, '00, Livermore Vly. $16.00 (B-Riverside)
Chardonnay, '01, Contra Costa Co. $12.00 (B-Orange)
Dry Riesling, '01, Arroyo Seco (S-State Fair)
Generic Red, 'NV, True Red, Lot 15, Lodi (S-L.A.)
Merlot, '99, Livermore Vly. $19.00 (5)
Petite Sirah, '99, Lodi $17.00 (6)
Pinot Noir, '99, Livermore Vly. $25.00 (S-Orange)
Red Rhone, '00, Mourvedre, Livermore Vly. $15.00 (S-Orange)
Sangiovese, '00, Lodi $14.00 (B-Orange)
Syrah, '99, Livermore Vly. $20.00 (4)
White Varietals, '01, Semillon, Livermore Vly. (S-State Fair)
Zinfandel, '99, Livermore Vly. $18.00 (6)

GLORIA FERRER

23555 Highway 121, Sonoma 95476
www.gloriaferrer.com

Chardonnay, '00, Carneros, Sonoma $20.00 (8)
Pinot Noir, '00, Carneros, Sonoma $24.00 (5)
Pinot Noir, '99, Carneros, Sonoma $24.00 (S-New World)
Sparkling Wine, '92, Brut, Carneros Cuvee $32.00 (6)
Sparkling Wine, '94, Brut, Royal Cuvee, Carneros $22.00 (7)
Sparkling Wine, 'NV, Blanc De Noir, Sonoma Co. $18.00 (6)
Sparkling Wine, 'NV, Brut, Sonoma Co. $18.00 (7)

FETZER

13325 So. Highway 101, Hopland 95449
www.fetzer.com

Cabernet Sauvignon, '98, Barrel Select, North Coast $20.00 (4)
Cabernet Sauvignon, '98, Napa Vly., Rsv. $40.00 (7)
Cabernet Sauvignon, '99, Central Coast 5 Rivers Ranch $13.00 (2)
Cabernet Sauvignon, '99, Valley Oaks, California $10.00 (4)
Chardonnay, '00, 5 Rivers Ranch, Central Coast $13.00 (4)
Chardonnay, '00, Mendocino Co. Barrel Select $14.00 (6)
Chardonnay, '00, Monterey Co., Rsv. (2)
Chardonnay, '01, Sundial, California $9.00 (7)
Dry Riesling, '01, Echo Ridge, California $8.00 (8)
Gewurztraminer, '01, Echo Ridge, California $8.00 (8)
Merlot, '00, Eagle Peak California $9.00 (3)
Merlot, '00, Sonoma Co., Barrel Select $14.00 (2)
Merlot, '99, Central Coast (S-Pac. Rim)
Merlot, '99, Central Coast 5 Rivers Ranch $13.00 (3)
Merlot, '99, Sonoma Co., Barrel Select $14.00 (3)
Pinot Noir, '00, Santa Maria Vly. 5 Rivers Ranch $13.00 (5)
Pinot Noir, '00, Santa Maria Vly., Bien Nacido Vnyd. Rsv. $40.00 (7)
Pinot Noir, '00, Sonoma Co., Barrel Select $20.00 (7)
Pinot Noir, '99, Santa Maria Vly., Bien Nacido Vnyd. Rsv. $28.00 (2)
Sauvignon Blanc, '01, Echo Ridge Sauvignon Blanc $9.00 (5)
Syrah, '99, Valley Oaks, California $9.00 (8)
White Zinfandel, '01, Echo Ridge, California $8.00 (8)
Zinfandel, '99, Barrel Select, Mendocino Co. $14.00 (7)
Zinfandel, '99, Valley Oaks, California $10.00 (4)

IELD STONE WINERY

10075 Highway 128, Healdsburg 95448

Cabernet Sauvignon, '98, Alexander Vly. Rsv. $40.00 (5)
Cabernet Sauvignon, '99, Alexander Vly. $24.00 (4)
Gewurztraminer, '00, Russian River Vly. (B-L.A.)
Petite Sirah, '98, Alexander Vly., Staten Rsv. $30.00 (S-Orange)
Sangiovese, '99, North Coast $18.00 (3)
Sauvignon Blanc, '01, Alexander Vly. $14.00 (G-Orange)

IFE VINEYARDS

P.O. Box 553, Saint Helena 94574

Zinfandel, '99, Chiles Vly., Dalraddy Vnyd. $25.00 (G-Orange)

ILSINGER VINEYARDS

39050 DePortola Rd., Temecula 92390

Cabernet Sauvignon, '99, Temecula Rsv. $21.00 (B-Orange)
Chardonnay, '00, Temecula Rsv. (G-State Fair)
Gewurztraminer, '01, Temecula Estate $8.00 (3)
Merlot, '00, Temecula (B-State Fair)
White Varietals, '01, Orange Muscat, California $9.00 (B-Riverside)

IRESTONE VINEYARD

5017 Zaca Station Rd., Los Olivos 93441
www.firestonevineyard.com

Chardonnay, '00, Santa Barbara Co. $16.00 (6)
Dry Riesling, '00, Central Coast $8.00 (S-New World)
Dry Riesling, '01, Central Coast $8.00 (B-W. Coast)
Gewurztraminer, '00, Santa Barbara Co. $10.00 (4)
Gewurztraminer, '01, Santa Barbara Co. $10.00 (2)
Merlot, '00, Santa Ynez Vly., Rsv. $30.00 (S-New World)

Merlot, '99, Santa Ynez Vly. 25th Anniversary $16.00 (5)
Sauvignon Blanc, '00, Santa Ynez Vly. $12.00 (6)
Sauvignon Blanc, '01, Santa Ynez Vly. (S-State Fair)
Syrah, '00, Santa Ynez Vly. $18.00 (3)

FLOODGATE VINEYARD

Address Not Available
www.floodgatevineyard.com

Pinot Gris, '01, Anderson Vly. $20.00 (S-Orange)
Pinot Noir, '00, Anderson Vly. $30.00 (2)

FLORA SPRINGS

1978 W. Zinfandel Lane, St Helena 94574
www.florasprings.com

Cabernet Sauvignon, '99, Napa Vly., Wild Boar Vnyd. $60.00 (4)
Merlot, '00, Napa Vly. Estate (G-L.A.)
Merlot, '99, Napa Vly., Rutherford, Windfall Vnyd. $40.00 (6)
Pinot Gris, '01, Napa Vly., Crossroads Vnyd. Pinot Grigio (2)
Red Italian, '99, Poggio Del Papa, Cypress Ranch $35.00 (8)
Red Meritage, '99, Trilogy, Napa Vly. $65.00 (4)
Sangiovese, '00, Cypress Ranch, Grandpa's Hill (S-L.A.)
Sangiovese, '00, Napa Vly. (S-Pac. Rim)
Sauvignon Blanc, '00, Soliloquy, Napa Valley-Oakville $22.50 (5)

THOMAS FOGARTY

3270 Alpine Road, Portola Valley 94028

Cabernet Sauvignon, '99, Napa Vly. $65.00 (B-San Fran)
Cabernet Sauvignon, '99, Santa Cruz Mtns. $45.00 (G-San Fran)
Chardonnay, '00, Santa Cruz Mtns. $24.00 (S-San Fran)
Gewurztraminer, '01, Monterey Co. $15.00 (B-San Fran)
Pinot Noir, '99, Santa Cruz Mtns. $23.00 (B-San Fran)

FOLEY ESTATES

1711 Alamo Pintado Rd., Solvang 93463
foleywines.com

Cabernet Sauvignon, '99, Santa Ynez, La Cuesta Vnyd. $35.00 (3)
Chardonnay, '00, Santa Barbara Co. Barrel Select $38.00 (3)
Chardonnay, '00, Santa Maria Vly., Bien Nacido Vnyd. $35.00 (2)
Pinot Noir, '00, Santa Barbara Co. Barrel Select $50.00 (4)
Pinot Noir, '00, Santa Maria Hills Vnyd. $38.00 (2)
Pinot Noir, '00, Santa Maria Vly., Dierberg Vnyd. $44.00 (B-Orange)

FOLIE A'DEUX

3070 St. Helena Highway, St Helena 94574
www.flavorweb.com/folie.htm

Cabernet Sauvignon, '98, La Grande Folie, Napa Vly. $65.00 (3)
Cabernet Sauvignon, '98, Napa Vly., Rsv. $36.00 (S-New World)
Cabernet Sauvignon, '99, Napa Vly. $26.00 (3)
Sangiovese, '99, Napa Vly. $22.00 (5)
Sparkling Wine, '98, Brut, Napa Vly., Wrotham Pinot $35.00 (3)
White Dessert, '99, Gewürtzraminer Icewine Frost $31.00 (3)
White Varietals, '00, Petite Folie, Menage a Trois $12.00 (4)
Zinfandel, '99, Amador Co. $18.00 (5)
Zinfandel, '99, Amador Co., DeMille Vnyd. $24.00 (4)
Zinfandel, '99, Amador Co., Harvey Vnyd. $28.00 (3)
Zinfandel, '99, Amador Co., The Wild Bunch Vnyd, $22.00 (5)
Zinfandel, '99, Fiddletown, Eschen Vnyd. Old Vine $24.00 (B-

FOPPIANO VINEYARDS

12707 Old Redwood Hwy., Healdsburg 95448
www.foppiano@aol.com

Cabernet Sauvignon, '00, Russian River Vly., Estate $18.00 (2)
Cabernet Sauvignon, '99, Russian River Vly., Estate $17.50 (2)
Chardonnay, '00, California Riverside Collection $7.50 (2)
Merlot, '97, Russian River Vly., Rsv. Estate $31.00 (3)
Merlot, '98, Sonoma Co. $18.00 (3)
Petite Sirah, '00, Sonoma Co. Estate $23.00 (3)
Petite Sirah, '99, Sonoma Co. Estate $20.50 (3)
Pinot Noir, '98, Russian River Vly., Estate (S-L.A.)
Pinot Noir, '99, Russian River Vly., Estate $21.00 (S-San Fran)
Sangiovese, '00, Alexander Vly. $18.00 (6)
Syrah, '97, California Riverside Collection $9.00 (Σ-New World)
White Zinfandel, 'NV, Riverside Collection $6.25 (S-Riverside)
Zinfandel, '00, Dry Creek Vly. $15.00 (5)
Zinfandel, '99, Dry Creek, Valera Vnyd. Rsv. $24.00 (S-W. Coast)

FORCHINI VINEYARDS

5141 Dry Creek Road, Healdsburg 95448

Cabernet Sauvignon, '99, Dry Creek Vly. Rsv. $26.00 (7)
Pinot Noir, '00, Russian River Vly. Rsv. $24.00 (S-New World)

FOREST GLEN WINERY

P.O. Box 789, Ceres 95307

Cabernet Sauvignon, '99, Oak Barrel Selection, California $10.00
Chardonnay, '00, Oak Barrel Fermented, California $10.00 (3)
Merlot, '00, Oak Barrel Selection $10.00 (2)
Pinot Gris, '00, California $10.00 (B-New World)
Pinot Gris, '01, California $10.00 (B-San Diego)
Sangiovese, '99, Oak Barrel Selection, California $10.00 (3)
Syrah, '00, Oak Barrel Selection, California $10.00 (7)
Syrah, '99, Oak Barrel Selection, California $10.00 (B-New World)

FORESTVILLE VINEYARD

7010 Trenton-Healdsburg Rd., Forestville 95436

Cabernet Sauvignon, '99, California (S-State Fair)
Chardonnay, '00, Russian River Vly. Rsv. $12.00 (4)
Chardonnay, '99, Sonoma Co. Rsv. $16.00 (B-New World)
Dry Riesling, '00, California $6.00 (B-Orange)
Merlot, '00, California (S-State Fair)
Sangiovese, '99, California $6.00 (G-New World)
Syrah, '00, California $6.00 (2)
White Zinfandel, '01, California (S-State Fair)
Zinfandel, '00, California $6.00 (2)

FOXHOLLOW VINEYARDS

P.O. Box 416, Sonoma 95476

Cabernet Sauvignon, '99, California, Barrel Select $9.00 (3)
Chardonnay, '99, California, Barrel Select $9.00 (2)
Merlot, '00, California, Barrel Select $9.00 (3)
Pinot Noir, '00, California, Barrel Select $9.00 (2)
Syrah, '00, California, Barrel Select $9.00 (5)

FRANCISCAN OAKVILLE ESTATE

1178 Galleron Rd., Rutherford 94573
www.franciscan.com

Cabernet Sauvignon, '99, Napa Vly. $27.00 (S-Orange)
Chardonnay, '00, Cuvée Sauvage, Wild Yeast Napa Vly. $35.00

Merlot, '00, Napa Vly. $22.00 (B-San Fran)
Red Meritage, '99, Magnificat Napa Vly. $45.00 (B-San Fran)

FRANK FAMILY VINEYARDS

Address Not Available

Cabernet Sauvignon, '95, FRL Cellars, Rsv. $165.00 (S-San Fran)
Cabernet Sauvignon, '96, FRL Cellars, Rsv. $150.00 (S-San Fran)
Cabernet Sauvignon, '98, Rsv. Rutherford $65.00 (B-San Fran)
Chardonnay, '00, Napa Vly. $29.00 (B-San Fran)

FRATELLI PERATA

1595 Arbor Rd., Paso Robles 93446

Cabernet Sauvignon, '97, Paso Robles Riserva $40.00 (2)
Cabernet Sauvignon, '98, Paso Robles $18.00 (2)
Merlot, '98, Paso Robles $18.00 (4)
Red Italian, '97, Tre Sorelle Paso Robles $35.00 (B-San Fran)

FREI BROTHERS WINERY

Address Not Available
www.freibros.com

Cabernet Sauvignon, '98, Alexander Vly. Rsv. $24.00 (2)
Cabernet Sauvignon, '99, Alexander Vly. Rsv. $24.00 (6)
Chardonnay, '00, Russian River Vly. $17.00 (5)
Merlot, '00, Dry Creek Vly. Rsv. $17.00 (6)
Pinot Noir, '00, Russian River Vly. Rsv. $24.00 (7)

FRENCH HILL WINERY

Address Not Available

Merlot, '00, El Dorado, Gold Hill Vnyd. $28.00 (2)
Red Italian, '00, Barbera, Amador Co. $26.00 (G-Orange)
Syrah, '00, El Dorado Rsv. (S-State Fair)
Zinfandel, '00, Amador Co. Bowman Vnyd. $22.00 (B-Riverside)

FRESNO STATE VINEYARDS

Address Not Available

Chardonnay, '00, Duarte Linden Hills Vnyd., California (B-L.A.)
Sangiovese, '00, California $10.00 (B-Orange)
Syrah, '00, California $10.00 (2)
Syrah, '99, John Diener Vnyd., 13.75% Alc. $13.00 (3)
Syrah, '99, John Diener Vnyd., 14.25% Alc. $13.00 (2)
White Zinfandel, '01, Fresno State Vnyd, California $6.00 (2)
Zinfandel, '00, Duarte Linden Hills Vnyd., Primitivo Rsv. $15.00 (2)

FREY VINEYARDS

14000 Tomki Rd., Redwood Valley 95470

Cabernet Sauvignon, '00, Redwood Vly., Org. $11.25 (B-W. Coast)
Merlot, '01, Redwood Vly., Biodynamic $19.00 (4)
Merlot, '01, Redwood Vly., Organic $17.00 (2)
Petite Sirah, '00, Mendocino Co., Organic $12.25 (3)
Syrah, '01, Mendocino Co., Organic (G-L.A.)
Zinfandel, '00, Mendocino Co., Organic $10.50 (2)

J. FRITZ WINERY

24691 Dutcher Creek, Cloverdale 95425

Chardonnay, '99, Russian River Vly. $22.00 (2)
Chardonnay, '99, Sonoma Co., Dutton Ranch (S-Pac. Rim)

THE GAINEY VINEYARD

P.O. Box 910, Santa Ynez 93460

Bordeaux, '99, Cabernet Franc, Santa Ynez Vly. $25.00 (S-Orange)
Chardonnay, '00, Santa Barbara Co. (B-L.A.)
Chardonnay, '01, Santa Ynez Vly. (S-Pac. Rim)
Dry Riesling, '00, Santa Ynez Vly. $12.00 (G-New World)
Dry Riesling, '01, Santa Ynez Vly. $12.00 (5)
Merlot, '98, Santa Ynez Vly. $20.00 (B-New World)
Merlot, '99, Santa Ynez Vly. $16.00 (3)
Sauvignon Blanc, '00, Santa Ynez Vly. $14.00 (4)

GALLEANO

42331 Wineville Rd., Mira Loma 91752

Red Rhone, '99, Ramon's Red, Cucamonga Vly. $9.00 (2)
Zinfandel, '00, Cucamonga Vly. Lot J6 (B-Orange)
Zinfandel, '99, Cucamonga Dos Rancheros $18.00 (B-Riverside)

GALLERON

Address Not Available

Merlot, '99, Napa Vly., Jaeger Vnyd. (Σ-State Fair)
Zinfandel, '00, Sonoma Co., Branham Rockpile (B-State Fair)

GALLO OF SONOMA

3387 Dry Creek Rd., Healdsburg 95448
www.gallosonoma.com

Cabernet Sauvignon, '90, Northern Sonoma Estate (G-L.A.)
Cabernet Sauvignon, '91, Northern Sonoma Estate $50.00 (2)
Cabernet Sauvignon, '92, Dry Creek Vly., Frei Vnyd. (B-L.A.)
Cabernet Sauvignon, '92, Northern Sonoma Estate $50.00 (2)
Cabernet Sauvignon, '93, Northern Sonoma Est. $55.00 (S-San Fran)
Cabernet Sauvignon, '94, Dry Creek Vly., Frei Vnyd. $18.00 (2)
Cabernet Sauvignon, '94, Northern Sonoma Estate $60.00 (2)
Cabernet Sauvignon, '96, Dry Creek Vly., Frei Vnyd. (S-L.A.)
Cabernet Sauvignon, '96, Dry Creek Vly., Stefani Vnyd. (S-L.A.)
Cabernet Sauvignon, '97, Alexander Vly., Barelli Creek $28.00 (7)
Cabernet Sauvignon, '97, Dry Creek Vly. Stefani Vnyd. $28.00 (4)
Cabernet Sauvignon, '97, Dry Creek Vly., Frei Vnyd. $28.00 (5)
Cabernet Sauvignon, '97, Northern Sonoma Estate $70.00 (4)
Cabernet Sauvignon, '98, Northern Sonoma $70.00 (S-W. Coast)
Cabernet Sauvignon, '99, Sonoma Rsv., Barrel Aged $13.00 (9)
Chardonnay, '00, Russian River Vly. Laguna Vnyd. $22.00 (3)
Chardonnay, '00, Sonoma Co. Rsv., Barrel Ferm. $11.00 (7)
Chardonnay, '98, Northern Sonoma Estate $45.00 (4)
Chardonnay, '99, Dry Creek Vly., Stefani Vnyd. $22.00 (8)
Chardonnay, '99, Northern Sonoma Estate $50.00 (2)
Chardonnay, '99, Russian River Vly. Laguna Vnyd. $24.00 (5)
Merlot, '99, Sonoma Co. $11.00 (3)
Pinot Gris, '00, Sonoma Coast $13.00 (4)
Pinot Gris, '01, Sonoma Coast $13.00 (4)
Pinot Noir, '00, Sonoma Co. Rsv., Barrel Aged $15.00 (8)
Red Italian, '00, Barbera, Alexander Vly. Barrelli Creek (S-San Fran)
Red Italian, '99, Barbera, AV, Barrelli Creek Vnyd. $22.00 (5)
Sangiovese, '99, Alexander Vly. $13.00 (7)
Zinfandel, '98, Alexander Vly., Barelli Creek Vnyd. $20.00 (2)
Zinfandel, '98, Dry Creek Vly., Frei Vnyd. $20.00 (5)

GAMBA VINEYARDS AND WINERY

Address Not Available

Zinfandel, '00, Russian River Vly. Old Vine $40.00 (G-Orange)

GAN EDEN

4950 Ross Road, Sebastopol 95472
www.ganeden.com

Cabernet Sauvignon, '97, Mendocino Co. Limited Rsv. $40.00 (5)
White Dessert, '00, Gewurztraminer, Monterey, Zabala $14.00 (6)

GEHRINGER BROTHERS ESTATE WINERY

Address Not Available

Chardonnay, '01, Dry Rock Vnyds. (B-L.A.)
White Varietals, '01, Classic Auxerrois (S-L.A.)
White Varietals, '01, Classic Ehrenfelser (S-L.A.)

GEYSER PEAK

22281 Chianti Rd., Geyserville 95441
www.geyserpeakwinery.com

Bordeaux, '99, Cabernet Franc, Alexander Vly. $20.00 (8)
Bordeaux, '99, Malbec, Alexander Vly. $20.00 (8)
Bordeaux, '99, Petite Verdot, Sonoma Co. $20.00 (9)
Cabernet Sauvignon, '98, Alexander Vly., Kuimelis Vnyd. $26.00 (2)
Cabernet Sauvignon, '98, Napa Vly., Vallerga Vnyd. $35.00 (4)
Cabernet Sauvignon, '98, Sonoma Co. Rsv. $40.00 (G-New World)
Cabernet Sauvignon, '99, Alexander Vly., Kuimelis Vnyd. $26.00 (6)
Cabernet Sauvignon, '99, Vallerga Vnyd. $35.00 (S-New World)
Cabernet Sauvignon, '99, Sonoma Co. $17.00 (5)
Cabernet Sauvignon, '99, Sonoma Co. Rsv. $40.00 (6)
Chardonnay, '00, Alexander Vly. Rsv. $23.00 (8)
Chardonnay, '00, Carneros-Sonoma Vly., Ricci Vnyd. $21.00 (9)
Chardonnay, '00, Russian River Vly. $16.00 (4)
Chardonnay, '00, Sonoma Co. $12.00 (5)
Dry Riesling, '01, California $9.00 (9)
Gewurztraminer, '01, California $9.00 (9)
Merlot, '98, Alexander Vly. Rsv. $40.00 (Σ-New World)
Merlot, '98, Sonoma Vly., Shorenstein Vnyd. $26.00 (3)
Merlot, '99, Alexander Vly. Rsv. $40.00 (3)
Merlot, '99, Sonoma Co. $17.00 (5)
Merlot, '99, Sonoma Co. Rsv. $32.00 (5)
Merlot, '99, Sonoma Vly., Shorenstein Vnyd. $26.00 (G-W. Coast)
Petite Sirah, '99, Alexander Vly., Winemaker's Selection $20.00 (4)
Red Meritage, '98, Rsv. Alexandre, Alexander Vly. $45.00 (5)
Red Meritage, '99, Rsv. Alexandre, Alexander Vly. $45.00 (6)
Sauvignon Blanc, '01, California $10.00 (8)
Syrah, '00, Sonoma Co. Shiraz $17.00 (8)
Syrah, '98, Sonoma Co. Shiraz Rsv. $40.00 (7)
Syrah, '99, Sonoma Co. Shiraz Rsv. $40.00 (6)
Viognier, '00, Alexander Vly., Sonoma Moment Vnyd. $19.00 (3)
White Dessert, '00, Riesling, Dry Creek Vly., LH Rsv. $19.00 (7)
White Dessert, '00, Riesling, Mendocino Co., LH Rsv. $19.00 (7)
Zinfandel, '00, Cucamonga Vly., DeAmbrogio Vnyd. $30.00 (3)
Zinfandel, '00, Sonoma Co. $17.00 (7)

GLEN ELLEN WINERY

21468 - 8th Street E., Sonoma 95476

Cabernet Sauvignon, '00, California $7.00 (B-San Fran)
Chardonnay, '00, California $7.00 (S-San Fran)

Sauvignon Blanc, '01, California $7.00 (B-San Fran)
White Zinfandel, '00, California $7.00 (2)

GNEKOW FAMILY WINERY

17347 E. Gawne Rd., Collegeville 95215

White Varietals, '00, YN, Blended Vnyd., California $4.00 (5)
Zinfandel, '00, Campus Oaks, Old Vine, Lodi (B-L.A.)

GODWIN

7010 Trenton-Healdsburg Rd., Forestville 95436
www.wimbledonwine.com

Merlot, '99, Alexander Vly., Moss Oak Vnyd. $35.00 (S-Orange)
Red Meritage, '00, Alexander Vly., Moss Oak $35.00 (S-San Fran)
Red Meritage, '99, Alexander Vly., Moss Oak Vnyd. $35.00 (7)

GOLD HILL

5660 Vineyard Lane, Coloma 95613

Cabernet Sauvignon, '99, El Dorado (G-State Fair)
Red Italian, '99, Barbera, El Dorado (S-State Fair)
Sparkling Wine, 'NV, Extra Dry, California (B-State Fair)

GRAESER

255 Petrified Forest Rd., Calistoga 94515

Bordeaux, '98, Cabernet Franc, Diamond Mtn. Estate (B-L.A.)
Red Meritage, '99, Red Table Wine, Diamond Mtn. (3)

GRAND CRU VINEYARDS

1 Vintage Lane, Glen Ellen 95442

Dry Riesling, '00, California $7.00 (B-New World)
Syrah, '00, California $7.00 (3)

GRANITE SPRINGS

5050 Granite Springs Winery Road, Somerset 95684

Chardonnay, '01, El Dorado (G-State Fair)
Merlot, '99, El Dorado $16.00 (G-Orange)
Petite Sirah, '00, Fair Play (B-State Fair)
Petite Sirah, '99, El Dorado $12.50 (2)
Sauvignon Blanc, '00, El Dorado $10.00 (S-Pac. Rim)
Sauvignon Blanc, '01, El Dorado $10.00 (G-Orange)
Syrah, '99, El Dorado $16.00 (2)
Zinfandel, '00, Fair Play (S-State Fair)
Zinfandel, '99, Sierra Foothills, La Falda de la Sierra $13.00 (2)

GREENWOOD RIDGE VINEYARDS

5501 Highway 128, Philo 95466
www.greenwoodridge.com

Cabernet Sauvignon, '99, Mendocino Ridge Estate $30.00 (7)
Chardonnay, '00, Mendocino, DuPratt Vnyd. $24.00 (S-New World)
Dry Riesling, '00, Mendocino Ridge Estate $12.00 (2)
Dry Riesling, '01, Mendocino Ridge Estate (4)
Merlot, '99, Mendocino Ridge Estate $24.00 (5)
Pinot Noir, '00, Anderson Vly. $24.00 (5)
Sauvignon Blanc, '00, Anderson Vly. $13.50 (4)
White Dessert, '01, Riesling, Late Harvest, Estate $24.00 (5)
Zinfandel, '00, Scherrer Vnyds., Sonoma Co. $24.00 (8)

GRGICH HILLS

1829 St. Helena Hwy., Rutherford 94573
www.grgich.com

Cabernet Sauvignon, '98, Napa Vly. $50.00 (4)
Chardonnay, '99, Napa Vly. $33.00 (7)

Merlot, '99, Napa Vly. $38.00 (5)
Sauvignon Blanc, '00, Fume Blanc, Napa Vly. $18.00 (3)
Sauvignon Blanc, '99, Fume Blanc, Napa Vly. $18.00 (2)
White Dessert, '00, Violetta, Napa Vly., Late Harvest $40.00 (3)
Zinfandel, '98, Miljenko's Old Vines, Napa Vly. (B-L.A.)
Zinfandel, '99, Napa and Sonoma Countries $25.00 (4)

GROVE STREET

1440 Grove St., Healdsburg 95448
www.grovestreetwinery.com

Cabernet Sauvignon, '99, Alexander Vly. $39.00 (7)
Cabernet Sauvignon, '99, Napa Vly. $39.00 (4)
Chardonnay, '99, Sonoma Co. $15.00 (6)

GUENOC

21000 Butts Canyon Rd., Middletown 95461
www.guenoc.com

Cabernet Sauvignon, '00, California $14.00 (5)
Cabernet Sauvignon, '97, Tephra Ridge $34.00 (S-San Diego)
Cabernet Sauvignon, '98, Lake Co., Tephra Ridge $40.50 (B-L.A.)
Cabernet Sauvignon, '98, Napa Vly., Beckstoffer, Rsv. $41.00 (6)
Cabernet Sauvignon, '98, North Coast $17.00 (5)
Chardonnay, '00, California $11.50 (B-Orange)
Chardonnay, '00, Guenoc Vly. $14.50 (3)
Chardonnay, '00, Guenoc Vly., G. Magoon Rsv. $27.00 (2)
Chardonnay, '99, Guenoc Vly. $15.00 (4)
Chardonnay, '99, Guenoc Vly., G. Magoon Rsv. $27.00 (4)
Petite Sirah, '98, Guenoc Vly. Serpentine Meadow $36.00 (6)
Petite Sirah, '98, North Coast $19.00 (5)
Petite Sirah, '99, North Coast $19.00 (5)
Red Meritage, '97, Langtry, North Coast $49.00 (B-Pac. Rim)
Red Meritage, '98, Langtry, Napa/Lake Co. $49.00 (7)
Red Meritage, '98, Napa & Lake Co. Victorian Claret $20.50 (2)
Sauvignon Blanc, '00, North Coast $14.00 (4)
Sauvignon Blanc, '01, California $10.00 (4)
White Meritage, '00, Langtry, Guenoc Vly. $21.00 (5)
Zinfandel, '99, California $11.50 (5)

EMILIO GUGLIELMO WINERY

1480 East Main Ave., Morgan Hill 95037
www.guglielmowinery.com

Cabernet Sauvignon, '99, Central Coast, Vnyd. Select. $10.00 (4)
Chardonnay, '00, Carneros Private Rsv. $16.00 (2)
Petite Sirah, '99, Santa Clara Vly. (B-State Fair)
Red Italian, '00, Barbera, Sonoma Co. Rsv. (S-State Fair)
Sangiovese, '00, Napa Vly. Private Rsv. $12.00 (4)
Zinfandel, '99, Santa Clara Vly., Rsv. $13.00 (2)

GUNDLACH-BUNDSCHU WINERY

2000 Denmark St., Sonoma 95476
www.gunbun.com

Cabernet Sauvignon, '97, Sonoma Vly., Rhinefarm Rsv. (S-L.A.)
Cabernet Sauvignon, '99, Sonoma Vly., Rhinefarm Vnyd. $30.00
Chardonnay, '00, Sonoma Vly., Rhinefarm Vnyd. $20.00 (5)
Gewurztraminer, '01, Sonoma Vly., Rhinefarm Vnyd. $18.00 (4)
Merlot, '99, Sonoma Vly., Rhinefarm Vnyd. $28.00 (6)
Pinot Noir, '00, Sonoma Vly., Rhinefarm Vnyd. $27.00 (3)
Zinfandel, '00, Sonoma Vly., Morse Vnyd. (G-L.A.)
Zinfandel, '00, Sonoma Vly., Rhinefarm Vnyd. $26.00 (4)

HACIENDA WINERY

P.O. Box 789, Ceres 95307

Cabernet Sauvignon, '99, Calif. Clair de Lune $7.00 (S-Riverside)
Chardonnay, '99, California Clair de Lune $7.00 (2)
Merlot, '00, California Clair de Lune $7.00 (2)
Pinot Noir, '99, California Clair de Lune (2)
Sauvignon Blanc, '99, California Clair de Lune $7.00 (Σ-W. Coast)
Sparkling Wine, 'NV, Brut, California $10.00 (2)
White Varietals, '99, Chenin Blanc, California $7.00 (B-San Diego)
White Zinfandel, '00, California Clair de Lune $6.00 (4)

HAGAFEN CELLARS

P.O. Box 3035, Napa 94558
www.hagafen.com

Cabernet Sauvignon, '99, Napa Vly. $36.00 (2)
Chardonnay, '00, Napa Vly. (B-Pac. Rim)
Dry Riesling, '01, Napa Vly. $15.00 (4)
Syrah, '99, Napa Vly. $27.00 (2)

HAHN ESTATES

37700 Foothill Rd., Soledad 93960
www.wimbledonwine.com

Chardonnay, '99, Monterey Co. (B-Pac. Rim)
Merlot, '98, Santa Lucia Highlands $12.00 (4)
Red Meritage, '99, Santa Lucia Highlands $18.00 (6)

ROBERT HALL WINERY

Address Not Available

Cabernet Sauvignon, '00, Paso Robles $18.00 (B-San Fran)
Merlot, '00, Paso Robles $18.00 (S-San Fran)
Sauvignon Blanc, '01, Paso Robles, Red Tail $14.00 (B-San Fran)

HANDLEY

P.O. Box 66, Philo 95466
www.handleycellars.com

Chardonnay, '00, Anderson Vly. Estate $16.00 (3)
Chardonnay, '00, Dry Creek Vly., Handley Vnyd. $18.00 (3)
Chardonnay, '99, Anderson Vly. Estate $16.00 (3)
Gewurztraminer, '00, Anderson Vly. $14.00 (2)
Gewurztraminer, '01, Anderson Vly. $14.00 (Σ-Riverside)
Pinot Gris, '01, Anderson Vly. $16.00 (5)
Pinot Noir, '00, Anderson Vly. (B-State Fair)
Pinot Noir, '00, Santa Lucia, River Road Vnyd. $25.00 (S-W. Coast)
Pinot Noir, '98, Anderson Vly. Rsv. $48.00 (B-New World)
Pinot Noir, '99, Anderson Vly. $25.00 (4)
Pinot Noir, '99, Anderson Vly. Rsv. $48.00 (3)
Sauvignon Blanc, '00, Anderson Vly., Ferrington Vnyd. $14.00 (4)
Sparkling Wine, '96, Brut, Anderson Vly. $28.00 (4)
Sparkling Wine, '97, Brut Anderson Vly. $28.00 (B-San Fran)
Sparkling Wine, '98, Brut Rose, Anderson Vly. $28.00 (3)
White Varietals, '01, Brightlighter White, Anderson Vly. $11.00 (2)

HANNA

4345 Occidental Rd., Santa Rosa 95401
www.flavorweb.com/hanna

Cabernet Sauvignon, '98, Sonoma Vly., Bismark Rnch (B-State Fair)
Cabernet Sauvignon, '99, Alexander Vly. $25.00 (2)

Chardonnay, '00, Russian River Vly. $19.00 (2)
Merlot, '99, Alexander Vly. $25.00 (2)
Pinot Noir, '99, Russian River Vly. $22.00 (B-W. Coast)
Sauvignon Blanc, '00, Slusser Road Vnyd. $16.00 (B-New World)
Sauvignon Blanc, '01, Russian River, Slusser Road Vnyd. $16.00 (3)
Syrah, '98, Sonoma Vly., Bismark Ranch $45.00 (B-San Fran)
Zinfandel, '99, Sonoma Vly., Bismark Ranch $49.00 (S-W. Coast)

HARMONY CELLARS

P.O. Box 2502, Harmony 93435
www.harmonycellars.net

Cabernet Sauvignon, '99, Paso Robles $16.00 (7)
Chardonnay, '00, San Luis Obispo Co. $15.00 (2)
Merlot, '00, Paso Robles $15.00 (2)
White Varietals, 'NV, White Table Wine $10.00 (B-New World)
Zinfandel, '00, Paso Robles $17.00 (B-San Fran)

HART WINERY

32580 Rancho Calif. Rd., Temecula 92390

Merlot, '00, Estate, Temecula $24.00 (3)
Red Rhone, '99, Grenache-Syrah, South Coast $14.00 (3)
Zinfandel, '99, Cucamonga Vly., Lopez Ranch $18.00 (S-Riverside)

HARTWELL VINEYARDS

Address Not Available

Cabernet Sauvignon, '99, Stag's Leap District $100.00 (S-San Fran)
Merlot, '99, Stags Leap District $60.00 (G-Riverside)

HAWLEY WINES

Address Not Available

Cabernet Sauvignon, '99, Dry Creek Vly. (2)
Merlot, '99, Bradford Mtn. $25.00 (4)
Viognier, '01, Placer Co. $20.50 (3)

HEITZ WINE CELLAR

500 Taplin Rd., Saint Helena 94574

Cabernet Sauvignon, '97, Napa, Trailside Vnyd. $70.00 (B-San Fran)
Chardonnay, '00, Napa Vly., Cellar Selection $30.00 (2)

HELLER ESTATE

18820 Cachagua Rd., Carmel Valley 93924
www.hellerestate.com

Cabernet Sauvignon, '97, Carmel Vly./Monterey Rsv. $100.00 (2)
Cabernet Sauvignon, '99, Carmel/Monterey $28.00 (S-San Fran)
Chardonnay, '98, Carmel Vly./Monterey (S-State Fair)
Merlot, '99, Carmel Vly./Monterey, Durney Vnyd. $26.00 (2)

HESS COLLECTION WINERY

4411 Redwood Road, Napa 94558
www.hesscollection.com

Cabernet Sauvignon, '98, Napa, Mt. Veeder $35.00 (S-Orange)
Cabernet Sauvignon, '99, California, Hess Select $14.00 (B-San
Cabernet Sauvignon, '99, Napa, Hess Estate $20.00 (S-San Fran)
Chardonnay, '00, Napa Vly., Hess Collection $20.00 (Σ-San Fran)
Syrah, '00, California, Hess Select $14.00 (B-San Fran)

HIDDEN CELLARS

1500 Ruddick-Cunningham Rd., Ukiah 95482
www.parducci.com

Cabernet Sauvignon, '97, Mendocino Co. $13.00 (G-San Diego)
Petite Sirah, '98, Mendocino Co. (B-L.A.)

Syrah, '98, Mendocino Co. $13.00 (S-Orange)
Zinfandel, '98, Mendocino Co. $15.00 (B-W. Coast)
Zinfandel, '98, Old Vines, Mendocino Co. $13.00 (2)
Zinfandel, '98, Sorcery, Mendocino Co. $19.00 (S-San Diego)

HIDDEN MOUNTAIN RANCH

5065 Adelaida Rd., Paso Robles 93446

Zinfandel, '99, Paso Robles Dante Dusi Vnyd. $22.00 (5)
Zinfandel, '99, Paso Robles Wine Bush Vnyd. East $16.00 (3)

WILLIAM HILL WINERY

1761 Atlas Peak Rd., Napa 94558
www.williamhillwinery.com

Cabernet Sauvignon, '98, Napa Vly. Rsv. $38.00 (S-Orange)
Cabernet Sauvignon, '99, Napa Vly. (S-L.A.)
Chardonnay, '00, Napa Vly. $16.00 (2)
Chardonnay, '00, Napa Vly. Rsv. $23.00 (3)

HOP KILN WINERY

6050 Westside Rd., Healdsburg 95448
www.hopkilnwinery.com

Chardonnay, '00, Russian River Vly., Griffin Vnyd. $18.00 (2)
Chardonnay, '01, North Coast $12.00 (3)
Dry Riesling, '01, Russian River Vly., Griffin Vnyd. (B-State Fair)
Zinfandel, '00, Russian River Vly. Late Harvest $16.00 (B-New World)
Zinfandel, '99, Russian River Vly. Old Windmill Vnyd. $20.00 (5)
Zinfandel, '99, Russian River Vly. Primitivo Vnyd, $18.00 (5)

HRM

Address Not Available
www.hanhestates.com

Cabernet Sauvignon, 'NV, Central Coast $8.00 (2)
Chardonnay, '00, Central Coast $8.00 (2)
Merlot, 'NV, Central Coast (S-State Fair)

VICTOR HUGO

Address Not Available

Cabernet Sauvignon, '99, Paso Robles $18.00 (7)
Petite Sirah, '00, Paso Robles $17.00 (4)
Petite Sirah, '99, Paso Robles $17.00 (S-Riverside)
Red Meritage, '99, Opulence Paso Robles $22.00 (6)
Syrah, '00, Paso Robles Estate $20.00 (3)
Syrah, '99, Paso Robles $19.50 (B-New World)
Viognier, '00, Paso Robles (B-Pac. Rim)
Zinfandel, '99, Paso Robles $17.00 (6)

HUNT CELLARS

Address Not Available
www.huntcellars.com

Cabernet Sauvignon, '99, Paso Robles, Destiny Vnyd. $24.00 (3)
Chardonnay, '00, Central Coast (B-L.A.)
Sauvignon Blanc, '00, Paso Robles, Destiny Vnyd. (B-State Fair)
Syrah, '99, California, Serenade $22.00 (3)
Zinfandel, '00, Paso Robles, Outlaw Ridge $35.00 (2)
Zinfandel, '00, Paso Robles, Zinphony 2 $30.00 (2)

HUNTINGTON

18700 Geyserville Ave., Geyserville 95441
www.wimbledonwine.com

Chardonnay, '00, Russian River Vly. $15.00 (B-W. Coast)

Merlot, '99, Sonoma Co. $18.00 (5)
Sauvignon Blanc, '01, Earthquake, Napa Vly. $12.00 (4)

HUSCH VINEYARDS

4400 Highway 128, Philo 95466
www.huschvineyards.com

Cabernet Sauvignon, '99, Mendocino, La Ribera Vnyd. $19.00 (2)
Chardonnay, '00, Mendocino Co. $14.00 (3)
Chardonnay, '99, Anderson Vly., Rsv. $25.00 (6)
Gewurztraminer, '00, Anderson Vly., Day Ranch (B-Pac. Rim)
Gewurztraminer, '01, Anderson Vly., Estate $12.00 (4)
Pinot Noir, '98, Anderson Vly., Rsv. (• -Pac. Rim)
Pinot Noir, '99, Anderson Vly., Estate $18.50 (B-New World)
Sauvignon Blanc, '00, Mendocino, La Ribera $18.00 (B-New World)
Sauvignon Blanc, '01, Mendocino Co., La Ribera Vnyd. $13.00 (4)
White Varietals, '00, Muscat, La Ribera $14.00 (Σ-New World)
White Varietals, '01, Chenin Blanc, La Ribera $9.00 (Σ-New World)
White Varietals, '01, Muscat, La Ribera $14.00 (B-State Fair)

I

ICARA CREEK WINERY

Address Not Available

Cabernet Sauvignon, '97, Alexander Vly., Hillside Vnyd. $60.00 (2)
Cabernet Sauvignon, '98, Alexander Vly., Hillside Vnyd. (S-L.A.)

IMAGERY SERIES

1883 London Ranch Rd., Glen Ellen 95442
www.imagerywinery.com

Bordeaux, '99, Barbera, Sonoma Vly. $33.00 (S-W. Coast)
Bordeaux, '99, Cabernet Franc, Alexander Vly. (G-L.A.)
Bordeaux, '99, Malbec, Alexander Vly. $33.00 (5)
Cabernet Sauvignon, '98, Alexander Vly., Ash Creek $50.00 (2)
Cabernet Sauvignon, '98, Sonoma Vly., Sunny Slope $50.00 (4)
Cabernet Sauvignon, '99, Alexander Vly., Ash Creek Vyd. (2)
Cabernet Sauvignon, '99, Sonoma Vly., Sunny Slope $50.00 (4)
Chardonnay, '99, Carneros, Ricci Vnyd. $25.00 (5)
Merlot, '99, Sonoma Vly., Sunny Slope Vyd. $35.00 (4)
Petite Sirah, '99, Artist Collection, Paso Robles $35.00 (6)
Red Italian, '99, Barbera, Sonoma Vly. (S-L.A.)
Red Italian, '99, Tuscan Blend, Sonoma Co. (G-L.A.)
Sangiovese, '99, Artist Collection Sonoma $25.00 (2)
White Varietals, '00, White Burgundy, Napa Vly. (2)
White Varietals, '99, Pinot Blanc, Santa Maria $21.00 (2)
White Varietals, '99, White Burgundy, Napa Vly. $25.00 (2)
Zinfandel, '99, Taylor Vnyd., Dry Creek Vly. $35.00 (3)

INCOGNITO

Address Not Available

Red Rhone, 'NV, Rhone Blends, Lodi $22.00 (2)
Viognier, '01, California $22.00 (2)

INDIAN SPRINGS VINEYARDS

16110 Indian Springs Rd., Penn Valley 95946
www.gv.net/~isv

Bordeaux, '99, Cabernet Franc, Nevada Co. $16.00 (6)
Cabernet Sauvignon, '99, Nevada Co. $20.00 (4)
Chardonnay, '00, Nevada Co. $14.50 (2)
Merlot, '99, Nevada Co. $18.00 (5)

Sangiovese, '99, Nevada Co. $16.00 (B-New World)
Syrah, '99, Nevada Co. $18.00 (5)

INDIGO HILLS

3387 Dry Creek Rd., Healdsburg 95448

Chardonnay, '00, Central Coast (G-L.A.)
Merlot, '99, San Francisco Bay Livermore Vly. $14.00 (3)
Pinot Noir, '99, Central Coast $12.00 (5)

INGLENOOK ESTATE CELLARS

1991 St. Helena Hwy., Rutherford 94573

Chardonnay, 'NV, California $8.00 (4)
Merlot, 'NV, California $8.00 (B-New World)
Sauvignon Blanc, 'NV, California $8.00 (2)
White Varietals, 'NV, Chardonnay/Pinot Grigio $8.00 (B-New World)

IRON HORSE VINEYARDS

9786 Ross Station Road, Sebastopol 95472

Sparkling Wine, '96, Brut, Sonoma, Green Vly. $25.00 (G-Orange)

IRONSTONE VINEYARDS

1894 Six-Mile Rd., Murphys 95247
www.ironstonevineyards.com

Bordeaux, '99, Cabernet Franc, California $9.00 (2)
Bordeaux, '99, Cabernet Franc, Sierra Foothills Rsv. $18.00 (3)
Cabernet Sauvignon, '99, California $10.00 (3)
Chardonnay, '00, California $10.00 (B-W. Coast)
Syrah, '00, California Shiraz $10.00 (5)
White Varietals, '01, Obsession Symphony $8.00 (5)
Zinfandel, '00, California $10.00 (5)
Zinfandel, '00, Lodi Rsv. $18.00 (B-San Fran)

J

J WINE COMPANY

11455 Old Redwood Hwy., Healdsburg 95448

Chardonnay, '99, Russian River Vly. Estate $32.00 (3)
Pinot Gris, '01, Russian River Vly. (S-State Fair)
Pinot Noir, '98, Russian River Vly., Nicole's Vnyd. $35.00 (4)
Pinot Noir, '99, Russian River Vly. Estate $20.00 (4)
Sparkling Wine, '97, Brut Russian River Vly. $28.00 (4)

JACKSON CELLARS

Address Not Available

Merlot, '99, Livermore Vly. $17.00 (G-Riverside)
Sangiovese, '00, Livermore Vly. $19.00 (S-Riverside)

JADE MOUNTAIN

Address Not Available
www.chalonewinegroup.com

Red Rhone, '99, La Provencale, California $17.50 (8)
Syrah, '99, Napa Vly. $27.00 (4)

TOBIN JAMES CELLARS

8950 Union Rd., Paso Robles 93446

Cabernet Sauvignon, '99, James Gang Rsv. $28.00 (B-Orange)
Chardonnay, '01, Paso Robles, Radiance $16.00 (B-Orange)
Red Meritage, '99, Private Stash, Paso Robles $38.00 (B-Orange)
White Dessert, '00, Muscat, James Gang Rsv. $20.00 (G-Orange)
Zinfandel, '99, Paso Robles, Ballistic $16.00 (S-Orange)

JANKRIS VINEYARD

Rt. 2, Box 40, Templeton 93465

Cabernet Sauvignon, '99, Dry Creek Vnyd. $13.00 (S-Riverside)
Chardonnay, '00, Central Coast $14.00 (3)
Merlot, '00, Mystere, Paso Robles $13.00 (4)
Red Rhone, '00, Cabernet/Syrah, Paso Robles (B-Pac. Rim)
Syrah, '00, Paso Robles Sojourn $14.50 (2)
Zinfandel, '99, Paso Robles Estate Select $13.00 (B-Riverside)

JEKEL VINEYARDS

40155 Walnut Avenue, Greenfield 93927
usawines.com/jekel

Cabernet Sauvignon, '98, Monterey, Sanctuary Rsv. (G-State Fair)
Cabernet Sauvignon, '99, Central Coast $16.00 (3)
Cabernet Sauvignon, '99, Monterey Co. $16.00 (2)
Chardonnay, '00, Monterey Co. (S-Pac. Rim)
Chardonnay, '00, Monterey Gravelstone $13.00 (5)
Chardonnay, '99, F O S, Monterey Co. Rsv. $22.00 (4)
Chardonnay, '99, Monterey Co. (Σ-Pac. Rim)
Chardonnay, '99, Monterey Gravelstone $22.00 (S-New World)
Dry Riesling, '00, Monterey Co., Sanctuary Est. $10.00 (6)
Dry Riesling, '01, Monterey Co., Sanctuary Est. $10.00 (2)
Merlot, '99, Monterey Co. $15.00 (3)
Pinot Noir, '00, Monterey Co., Sanctuary Est. $15.00 (6)
Red Meritage, '98, Monterey Co., Sanctuary Est. $28.00 (4)
Syrah, '99, Monterey Co. $15.00 (7)
White Dessert, '00, Riesling, Monterey Co., Late Harvest $22.00 (8)

JEPSON

10400 So. Highway 101, Ukiah 95482
www.jepsonwine.com

Chardonnay, '99, Mendocino Co. Est. Select $15.00 (S-San Diego)
Merlot, '98, Mendocino Co. $18.00 (2)
Merlot, '99, Mendocino Co. (B-State Fair)
Syrah, '00, Mendocino Co. Estate Select $22.00 (5)

JESSIE'S GROVE WINERY

Address Not Available
www.jgwinery.com

Red Rhone, '00, Carignane, Lodi $15.00 (8)
Zinfandel, '00, Lodi Royal-tee Vnyd. $25.00 (5)
Zinfandel, '00, Lodi, Old Vine, Vintners Choice $15.00 (7)
Zinfandel, '00, Lodi, Westwind Vyd., Old Vine $22.00 (7)

JEWEL

Address Not Available

Merlot, '00, California (S-State Fair)
Red Italian, '00, Duetto, California $10.00 (B-Orange)
Syrah, '00, California $10.00 (S-San Fran)

JODAR

2393 Gravel Rd., Placerville 95667
www.jodarwinery.com

Cabernet Sauvignon, '99, El Dorado, Estate (B-Pac. Rim)
Chardonnay, '99, El Dorado, Estate Rsv. (B-L.A.)
Sangiovese, '00, El Dorado $16.00 (2)

JORY

P.O. Box 1495, Los Gatos 95031

Chardonnay, '00, Central Coast, El Nino Grande (G-Pac. Rim)
Syrah, '00, Central Coast $19.00 (2)
Syrah, '00, Paso Robles, Lock Vnyd. (2)

JUSTIN

11680 Chimney Rock Rd., Paso Robles 93446

Red Meritage, '99, Isoceles, Paso Robles, Estate $48.00 (2)
Syrah, '99, Paso Robles, Halter Vyd. $22.50 (2)

K

ROBERT KEENAN

3660 Spring Mtn. Rd., St Helena 94574

Cabernet Sauvignon, '98, Napa Vly. $36.00 (3)
Cabernet Sauvignon, '99, Napa Vly. (B-State Fair)
Merlot, '99, Napa Vly. $30.00 (6)

KEMPTON CLARK

Address Not Available
www.rhphillips.com

Petite Sirah, '99, Dunnigan Hills $10.00 (6)
Zinfandel, '99, Mad Zin, California $10.00 (5)

KENDALL-JACKSON WINERY

421 Aviation Blvd., Santa Rosa 95403
www.kj.com

Bordeaux, '99, Cabernet Franc, Vintner's Rsv., California $15.00 (7)
Cabernet Sauvignon, '97, Alexander Vly., Buckeye $43.00 (2)
Cabernet Sauvignon, '97, GE, Alexander Vly. $49.00 (S-New World)
Cabernet Sauvignon, '97, Great Estates, Napa Vly. $49.00 (6)
Cabernet Sauvignon, '97, Stature Napa Vly. $125.00 (2)
Cabernet Sauvignon, '98, Grand Rsv., California $40.00 (3)
Cabernet Sauvignon, '98, Great Estates, Alexander Vly. $49.00 (5)
Cabernet Sauvignon, '98, Great Estates, Napa Vly. $49.00 (7)
Cabernet Sauvignon, '98, Vintner's Rsv., California $16.00 (5)
Cabernet Sauvignon, '99, Grand Rsv., California $30.00 (7)
Chardonnay, '00, Grand Rsv., California $20.00 (3)
Chardonnay, '00, Great Estates, Arroyo Seco $37.00 (6)
Chardonnay, '00, Great Estates, Santa Barbara $28.00 (5)
Chardonnay, '00, Santa Maria Vly., Camelot Bench, Estate Series
Chardonnay, '00, Vintner's Rsv., California $12.00 (7)
Chardonnay, '98, Great Estates, Sonoma Coast $28.00 (3)
Chardonnay, '99, Great Estates, Monterey Co. $28.00 (5)
Chardonnay, '99, Great Estates, Sonoma Coast $28.00 (7)
Chardonnay, '99, Great Estates, Sonoma Vly. $37.00 (6)
Dry Riesling, '00, Vintner's Rsv., California $10.00 (S-New World)
Dry Riesling, '01, Vintner's Rsv., California $10.00 (4)
Gewurztraminer, '00, Vintner's Rsv., California $10.00 (B-New World)
Merlot, '97, Alexander Vly. Single Vnyd. Series Buckeye $32.00 (6)
Merlot, '98, Grand Rsv., California $30.00 (3)
Merlot, '98, Great Estates, Sonoma Co. $35.00 (9)
Merlot, '99, Grand Rsv., California $30.00 (9)
Merlot, '99, Great Estates, Sonoma Co. $35.00 (B-State Fair)
Merlot, '99, Vintner's Rsv., California $16.00 (7)
Petite Sirah, '00, Vintner's Rsv., California $16.00 (3)
Pinot Noir, '00, Vintner's Rsv., California $14.00 (8)

Pinot Noir, '99, Great Estates, Monterey Co. $32.00 (9)
Red Meritage, '00, Collage Cabernet Sauvignon/Merlot $10.00 (4)
Red Meritage, '97, Grand Rsv., California $40.00 (6)
Red Rhone, '00, Collage, Shiraz/Cabernet $10.00 (8)
Red Rhone, '99, Collage, Shiraz/Zinfandel $10.00 (4)
Sangiovese, '99, Vintner's Rsv., California $15.00 (8)
Sauvignon Blanc, '00, Fume Blanc Vintner's Rsv. $10.00 (6)
Sauvignon Blanc, '00, Grand Rsv., California $16.00 (6)
Sauvignon Blanc, '00, Vintner's Rsv., California $10.00 (6)
Sauvignon Blanc, '01, Vintner's Rsv. California $10.00 (S-San Fran)
Syrah, '99, Grand Rsv., California $18.00 (5)
Syrah, '99, Vintner's Rsv., California $12.00 (5)
Viognier, '00, Grand Rsv., California $20.00 (4)
Viognier, '00, Vintner's Rsv., California $14.00 (3)
White Meritage, '00, Grand Rsv., California $13.00 (7)
White Varietals, '00, Marsanne, Vintner's Rsv. $16.00 (9)
White Varietals, '00, Pinot Blanc, Vintner's Rsv. $13.00 (4)
White Varietals, '00, Semillon, Vintner's Rsv. $10.00 (6)
White Varietals, '01, Muscat Canelli, Vintner's Rsv. $10.00 (3)
Zinfandel, '00, Great Estates, Mendocino Co. $30.00 (2)
Zinfandel, '00, Vintner's Rsv., California $12.00 (5)
Zinfandel, '98, Grand Rsv., California $17.00 (7)
Zinfandel, '99, Vintner's Rsv., California $12.00 (B-New World)

KATHRYN KENNEDY

13180 Pierce Rd., Saratoga 95070
www.kathrynkennedywinery.com

Cabernet Sauvignon, '99, Estate, Santa Cruz Mtns. $125.00 (3)
Syrah, '99, Santa Cruz Mtns., Maridon Vnyd. $85.00 (G-Orange)

KENWOOD VINEYARDS

9592 Sonoma Highway, Kenwood 94552
www.kenwoodvineyards.com

Cabernet Sauvignon, '98, Sonoma Co. $20.00 (B-New World)
Cabernet Sauvignon, '99, Sonoma Co. $20.00 (3)
Cabernet Sauvignon, '99, Sonoma, Jack London Vnyd. $35.00 (3)
Chardonnay, '00, Russian River Vly. Rsv. $20.00 (3)
Chardonnay, '00, Sonoma Co. $15.00 (B-Riverside)
Merlot, '98, Sonoma Vly., Massara Vnyd. $25.00 (S-W. Coast)
Merlot, '99, Sonoma Co. $17.00 (2)
Merlot, '99, Sonoma Vly. Jack London Vnyd. $30.00 (3)
Pinot Noir, '00, Russian River Vly. $17.00 (5)
Pinot Noir, '99, Russian River Vly. Rsv. Olivet $30.00 (4)
Sauvignon Blanc, '00, Sonoma Co. $12.00 (4)
Sauvignon Blanc, '00, Sonoma Co. Rsv. $15.00 (4)
Zinfandel, '99, Sonoma Co. $16.00 (8)
Zinfandel, '99, Sonoma, Jack London Vnyd. $20.00 (G-New World)
Zinfandel, '99, Sonoma Vly., Nun's Canyon Vnyd. $20.00 (2)

KIRKLAND RANCH WINERY

Address Not Available
www.kirklandranchwinery.com

Cabernet Sauvignon, '99, Napa Vly. $45.00 (B-San Fran)
Chardonnay, '00, KRV Block 13 Napa Vly. $30.00 (B-San Fran)
Chardonnay, '00, KRV Napa Vly. $22.00 (2)
Merlot, '99, Napa Vly. $30.00 (4)
Merlot, '99, Napa Vly. Estate $35.00 (2)
Pinot Noir, '00, Napa Vly. $30.00 (2)

KOEHLER WINERY

Address Not Available

Chardonnay, '00, Santa Barbara Co., Estate $15.00 (2)
Chardonnay, '00, Santa Barbara, Winemaker Select $20.00 (2)
Dry Riesling, '00, Santa Barbara Co. $11.00 (B-Orange)
Pinot Noir, '00, Monterey Co. $26.00 (2)
White Meritage, '01, Santa Barbara Co., Estate (B-L.A.)

KORBEL

13250 River Rd., Guerneville 95446
www.korbel.com

Sparkling Wine, '95, Le Premier, Vintage Rsv. (S-L.A.)
Sparkling Wine, '97, Blanc De Noir, Sonoma, Russian River Vly. (2)
Sparkling Wine, '99, Natural, Sonoma Co. $13.00 (7)
Sparkling Wine, 'NV, Blanc De Noir, California $11.00 (7)
Sparkling Wine, 'NV, Brut Rose, California $11.00 (6)
Sparkling Wine, 'NV, Brut, California $11.00 (3)
Sparkling Wine, 'NV, Chardonnay Champagne, Calif. $12.00 (3)
Sparkling Wine, 'NV, Dry, California $10.00 (S-Riverside)
Sparkling Wine, 'NV, Extra Dry, California $11.00 (3)
Sparkling Wine, 'NV, Sonoma Co. Muscat Rouge $13.00 (2)

CHARLES KRUG

2800 St. Helena Hwy., St Helena 95474

Cabernet Sauvignon, '99, Napa Vly. (S-State Fair)
Chardonnay, '00, Carneros Napa Vly. Rsv. (S-State Fair)
Chardonnay, '00, Napa Vly. (B-State Fair)
Red Meritage, '99, Napa Vly., Rsv. Generations (S-State Fair)
Sauvignon Blanc, '01, Napa Vly. (B-State Fair)

KUNDE ESTATE WINERY

10155 Sonoma Hwy., Kenwood 95452
www.kunde.com

Cabernet Sauvignon, '98, Sonoma Vly., Drummond Vnyd. (B-L.A.)
Chardonnay, '00, Sonoma Vly. Estate $16.00 (B-Orange)
Chardonnay, '99, Kinneybrook Vnyd. $22.00 (B-W. Coast)
Chardonnay, '99, Sonoma Vly. Rsv. $35.00 (2)
Sauvignon Blanc, '01, Sonoma Vly., Magnolia Lane (2)

KYNSI WINERY

Address Not Available

Pinot Noir, '99, Santa Maria Vly., Julia's Vnyd. (B-State Fair)
Syrah, '99, Edna Vly., Paragon Vnyd. (Σ-State Fair)

L

LA CREMA

3690 Laughlin Rd., Windsor 95492

Chardonnay, '00, Russian River Vly. $30.00 (2)
Chardonnay, '00, Sonoma Coast $18.00 (4)
Chardonnay, '99, Russian River Vly. $30.00 (7)
Pinot Noir, '00, Anderson Vly. $26.00 (3)
Pinot Noir, '00, Carneros Napa $26.00 (4)
Pinot Noir, '00, Russian River Vly. $35.00 (Σ-San Fran)
Pinot Noir, '00, Sonoma Coast $22.00 (7)
Pinot Noir, '99, Anderson Vly. $22.00 (S-New World)
Pinot Noir, '99, Carneros $22.00 (S-New World)
Pinot Noir, '99, Russian River Vly. $35.00 (7)
Syrah, '00, Sonoma $26.00 (S-San Fran)

Viognier, '01, Sonoma Vly. $24.00 (B-State Fair)
Zinfandel, '98, Sonoma Co. $22.00 (6)

LAETITIA

453 Deutz Dr., Arroyo Grande 93420
www.laetitiawine.com

Pinot Noir, '00, Arroyo Grande Vly. $25.00 (3)
Sparkling Wine, 'NV, Brut Cuvee, Central Coast (S-L.A.)
White Varietals, '00, Pinot Blanc, Arroyo Grande $25.00 (2)

LAFOND

Address Not Available
www.lafondwinery.com

Chardonnay, '00, Santa Ynez Vly., Santa Rita Hills $18.00 (2)
Pinot Noir, '00, Santa Ynez Vly., Santa Rita Hills $18.00 (4)
Pinot Noir, '98, Santa Ynez Vly., Lafond Vnyd. $30.00 (B-Orange)
Syrah, '00, Santa Ynez Vly., Santa Rita Hills $18.00 (3)
Syrah, '99, Santa Ynez Vly., Lafond Vnyd. $30.00 (S-Orange)

LAGO DI MERLO

Address Not Available

Merlot, '99, Dry Creek Vly. $23.00 (S-W. Coast)
Syrah, '00, Dry Creek Vly. $29.00 (B-W. Coast)
Zinfandel, '00, Dry Creek $29.00 (G-W. Coast)

LAKE SONOMA WINERY

P.O. Box 263, Healdsburg 95448
www.lakesonomawinery.net

Cabernet Sauvignon, '98, Alexander Vly. $21.00 (5)
Chardonnay, '00, Russian River Vly. $15.00 (6)
Zinfandel, '99, Dry Creek Vly. $15.00 (S-New World)
Zinfandel, '99, Dry Creek Vly., Saini Farms Old Vine $20.00 (7)

LAKEVILLE CELLARS

Address Not Available

Zinfandel, '99, Napa Vly. $15.00 (G-New World)

LAMBERT BRIDGE WINERY

4085 W. Dry Creek Rd., Healdsburg 95448
www.lambertbridge.com

Chardonnay, '00, Sonoma Co. $20.00 (2)
Merlot, '99, Sonoma Co. $24.00 (5)
Zinfandel, '00, Dry Creek Vly. $24.00 (B-Riverside)

LATCHAM VINEYARDS

2860 Omo Ranch Rd., Mount Aukum 95656

Bordeaux, '99, Cabernet Franc, Fair Play Estate $15.00 (5)
Cabernet Sauvignon, '99, Fair Play, Chiu Vnyd. $16.00 (G-Orange
Chardonnay, '00, Fair Play (B-Pac. Rim)
Red Italian, '00, Barbera, Sierra Foothills $20.00 (B-San Fran)
Red Italian, '99, Barbera, Sierra Foothills $18.00 (B-New World)
Sauvignon Blanc, '01, El Dorado $12.00 (3)
White Varietals, '01, Muscat Canelli, Oliver Vnyd. $12.00 (S-Orang
Zinfandel, '00, Fair Play (S-State Fair)
Zinfandel, '00, Fair Play Rsv. (G-State Fair)
Zinfandel, '99, El Dorado $16.00 (2)

LAURIER

6342 Bystrum Road, Ceres 95307

Chardonnay, '00, Los Carneros, Sonoma $16.00 (7)
Merlot, '00, Dry Creek Vly. $16.00 (B-San Fran)

Pinot Noir, '97, Sonoma Co. (S-L.A.)

LAVA CAP

2221 Fruitridge Rd., Placerville 95667
www.lavacap.com

Merlot, '99, El Dorado (B-State Fair)
Merlot, '99, El Dorado, Stromberg (B-State Fair)
Red Italian, '99, Barbera, Sierra Foothills Rsv. (S-State Fair)
Syrah, '99, El Dorado Rsv. $20.00 (2)
White Varietals, '00, Muscat Canelli, Sierra Foothills (G-State Fair)
White Varietals, '00, Semillon, El Dorado, Granite Hill (S-State Fair)

LE DUCQ VINEYARDS

3120 North St. Helena Hwy, Saint Helena 94574

Cabernet Sauvignon, '99, Napa Vly. $40.00 (G-New World)

LEANING OAK

Address Not Available

Bordeaux, '98, Cabernet Franc, Napa Vly. $28.00 (4)
Cabernet Sauvignon, '98, Napa Vly. $24.00 (S-W. Coast)
Chardonnay, '00, Napa Vly. (B-State Fair)
Merlot, '98, Napa Vly. $24.00 (B-San Fran)
Sauvignon Blanc, '00, Napa Vly. $15.00 (B-W. Coast)
Zinfandel, '99, Sonoma Co., Old Vine Gold Vnyds. $20.00 (G-San

LEDSON WINERY & VINEYARDS

7335 Sonoma Hwy., Santa Rosa 95409

Dry Riesling, '00, Monterey Co. $16.00 (S-Orange)
Merlot, '99, Sonoma Vly. $36.00 (2)
Sauvignon Blanc, '00, Napa Vly. $18.00 (B-Orange)
White Varietals, '00, Orange Muscat, Monterey $16.00 (S-Orange)
Zinfandel, '99, Russian River Vly. Old Vine $36.00 (2)

LINCOURT

343 N. Refugio Rd., Santa Ynez 93460

Chardonnay, '00, Santa Barbara Co. $18.00 (3)
Pinot Noir, '00, Santa Barbara Co. $22.00 (3)
Syrah, '00, Santa Barbara Co. $20.00 (2)

LIONS PEAK

Address Not Available

Cabernet Sauvignon, '98, Paso Robles $24.00 (3)
Red Meritage, '99, Lioness, Paso Robles (B-State Fair)
Viognier, '01, California $14.00 (4)
Zinfandel, '99, Paso Robles $18.00 (B-W. Coast)

LOCKWOOD VINEYARD

1044 Harkins Road, Salinas 93901
www.lockwood-wine.com

Cabernet Sauvignon, '99, Monterey Co. Estate $17.00 (5)
Chardonnay, '00, Monterey Co., San Lucas $15.00 (2)
Chardonnay, '98, Monterey Co. Rsv. $35.00 (2)
Chardonnay, '99, Monterey Co. Estate $15.00 (B-New World)
Merlot, '97, Monterey Co. Rsv. (B-L.A.)
Merlot, '99, Monterey Co. Estate $17.00 (3)
Red Meritage, '97, Monterey Co. Rsv. $45.00 (2)
Sauvignon Blanc, '00, Monterey Co. Estate $11.00 (Σ-Riverside)
Syrah, '99, Monterey Co. Estate $16.00 (2)

J. LOHR ESTATE

1000 Lenzen Ave., San Jose 95126
www.jlohr.com

Cabernet Sauvignon, '00, Seven Oaks, P.R. $15.00 (S-San Fran)
Cabernet Sauvignon, '98, Paso Robles Hilltp Vnyd. $32.00 (5)
Cabernet Sauvignon, '99, Cypress California $10.00 (S-San Fran)
Cabernet Sauvignon, '99, Seven Oaks, Paso Robles $15.00 (2)
Chardonnay, '00, Arroy Seco Riverstone Estates $15.00 (6)
Chardonnay, '00, Cypress California $10.00 (2)
Chardonnay, '01, Painter Bridge California $7.00 (2)
Chardonnay, '99, Arroyo Seco Arroyo Vista Vnyd. $25.00 (6)
Dry Riesling, '01, Monterey Co., Bay Mist $8.00 (9)
Merlot, '00, Cypress California $10.00 (S-San Fran)
Merlot, '99, Paso Robles, Los Osos $15.00 (2)
Red Meritage, '98, POM (S-W. Coast)
Red Rhone, '00, Painter Bridge, Syrah/Zinfandel $7.00 (2)
Sauvignon Blanc, '01, Napa Vly., Carol's Vnyd. (B-L.A.)
Syrah, '00, Paso Robles, South Ridge (S-State Fair)
Syrah, '99, Paso Robles, South Ridge $15.00 (4)
Zinfandel, '00, Cypress, California $10.00 (2)
Zinfandel, '99, Lodi, Bramblewood $20.00 (6)

LOLONIS

1905 Road D, Redwood Valley 95470
www.lolonis.com

Red Rhone, 'NV, Carignane, Redwood Vly. $14.00 (B-Orange)
Zinfandel, '99, Redwood Vly. Estate, Organic $18.00 (2)

LUCAS & LEWELLEN

Address Not Available

Chardonnay, '00, Santa Barbara Co., Old Adobe Vnyd. $24.00 (2)
Chardonnay, '01, Virgin, Central Coast (B-L.A.)
Pinot Noir, '99, Santa Barbara Co., Old Adobe Vnyd. Rsv. (B-L.A.)
Red Italian, '00, Barbera, Santa Barbara Co. $14.00 (2)
Red Italian, '00, Dolcetto, Santa Barbara $12.00 (B-New World)
Sauvignon Blanc, '01, Santa Barbara Co. $12.00 (B-Orange)
Sauvignon Blanc, '01, Virgin, Central Coast $13.00 (3)
White Dessert, '99, Sauvignon Blanc $18.00 (S-W. Coast)

M

MACMURRAY RANCH

Address Not Available

Pinot Noir, '00, Russian River Vly. $32.00 (B-Orange)
White Varietals, '01, Russian River Vly. $23.00 (G-Orange)

MADDALENA VINEYARD

737 Lamar Street, Los Angeles 90031
www.riboliwines.com

Cabernet Sauvignon, '99, Central Coast $10.00 (B-Orange)
Dry Riesling, '01, Monterey Co. $10.00 (6)
Merlot, '00, Central Coast South (B-State Fair)
Pinot Gris, '00, Monterey Co., Loma Vista Pinot Grigio $10.00 (2)
White Varietals, '01, Muscat, Paso Robles $10.00 (B-San Diego)

MADONNA ESTATE

Address Not Available

Chardonnay, '00, California Estate, Organic $22.00 (B-New World)
Pinot Gris, '01, Carneros Pinot Grigio $22.00 (2)

Pinot Noir, '00, Carneros $26.00 (2)
Pinot Noir, '99, Carneros "Rsv." (S-Pac. Rim)

MADRONA

P.O. Box 454, Gatlin Rd., Camino 95709

Bordeaux, '00, Cabernet Franc, El Dorado Est. $15.00 (2)
Gewurztraminer, '01, El Dorado $10.00 (S-Riverside)
Red Meritage, '98, El Dorado Rsv. Estate $25.00 (B-Riverside)
Zinfandel, '00, El Dorado Estate $14.00 (3)
Zinfandel, '99, El Dorado Rsv. Estate $20.00 (2)

MARCELINA VINEYARDS

3387 Dry Creek Rd., Healdsburg 95448

Cabernet Sauvignon, '98, Napa Vly. $30.00 (5)
Chardonnay, '00, Carneros $22.00 (4)
Merlot, '99, Napa Vly. $30.00 (2)
Pinot Noir, '00, Carneros $32.00 (B-Orange)

MARIAH

Address Not Available

Syrah, '99, Mendocino Ridge $30.00 (4)
Zinfandel, '99, Mendocino Ridge $31.00 (4)

MARKHAM

2812 N. St. Helena Hwy., St Helena 94574

Cabernet Sauvignon, '98, Napa Vly. $26.00 (S-Orange)
Merlot, '99, Napa Vly. $21.00 (3)

MARTIN & WEYRICH WINERY

Address Not Available
www.martinweyrich.com

Chardonnay, '00, Edna Vly., Edna Ranch $18.00 (3)
Red Italian, '99, Nebbiolo Il Vecchio, Paso Robles $24.00 (4)
Red Italian, '99, Nebbiolo, Paso Robles (B-State Fair)
White Dessert, '00, Moscato Allegro, Calif. $12.00 (S-San Diego)
White Dessert, '01, Moscato Allegro, California $12.00 (4)
Zinfandel, '99, Paso Robles, Dante Dusi Rsv. $24.00 (2)
Zinfandel, '99, Paso Robles, La Primitiva $18.00 (B-San Fran)

LOUIS M. MARTINI

254 St. Helena Hwy., N., St Helena 94574

Cabernet Sauvignon, '98, Monte Rosso Vyd. $50.00 (B-New World)
Cabernet Sauvignon, '99, California $12.00 (2)
Cabernet Sauvignon, '99, Sonoma, Monte Rosso Vnyd. $50.00 (5)
Chardonnay, '00, Russian River Vly., Del Rio Vnyd. $22.00 (6)
Gewurztraminer, '00, Russian River Vly., Del Rio Vnyd. $15.00 (4)
Merlot, '98, Napa Vly., Ghost Pines Cuvee $27.00 (6)
Merlot, '99, Russian River Vly., Del Rio Vnyd. $22.00 (2)
Red Italian, '98, Barbera, Lake Co. $12.00 (3)
Red Italian, '98, Barbera, Napa Co. (B-Pac. Rim)
Sangiovese, '99, Dunnigan Hills $15.00 (2)
White Varietals, '00, Folle Blanc, Sonoma, Monte Rosso $15.00 (2)
Zinfandel, '99, Gnarly Vine $50.00 (B-W. Coast)
Zinfandel, '99, Sonoma Vly., Monte Rosso Vnyd. $35.00 (2)

MAZZOCCO

1400 Lytton Springs Rd., Healdsburg 95448

Chardonnay, '00, Sonoma, River Lane Vnyds. $18.00 (B-W. Coast)
Red Meritage, '97, Dry Creek Vly. Matrix Estate $40.00 (3)
Zinfandel, '98, Dry Creek Vly. $16.00 (B-San Diego)

MC CRAY RIDGE

Address Not Available

Merlot, '99, Two Moon Vnyd., Dry Creek Vly. $28.00 (4)

MC ILROY WINES

8375 Westside Road, Healdsburg 95448

Bordeaux, '99, Cabernet Franc, RRV, Salzgeber Vnyd. $24.00 (2)
Chardonnay, '00, Russian River Vly., Aquarius Ranch $22.00 (6)
Chardonnay, '00, Russian River Vly., Signature Edition $34.00 (2)
Merlot, '00, Russian River Vly., Aquarius Ranch (B-State Fair)
Pinot Noir, '00, Russian River Vly., Aquarius Ranch $24.00 (3)
Pinot Noir, '99, Russian River Vly., Aquarius Ranch (B-Pac. Rim)
White Dessert, '00, Gewurztraminer, Aquarius Ranch $15.00 (2)
Zinfandel, '00, Russian River Vly., Porter Bass Vyds. (B-L.A.)
Zinfandel, '98, Russian River, Porter Bass $21.00 (B-New World)
Zinfandel, '99, Russian River Vly., Porter Bass Vyds. $24.00 (4)

MC MANIS FAMILY VINEYARDS

Address Not Available

Cabernet Sauvignon, '00, California $9.00 (B-Riverside)
Cabernet Sauvignon, '01, California $9.00 (2)
Chardonnay, '01, River Junction $9.00 (3)
Merlot, '00, California $9.00 (2)
Merlot, '01, California $9.00 (2)
Syrah, '00, California $9.00 (2)

MC NAB RIDGE

2350 McNab Ranch Rd., Ukiah 95482

Cabernet Sauvignon, '99, Mendocino Co. Rsv. $18.00 (2)
Chardonnay, '00, Mendocino Co. (S-State Fair)

MEADOR ESTATE

Address Not Available
www.ventanawines.com

Chardonnay, '99, Block 9, Arroyo Seco $30.00 (4)
Sauvignon Blanc, '01, Block 3, Arroyo Seco (B-L.A.)
Syrah, '00, Monterey, Arroyo Seco, Maverick (B-State Fair)
Syrah, '98, Monterey, Arroyo Seco, Maverick $50.00 (3)
White Varietals, '00, Chenin Blanc, Arroyo Seco $18.00 (5)

MERIDIAN VINEYARDS

P.O. Box 3289, Paso Robles 93447
www.meridianvineyards.com

Cabernet Sauvignon, '97, Monterey Co., Coastal Rsv. $28.00 (5)
Cabernet Sauvignon, '98, California $13.00 (S-New World)
Cabernet Sauvignon, '98, Paso Robles $18.00 (B-Orange)
Cabernet Sauvignon, '99, California $11.00 (4)
Chardonnay, '00, Santa Barbara Co. $10.00 (5)
Chardonnay, '99, Rsv., Edna Vly. $14.00 (4)
Chardonnay, '99, Santa Barbara Co., Limited $22.00 (8)
Gewurztraminer, '00, Santa Barbara Co. $8.00 (3)
Merlot, '99, California $11.00 (6)
Merlot, '99, Paso Robles $18.00 (2)
Petite Sirah, '99, Paso Robles, Limited Release $18.00 (6)
Pinot Gris, '00, Pinot Grigio $11.00 (S-W. Coast)
Pinot Noir, '00, Santa Barbara Co. $11.00 (8)
Sauvignon Blanc, '00, California $8.00 (4)
Syrah, '99, California Shiraz $11.00 (5)
Syrah, '99, Paso Robles $15.00 (7)

ERRYVALE

1000 Main St., Saint Helena 94574
www.merryvale.com

Cabernet Sauvignon, '99, Napa Vly. Rsv. (G-State Fair)
Chardonnay, '00, Carneros Rsv. $35.00 (S-San Fran)
Chardonnay, '00, Russian River Vly., Dutton Ranch (S-State Fair)
Merlot, '99, Napa Vly. Rsv. $39.00 (3)

ETTLER FAMILY VINEYARDS

Address Not Available
www.mettlerwine.com

Cabernet Sauvignon, '00, Lodi $24.00 (S-San Fran)
Cabernet Sauvignon, '99, Lodi $24.00 (3)

ICHAEL-DAVID PHILLIPS

4580 W. Hwy 12, Lodi 95242

Cabernet Sauvignon, '00, Lodi $24.00 (3)
Merlot, '00, Lodi $20.00 (4)
Syrah, '99, Lodi $20.00 (B-New World)
Viognier, '00, California $15.00 (B-New World)
White Varietals, '00, Symphony, Lodi (B-State Fair)
White Varietals, '00, Zinphony, Lodi (S-State Fair)
White Varietals, '01, Symphony, Lodi (S-State Fair)
Zinfandel, '00, Lodi Estates $11.00 (S-Riverside)
Zinfandel, '00, Lodi, Maley Vnyd. $24.00 (5)
Zinfandel, '00, Lodi, Old Vine $20.00 (3)
Zinfandel, '00, Lodi, Seven Deadly Zins $17.00 (4)
Zinfandel, '99, Lodi, Old Vine $19.00 (B-New World)

ICHEL-SCHLUMBERGER

4155 Wine Creek Road, Healdsburg 95448
www.michelschlumberger.com

Cabernet Sauvignon, '97, Dry Creek Vly. Rsv. $65.00 (5)
Cabernet Sauvignon, '99, Dry Creek Vly. $29.00 (8)
Chardonnay, '00, Dry Creek Vly. $22.00 (2)
Chardonnay, '98, Dry Creek Vly. Rsv. (B-Pac. Rim)
Merlot, '99, Dry Creek Vly. $22.00 (4)
Syrah, '99, North Coast $22.00 (4)
White Varietals, '01, Pinot Blanc, Dry Creek Vly. $18.00 (B-San Fran)

IDNIGHT CELLARS

2867 Township Rd., Paso Robles 93446

Cabernet Sauvignon, '99, Nebula, Paso Robles $25.00 (5)
Chardonnay, '00, Equinox, Paso Robles $16.00 (3)
Merlot, '99, Eclipse, Paso Robles $20.00 (7)
Merlot, '99, Paso Robles Estate $22.00 (2)
Red Meritage, '98, Mare Nectaris, Paso Robles $32.00 (6)
Sangiovese, '99, Starlight, Paso Robles $20.00 (3)
Syrah, '00, Nocturne, Paso Robles $24.00 (6)

ILL CREEK VINEYARDS

1401 Westside Rd., Healdsburg 95448
www.mcvonline.com

Cabernet Sauvignon, '98, Sonoma Co. $19.50 (2)
Chardonnay, '99, Dry Creek Vly. $15.00 (3)
Chardonnay, '99, Dry Creek Vly. Barrel Select $20.00 (S-Riverside)
Gewurztraminer, '00, Dry Creek Vly. Estate $13.00 (5)
Merlot, '99, Dry Creek Vly. Estate $18.50 (6)
Sauvignon Blanc, '00, Dry Creek Vly. Estate $14.00 (2)

Zinfandel, '98, Dry Creek Vly. (B-L.A.)
Zinfandel, '99, Russian River, Matteucci Vyds. $26.00 (3)

MILLIAIRE

276 Main Street, Murphys 95247

Cabernet Sauvignon, '97, Sierra Foothills, Clairmont (S-L.A.)
Gewurztraminer, '00, Sierra Foothills $12.00 (S-Orange)
Syrah, '99, Sierra Foothills $14.00 (B-Orange)
Zinfandel, '98, Sierra Foothills, Bicocca (B-State Fair)
Zinfandel, '98, Sierra Foothills, Clockspring $16.00 (B-San Fran)
Zinfandel, '98, Sierra Foothills, Ghirardelli $18.00 (2)

MINER FAMILY VINEYARDS

Address Not Available
www.minerwines.com

Cabernet Sauvignon, '99, Oakville, Napa $60.00 (B-San Fran)
Chardonnay, '00, Napa Vly. $30.00 (S-San Fran)
Merlot, '99, Napa Vly., Stagecoach Vnyd. $35.00 (S-San Fran)
Sangiovese, '00, Mendocino, Gibson Ranch $20.00 (B-San Fran)

MIRASSOU

3000 Aborn Rd., San Jose 95135
www.mirassou.com

Cabernet Sauvignon, '99, Central Coastal Selection $11.00 (6)
Chardonnay, '00, Monterey Co., Coastal Selection $10.00 (5)
Chardonnay, '00, Monterey Co., Zabala Vnyd. $24.00 (6)
Chardonnay, '99, Showcase Selection $30.00 (B-San Fran)
Dry Riesling, '01, Monterey Coastal Selection $7.00 (B-Orange)
Merlot, '98, Monterey Co., Harvest Rsv. $15.00 (2)
Merlot, '99, Monterey Co., Coastal Selection $10.00 (2)
Pinot Noir, '99, Monterey Co., Coastal Selection $11.00 (4)
Pinot Noir, '99, Monterey Co., Harvest Rsv. $15.00 (6)
Pinot Noir, '99, Monterey Co., Showcase Selection $30.00 (5)
Sparkling Wine, 'NV, Blanc De Blanc, Monterey Co. $24.00 (4)
Syrah, '99, Monterey Co., Harvest Rsv. $15.00 (3)
White Varietals, '00, Pinot Blanc, Coastal Selection $9.00 (7)
White Varietals, '00, Pinot Blanc, Mission Vnyd. $24.00 (3)

MISSION VIEW VINEYARDS

P.O. Box 129, San Miguel 93451
www.prettysmith.com

Cabernet Sauvignon, '99, Paso Robles (G-State Fair)
Chardonnay, '00, Paso Robles $12.00 (G-San Fran)
Zinfandel, 'NV, Paso Robles (S-State Fair)

CHARLES B. MITCHELL VINEYARDS

8221 Stoney Creek Rd., Somerset 95684

Bordeaux, '00, Malbec, El Dorado (S-State Fair)
Cabernet Sauvignon, '00, El Dorado Rsv. $25.00 (4)
Cabernet Sauvignon, '00, Fair Play, Rsv. (B-State Fair)
Dry Riesling, '00, El Dorado $10.00 (B-Orange)
Merlot, '99, California, Hillside Vnyd. $15.00 (B-New World)
Red Italian, '00, Barbera, Lodi (B-State Fair)
Red Italian, 'NV, Bella Rossa, California $15.00 (3)
Red Rhone, 'NV, Cotes du Cosumnes, Calif. $10.00 (S-Orange)
Syrah, '00, El Dorado Rsv. $25.00 (4)

ROBERT MONDAVI COASTAL

841 Latour Ct., Napa 94558
www.robertmondavi.com

Chardonnay, '00, Central Coast $11.00 (2)
Dry Riesling, '01, Central Coast $9.00 (2)
Pinot Noir, '00, Central Coast $13.00 (B-Orange)
Syrah, '00, Central Coast $11.00 (2)
Zinfandel, '00, Central Coast $9.00 (B-New World)

LA FAMIGLIA DI ROBERT MONDAVI

P.O. Box 363, Oakville 94562
www.robertmondavi.com

Pinot Gris, '00, California $18.00 (G-New World)
Red Italian, '99, Barbera, California $20.00 (2)
Red Rhone, '99, Rhone Blend, Napa Vly. $40.00 (S-New World)
White Varietals, '00, Moscato Bianco California $16.00 (2)

MONTERRA WINERY

12001 S. Hwy. 99, Manteca 95336

Cabernet Sauvignon, '00, Monterey Co. $13.00 (4)
Cabernet Sauvignon, '99, Monterey Co. $10.00 (S-New World)
Chardonnay, '00, Monterey Co. $13.00 (5)
Merlot, '00, Monterey Co. $13.00 (3)
Merlot, '99, Monterey Co. $10.00 (∑-New World)
Syrah, '99, Monterey Co. $13.00 (5)
White Varietals, '00, Encore, San Bernabe Vnyd. (S-State Fair)

MONTEVINA

20680 Shenandoah School, Plymouth 95669
www.montevina.com

Pinot Gris, '01, Amador Co. Pinot Grigio $10.00 (3)
Red Italian, '98, Barbera, Terra D'Oro, Amador Co. $18.00 (6)
Red Italian, '99, Barbera, Amador Co. $12.00 (7)
Sangiovese, '98, Amador Co. $12.00 (2)
Sangiovese, '99, Terra D'oro, Amador Co. $18.00 (6)
Sauvignon Blanc, '00, Fume Blanc, Amador Co. $7.00 (2)
Sauvignon Blanc, '01, California (S-State Fair)
Syrah, '99, Terra D'oro, Amador Co. $18.00 (6)
White Zinfandel, '00, Amador Co. $6.50 (2)
White Zinfandel, '01, Amador Co. $7.00 (5)
Zinfandel, '98, Amador Co., Deaver Vnyd. $29.00 (2)
Zinfandel, '98, Terra D'oro Estate, Amador Co. $18.00 (4)
Zinfandel, '99, Amador Co. $12.00 (2)
Zinfandel, '99, Terra d'Oro, Amador Co. $18.00 (4)
Zinfandel, '99, Terra d'Oro, Amador Co., Home Vnyd. $24.00 (6)
Zinfandel, '99, Terra d'Oro, Amador Co., SHR $24.00 (5)

MONTHAVEN

401 St. Helena Hwy., So., Saint Helena 94574

Cabernet Sauvignon, '99, California $10.00 (2)
Chardonnay, '00, California Coastal (S-State Fair)
Zinfandel, '99, Coastal, California $10.00 (2)

MONTICELLO CORLEY FAMILY VINEYARD

4242 Big Ranch Road, Napa 94558
www.monticellovineyards.com

Cabernet Sauvignon, '99, Napa Vly., Jefferson Cuvee $34.00 (3)
Cabernet Sauvignon, '99, Napa Vly., Rsv. $85.00 (B-San Fran)
Chardonnay, '00, Napa Vly., Estate $24.00 (3)

Merlot, '99, Napa Vly., Estate $28.00 (S-San Diego)
Pinot Noir, '00, Napa Vly., Estate $34.00 (2)

MONTPELLIER VINEYARDS

P.O. Box 789, Ceres 95307

Cabernet Sauvignon, '99, California $7.00 (5)
Chardonnay, '00, California $7.00 (2)
Chardonnay, '99, California $7.00 (G-New World)
Merlot, '00, California $7.00 (3)
Pinot Gris, '99, California $7.00 (B-San Diego)
Pinot Noir, '99, California $7.00 (B-Orange)
Red Italian, '99, Tuscan Blend, California $7.00 (2)
Red Meritage, '98, Cabernet/Merlot, Calif. $7.00 (B-New World)
Red Rhone, '98, Shiraz/Cabernet, California $7.00 (B-New World)
Syrah, '00, California $7.00 (6)
Viognier, '00, California $7.00 (5)
White Varietals, '99, Semillion/Chardonnay, California $7.00 (2)
White Zinfandel, '00, California $6.00 (4)
Zinfandel, '98, California (B-Pac. Rim)
Zinfandel, '99, California $7.00 (S-New World)

MOSBY

9496 Santa Rosa Rd., Buellton 93427

Pinot Gris, '01, Santa Barbara Co. Pinot Grigio $14.00 (S-Orange)
Red Italian, '00, Dolcetto, Santa Barbara Co. $14.00 (2)
Red Italian, '00, Teroldego, Santa Barbara Co. $28.00 (4)

MOSS CREEK

6015 Steele Canyon Rd., Napa 95448

Cabernet Sauvignon, '97, Napa Vly., Raney Rock $65.00 (2)
Zinfandel, '98, Napa Vly. $34.00 (2)

MOUNT PALOMAR WINERY

33820 Rancho Calif. Rd., Temecula 92591
www.mountpalomar.com

Red Italian, '99, Castelletto, Trovato, Temecula Vly. $18.00 (4)
Red Italian, '99, Super Tuscan, Temecula $15.00 (B-New World)
Red Meritage, '97, Estate, Temecula $18.00 (4)
White Varietals, '00, Cortese - Castelletto, Temecula $18.00 (5)

MUMM CUVEE NAPA

8445 Silverado Trail, Napa 94558
www.mumm.com

Sparkling Wine, '96, Brut, DVX, Napa Vly. $50.00 (3)
Sparkling Wine, '97, Blanc De Blanc, Napa Vly. $22.00 (5)
Sparkling Wine, '97, Brut, DVX, Napa Vly. $45.00 (S-Orange)
Sparkling Wine, 'NV, Blanc De Noir, Napa Vly. $18.00 (4)
Sparkling Wine, 'NV, Brut Prestige, Napa Vly. $18.00 (3)

MURPHY-GOODE

4001 Hwy. 128, Geyserville 95441
www.wines.com\murphy-goode\win

Cabernet Sauvignon, '99, Alexander Vly. $22.00 (3)
Chardonnay, '00, Sonoma Co. $15.00 (2)
Sauvignon Blanc, '00, Fume Rsv., Alexander Vly. $17.00 (2)
Zinfandel, '00, Liar's Dice, Sonoma Co. $20.00 (7)

MURRIETA'S WELL

5565 Tesla Rd., Livermore 94550
www.murrietaswell.com

Red Meritage, '97, Red Vendimia, Livermore Vly. $35.00 (2)
Red Meritage, '98, Red Vendimia, Livermore Vly. $35.00 (4)
White Meritage, '99, White Vendimia, Livermore Vly. $22.00 (2)
Zinfandel, '97, Livermore Vly. $29.00 (B-San Fran)

N

NAPA CELLARS

7481 St. Helena Hwy., Oakville 94562

Chardonnay, '00, Napa Vly. (B-State Fair)
Merlot, '00, Napa Vly. (S-State Fair)
Syrah, '00, Napa Vly. (S-State Fair)
Zinfandel, '00, Napa Vly. (G-State Fair)

NAPA RIDGE

P.O. Box 111, St Helena 94574

Cabernet Sauvignon, '97, Napa Vly. Rsv. $20.00 (8)
Cabernet Sauvignon, '99, Lodi $9.00 (5)
Cabernet Sauvignon, '99, Napa Vly. $12.00 (3)
Chardonnay, '00, Napa Vly. $12.00 (3)
Chardonnay, '00, North Coast (2)
Chardonnay, '97, Napa Vly. Rsv. (Σ-L.A.)
Chardonnay, '98, North Coast $9.00 (2)
Merlot, '00, Napa Vly. $12.00 (5)
Merlot, '97, Napa Vly. Rsv. $20.00 (2)
Merlot, '98, Lodi $9.00 (B-Riverside)
Pinot Noir, '00, North Coast $9.00 (4)
Syrah, '98, Stanislaus Co. Shiraz $9.00 (B-W. Coast)
White Varietals, '98, Semillon, Napa Vly. $9.00 (2)
White Varietals, '98, White Blend, North Coast $9.00 (B-New World)
Zinfandel, '97, North Coast $9.00 (2)

NATHANSON CREEK CELLARS

Address Not Available

Cabernet Sauvignon, 'NV, California $6.00 (2)
Chardonnay, '00, California $6.00 (S-Riverside)
Merlot, 'NV, California $6.00 (B-Riverside)

NAVARRO VINEYARDS

5601 Highway 128, Philo 95466
www.navarrowine.com

Cabernet Sauvignon, '98, Mendocino Co. $25.00 (B-New World)
Chardonnay, '00, Anderson Vly. Premiere Rsv. $18.00 (7)
Chardonnay, '00, Mendocino Co. $14.00 (8)
Dry Riesling, '00, Anderson Vly. $14.00 (2)
Gewurztraminer, '00, Estate, Anderson Vly. $14.00 (6)
Petite Sirah, '99, Mendocino Co. $20.00 (S-New World)
Pinot Gris, '01, Anderson Vly. $16.00 (2)
Pinot Noir, '00, Anderson Vly. Methode Ancienne $19.00 (8)
Pinot Noir, '00, Anderson Vly., Deep End Blend (S-State Fair)
Pinot Noir, '00, Mendocino $15.00 (4)
Pinot Noir, '99, Anderson Vly., Deep End Blend $38.00 (3)
Red Rhone, '99, Mourvedre, Mendocino $20.00 (2)
Sauvignon Blanc, '01, Mendocino, Cuvee 128 $14.00 (7)
White Dessert, '00, Gewurztraminer, Anderson Vly. $25.00 (3)

White Dessert, '00, Riesling, SLH, Anderson Vly. $25.00 (3)
White Dessert, '01, Gewurztraminer, Cluster Select $49.00 (2)
White Dessert, '01, White Riesling, Cluster Select $49.00 (3)
White Varietals, '01, Chenin Blanc, Old Vine Cuveé $9.75 (4)
White Varietals, '01, Edelzwicker Mendocino $10.00 (2)
White Varietals, '01, Traminer Anderson Vly. $10.00 (S-San Fran)
Zinfandel, '00, Mendocino Co. $19.00 (3)

NEESE VINEYARDS

Address Not Available

Zinfandel, '00, Redwood Vly. $17.00 (3)

NEVADA CITY WINERY

321 Spring St., Nevada City 95959

Bordeaux, '00, Cabernet Franc, Sierra Foothills (2)
Cabernet Sauvignon, '99, Sierra Foothills $16.00 (5)
Petite Sirah, '99, Sierra Foothills $21.00 (B-Riverside)
Red Meritage, '99, Sierra Foothills Vin Cing $14.00 (3)
Red Rhone, '99, Solaire, California $16.00 (4)
Syrah, '00, Sierra Foothills $18.00 (4)
Zinfandel, '99, Sierra Foothills $15.00 (3)

NEWLAN VINEYARDS & WINERY

5225 Solano Avenue, Napa 94558

White Dessert, '00, White Riesling, Napa Vly. $25.00 (3)
Zinfandel, '00, Napa Vly. $22.00 (B-Orange)

NICHOLS

4910 Edna Rd., San Luis Obispo 93401

Chardonnay, '99, Edna Vly., Paragon Vnyd. (G-L.A.)
Merlot, '98, Paso Robles $26.00 (B-Riverside)
Pinot Noir, '99, Edna Vly., Paragon Vnyd. $28.00 (B-Orange)
Zinfandel, '98, Central Coast, Cienaga Vnyd. $26.00 (S-Orange)

NOB HILL TRADING CO.

Address Not Available

Chardonnay, '00, Sonoma Co. (S-State Fair)
Merlot, '00, Alexander Vly. (B-State Fair)
Red Meritage, '00, Meritage Alexander Vly. $25.00 (2)

NORMAN VINEYARDS

7450 Vineyard Drive, Paso Robles 93446
www.normanvineyards.com

Cabernet Sauvignon, '99, Paso Robles Est. $19.00 (G-New World)
Red Meritage, '99, No Nonsense, Paso Robles $18.00 (6)
White Zinfandel, '01, Paso Robles $8.00 (B-Orange)
Zinfandel, '00, Paso Robles Clevenger Ranch $18.00 (B-Riverside)
Zinfandel, '00, Paso Robles, The Monster $18.00 (3)
Zinfandel, '99, Cucamonga Vly. Old Vine $16.00 (B-Riverside)
Zinfandel, '99, Paso Robles $18.00 (S-New World)

O

OAK GROVE VINEYARDS

Address Not Available

Chardonnay, '00, Private Rsv., California $10.00 (2)
Merlot, '00, California $10.00 (B-San Fran)

OAKSTONE

6440 Slug Gulch Rd., Fair Play 95684
http://innercite.com/~oakstone

Cabernet Sauvignon, '99, Fair Play, De Cascabel (S-State Fair)
Merlot, '99, Fair Play, De Cascabel Vnyd. $16.00 (2)
Red Italian, '00, Charbono, Fair Play Rsv. $20.00 (S-Orange)
Red Meritage, '00, Fair Play, De Cascabel Vnyd. (B-State Fair)
Syrah, '00, El Dorado, Boa Vista Vnyd. $14.00 (B-Orange)
Zinfandel, '99, Sierra Foothills (S-State Fair)

OBESTER

12341 San Mateo Rd., Half Moon Bay 94019

Cabernet Sauvignon, '00, Napa Vly. $17.00 (G-San Diego)

ORFILA VINEYARDS

13455 San Pasqual Rd., Escondido 92025
www.orfila.com

Chardonnay, '99, California Coastal Rsv. $18.00 (4)
Dry Riesling, '00, Monterey Co. / San Diego $11.00 (S-Orange)
Merlot, '98, California Coastal $16.00 (2)
Merlot, '99, San Diego Co. Rsv. $27.00 (5)
Pinot Noir, '98, Arroyo Grande Vly. $35.00 (S-San Diego)
Pinot Noir, '99, Edna Vly. $35.00 (G-San Diego)
Pinot Noir, '99, San Luis Obispo/Edna Vly. $35.00 (5)
Sangiovese, '98, San Pasqual Vly., Di Collina $20.00 (6)
Syrah, '97, San Pasqual Vly., Val De La Mer $24.00 (B-San Diego)
Syrah, '98, San Pasqual Vly., Val De La Mer $24.00 (2)
Syrah, '99, San Pasqual Vly., Val De La Mer $24.00 (4)
White Varietals, '97, Viognier Cuveé, San Pasquel Vly. (G-State Fair)
White Varietals, 'NV, Lotus, San Pasqual Vly. $28.00 (6)

P

PACIFIC ECHO

8501 Hwy. 128, Philo 95466

Sparkling Wine, 'NV, Brut, Mendocino Co. $16.00 (G-Orange)

PACIFIC STAR WINERY

33000 North Highway 1, Fort Bragg 95437

Generic Red, '99, Dad's Daily Red, California $12.00 (B-Orange)
Petite Sirah, '99, Mendocino Co. Rsv. $26.00 (S-Orange)
Zinfandel, '99, Mendocino, B-Bar-X Ranch Rsv. $24.00 (B-Orange)

PARADISE RIDGE

4545 Thomas Lake Harris Dr., Santa Rosa 95403
www.paradiseridgewinery.com

Cabernet Sauvignon, '99, Sonoma $27.00 (2)
Merlot, '99, Sonoma Co., Ladi's Vnyd. (S-State Fair)
Sauvignon Blanc, '01, Sonoma Co., Grandview Vnyd. $14.00 (2)
Syrah, '00, Sonoma Co., Ladi's Vnyd. $24.00 (2)

PARAISO SPRINGS VINEYARDS

38060 Paraiso Springs Rd., Soledad 93960

Chardonnay, '99, Monterey, Santa Lucia Highlands (S-State Fair)
Pinot Noir, '98, Monterey, Santa Lucia Highlands $16.00 (2)
Syrah, '99, Monterey Co., Santa Lucia Highlands (G-Pac. Rim)

PARDUCCI WINE CELLARS

501 Parducci Rd., Ukiah 95482

Cabernet Sauvignon, '99, Mendocino, Vintner Select $11.00 (2)

Chardonnay, '00, Mendocino Co., Vintner Select $10.00 (3)
Merlot, '99, Mendocino Co., Vintner Select $9.00 (2)
Petite Sirah, '99, California, Vintner Select $10.00 (3)
Pinot Noir, '00, Mendocino Co., Vintner Select $9.00 (S-Orange)
Sauvignon Blanc, '01, Lake Co. $8.00 (2)

FESS PARKER WINERY

6200 Foxen Canyon Rd., Los Olivos 93441
www.fessparker.com

Chardonnay, '00, Marcella's Vnyd. $26.00 (B-San Fran)
Pinot Noir, '00, Santa Barbara Co. $22.00 (G-Orange)
Pinot Noir, '00, Santa Barbara, Marcella's Vnyd. $45.00 (B-San Fran)

PEACHY CANYON WINERY

Rt. 1, Box 115C, Paso Robles 93446
www.peachycanyonwinery.com

Cabernet Sauvignon, '99, Westside $25.00 (B-New World)
Zinfandel, '99, Paso Robles Estate $30.00 (B-New World)
Zinfandel, '99, Paso Robles, Mustang Springs $26.00 (S-New World)
Zinfandel, '99, Paso Robles, Westside $19.00 (B-New World)

J. PEDRONCELLI

1220 Canyon Rd., Geyserville 95441

Cabernet Sauvignon, '00, Sonoma Co., Vintage Select (2)
Cabernet Sauvignon, '99, Alexander Vly., Morris Fay Vnyd. $16.00
Cabernet Sauvignon, '99, Dry Creek Vly., Three Vnyds. $15.00 (2)
Chardonnay, '00, Dry Creek Vly., F. Johnson Vnyd. $14.00 (3)
Chardonnay, '00, Vintage Selection $10.00 (S-W. Coast)
Merlot, '99, Dry Creek Vly. Bench Vnyd. $14.00 (2)
Pinot Noir, '00, Dry Creek Vly., F. Johnson Vnyd. $14.00 (6)
Sangiovese, '99, Dry Creek Vly. Alto Vnyd. $14.00 (B-Riverside)
Sauvignon Blanc, '00, Dry Creek Vly. East Side Vnyd. $10.00 (2)
White Zinfandel, '01, Zinfandel Rose, Vintage Selection $8.50 (2)
Zinfandel, '00, Dry Creek Vly., Mother Clone (B-State Fair)
Zinfandel, '00, Sonoma Co., Vintage Select $11.00 (B-Orange)
Zinfandel, '01, Sonoma Co., Vintage Select (2)

PEIRANO ESTATE VINEYARDS

21831 N. Hwy.99, Acampo 95220
www.peirano.com

Cabernet Sauvignon, '99, Lodi Estate $10.00 (5)
Chardonnay, '99, Lodi Estate $10.00 (5)
Merlot, '98, Lodi Six-Clones $10.00 (3)
Sauvignon Blanc, '99, Lodi Estate $9.00 (6)
Syrah, '98, Lodi Estate $11.00 (7)
Viognier, '99, Lodi Estate $11.00 (2)
Zinfandel, '97, Old Vine, Lodi Estate $11.00 (2)

PEJU PROVINCE

8466 St. Helena Hwy., Rutherford 94573
www.peju.com

Cabernet Sauvignon, '99, Napa Vly. (G-L.A.)
Cabernet Sauvignon, '99, Napa Vly. Rsv. (S-L.A.)

PELICAN RANCH

Address Not Available

Chardonnay, '00, Napa Carneros, Mitsuko's Vnyd. $19.00 (2)
Chardonnay, '00, Santa Lucia, Sleepy Hollow $19.00 (G-Orange)
Pinot Noir, '99, Santa Lucia, Sleepy Hollow Vnyd. $24.00 (4)

ROBERT PEPI WINERY

P.O. Box 328, Oakville 94562
www.pepi.com

Chardonnay, '01, Napa Vly. $14.00 (5)
Pinot Gris, '00, Willamette Vly. Pinot Grigio $12.00 (5)
Red Italian, '00, Barbera, California $16.00 (7)
Red Italian, '98, Colline Di Sassi, Napa Vly. $25.00 (4)
Sangiovese, '99, California $12.00 (5)
Sauvignon Blanc, '00, Two Heart Canopy, California $12.00 (6)

PEPPER LANE WINERY

Address Not Available

Chardonnay, '00, South Coast (S-L.A.)
Merlot, '00, California $12.00 (2)

PEPPERWOOD GROVE

P.O. Box 1607, Sonoma 95476

Bordeaux, '99, Cabernet Franc, California $9.00 (9)
Cabernet Sauvignon, '00, California $9.00 (4)
Chardonnay, '00, California $9.00 (B-San Fran)
Merlot, '00, Calfornia $9.00 (5)
Merlot, '99, California $7.00 (3)
Pinot Gris, '00, California Pinot Grigio $7.00 (2)
Pinot Noir, '00, California $9.00 (4)
Syrah, '00, California $9.00 (6)
Syrah, '99, California $8.00 (B-New World)
Viognier, '00, California $7.00 (4)
Zinfandel, '99, California $7.00 (5)

PERRY CREEK VINEYARDS

7400 Perry Creek Rd., Somerset 95684
www.perrycreek.com

Cabernet Sauvignon, '98, El Dorado Estate $14.00 (S-Riverside)
Cabernet Sauvignon, '99, El Dorado Estate $14.00 (8)
Chardonnay, '00, El Dorado Estate $12.00 (3)
Merlot, '99, El Dorado Estate $12.00 (2)
Red Rhone, '00, Coteau De Michel, California $16.00 (5)
Sangiovese, '98, El Dorado Estate $16.00 (B-New World)
Syrah, '98, El Dorado Estate $16.00 (3)
Syrah, '99, El Dorado Estate $16.00 (6)
Viognier, '00, El Dorado Estate $16.00 (2)
White Varietals, '01, Muscat, El Dorado Estate $9.00 (6)
Zinfandel, '00, El Dorado (S-State Fair)
Zinfandel, '00, El Dorado, Spanish Creek Ranch (G-State Fair)
Zinfandel, '00, Sierra Foothills, Zin Man $12.00 (7)
Zinfandel, '99, Sierra Foothills, Potter Vnyd. $24.00 (3)
Zinfandel, '99, Sierra Foothills, Zin Man $12.00 (2)

PEZZI-KING VINEYARDS

3510 Unocal Place, Ste. 208, Santa Rosa 95403
www.pezziking.com

Sauvignon Blanc, '00, Fume Blanc, North Coast $13.00 (2)
Zinfandel, '00, Dry Creek Vly., Maple Vnyd. (B-L.A.)
Zinfandel, '99, Dry Creek Vly. Old Vines $23.00 (S-Orange)

JOSEPH PHELPS VINEYARDS

200 Taplin Road, St Helena 94574
www.jpvwines.com

Red Meritage, '99, Insignia, Napa Vly. $95.00 (G-Orange)

PHILLIPS FARMS VINEYARDS

4580 W. Hwy 12, Lodi 95242
www.phillipsvineyards.com

Cabernet Sauvignon, '00, Lodi $24.00 (S-San Fran)
Chardonnay, '00, Lodi Rsv. $15.00 (B-San Fran)
Merlot, '00, Lodi $20.00 (B-San Fran)
Viognier, '00, California $18.00 (B-San Fran)
Zinfandel, '00, Lodi, Maley Vnyd. $24.00 (B-San Fran)

R. H. PHILLIPS

26836 County Rd. 12A, Esparto 95627
www.rhphillips.com

Bordeaux, '99, Malbec, Toasted Head, Dunnigan Hills $17.00 (4)
Cabernet Sauvignon, '00, Dunnigan Hills, Estate $9.00 (2)
Cabernet Sauvignon, '99, California (B-L.A.)
Chardonnay, '00, California $9.00 (S-New World)
Chardonnay, '00, Toasted Head, Dunnigan Hills $14.00 (B-Orange)
Chardonnay, '99, Toasted Head, Giguiere Ranch $25.00 (3)
Merlot, '99, Toasted Head, Dunnigan Hills $17.00 (B-New World)
Red Meritage, '99, Toasted Head, Dunnigan Hills (S-State Fair)
Red Rhone, '99, Syrah/Cab, Toasted Head $17.00 (6)
Sauvignon Blanc, '01, Dunnigan Hills, Estate $8.00 (2)
Syrah, '00, Dunnigan Hills, Estate (S-State Fair)
Syrah, '00, EXP, Dunnigan Hills $14.00 (6)
Syrah, '99, EXP, Dunnigan Hills $25.00 (4)
Viognier, '00, EXP, Dunnigan Hills $14.00 (5)
Viognier, '01, EXP, Dunnigan Hills (B-State Fair)

PHOENIX VINEYARDS

3175 Dry Creek Road, Napa 94558

Chardonnay, '00, Napa Vly. Rsv. $18.00 (3)
Red Meritage, '99, Napa Vly. Rancho Napa $37.00 (2)

PIETRA SANTA

10034 Cienaga Rd., Hollister 95023
www.pietrasantawinery.com

Red Italian, '98, Sassolino, Cienega Vly. (B-Pac. Rim)
Red Italian, '99, Dolcetto, Cienega Vly. $20.00 (3)
Sangiovese, '99, Cienega Vly. $24.00 (3)

PINE RIDGE

5901 Silverado Trail, Napa 94558
www.pineridgewine.com

Cabernet Sauvignon, '99, Stag's Leap District $60.00 (B-San Fran)
Chardonnay, '00, Carneros, Dijon Clones $25.00 (Σ-San Fran)

MICHAEL POZZAN WINERY

P.O. Box 2121, Orinda 94563

Cabernet Sauvignon, '97, Alexander Vly., Special Rsv. $12.00 (S-
Cabernet Sauvignon, '99, Napa Vly., Matthew's Cuvee $15.00 (2)
Chardonnay, '00, Sonoma Co., Special Rsv. (S-Pac. Rim)
Merlot, '99, Alexander Vly., Special Rsv. (S-Pac. Rim)
Merlot, '99, California, Barrel Select (B-Pac. Rim)
Pinot Noir, '00, Napa Vly., Special Rsv. $10.00 (G-New World)
Red Meritage, '98, Napa Vly. (S-Pac. Rim)
Sangiovese, '99, Napa Vly., Special Rsv. $8.00 (3)
Syrah, '98, Napa Vly., Special Rsv. $15.00 (2)

Q

QUADY

13181 Rd. 24, Madera 93637

White Dessert, '01, Electra Orange Muscat, California $8.00 (6)

QUAIL RIDGE

1155 Mee Lane, Rutherford 94573

Cabernet Sauvignon, '99, Rsv., Napa Vly. $60.00 (2)
Zinfandel, '00, Old Vines, Napa Vly. $25.00 (3)

QUINTA DA SONORA

Address Not Available

White Varietals, '01, Verdelho, California $13.00 (G-Orange)

QUIVIRA

4900 W. Dry Creek Rd., Healdsburg 95448
www.quivirawine.com

Red Rhone, '00, Dry Creek Cuvee $19.00 (5)
Sauvignon Blanc, '00, Dry Creek Vly., Fig Tree Vnyd. $17.00 (3)
Zinfandel, '00, Dry Creek Vly., Anderson Ranch $35.00 (S-L.A.)
Zinfandel, '99, Dry Creek Vly. $20.00 (2)
Zinfandel, '99, Dry Creek Vly., Dieden Vnyd. $35.00 (3)
Zinfandel, '99, Dry Creek Vly., Wine Creek Ranch $35.00 (2)

QUPÉ

4665 Santa Maria Mesa Rd., Santa Maria 93454

Red Rhone, '00, Los Olivos Cuveé, Santa Ynez $20.00 (S-Orange)
Syrah, '00, Central Coast $14.00 (B-Orange)
White Varietals, '01, Marsanne, Santa Ynez Vly. $15.00 (B-Orange)

R

RANCHO SISQUOC

6600 Foxen Canyon Rd., Santa Maria 93454

Bordeaux, '99, Malbec, Santa Barbara, Flood Vnyd. $30.00 (3)
Chardonnay, '00, Santa Barbara, Flood Family Vnyd. $18.00 (2)
Pinot Noir, '00, Santa Barbara, Flood Family Vnyd. $30.00 (3)
Red Meritage, '99, Santa Barbara, Flood Family Vnyd. $40.00 (2)

RANCHO ZABACO

2777 Cleveland Ave., #104, Santa Rosa 95403
www.ranchozabaco.com

Pinot Gris, '00, Sonoma Coast $16.00 (2)
Pinot Gris, '01, Sonoma Coast $16.00 (6)
Sauvignon Blanc, '01, Russian River Vly., Rsv. $18.00 (6)
Syrah, '99, Sonoma Co. $18.00 (4)
Zinfandel, '00, Dancing Bull, California $12.00 (8)
Zinfandel, '00, Dry Creek Vly. $25.00 (B-W. Coast)
Zinfandel, '00, Dry Creek Vly., Chiotti Vnyds. $25.00 (2)
Zinfandel, '00, Sonoma Co. Heritage Vines $15.00 (2)
Zinfandel, '99, Dry Creek Vly. $18.00 (8)
Zinfandel, '99, Dry Creek Vly. Stefani Vnyd. $25.00 (4)
Zinfandel, '99, Sonoma Co. Heritage Vines $15.00 (S-New World)

RAVENSWOOD

18701 Gehricke Rd., Sonoma 95476
www.ravenswood-wine.com

Red Italian, '99, Rancho Salina, Sonoma Vly. $27.00 (B-San Fran)
Red Meritage, '99, Sonoma Vly., Gregory Vnyd. $25.00 (B-San

Red Rhone, '99, Icon, Sonoma Co. $20.00 (2)
Zinfandel, '00, Napa Vly. $15.00 (B-Orange)
Zinfandel, '00, Sonoma Vly., Monte Rosso Vnyd. $30.00 (B-Orange)
Zinfandel, '99, Amador Co. $13.75 (S-Orange)
Zinfandel, '99, Lodi $13.00 (2)
Zinfandel, '99, Mendocino Co. $14.00 (2)
Zinfandel, '99, Napa Vly. $15.00 (B-San Fran)
Zinfandel, '99, Sonoma Co. $15.00 (S-San Fran)

MARTIN RAY

P.O. Box 43, Graton 95444

Cabernet Sauvignon, '99, Napa, Sonoma & Mendocino (S-L.A.)
Merlot, '99, Sonoma Co., Mariage (S-L.A.)
Pinot Noir, '99, North Coast, La Montana (S-L.A.)

RAYE'S HILL

Address Not Available

Pinot Noir, '98, Anderson Vly. $24.00 (3)
Pinot Noir, '99, Russian River Vly. $20.00 (S-W. Coast)

RAYMOND

849 Zinfandel Lane, St Helena 94574
www.raymondwine.com

Cabernet Sauvignon, '97, Generations $80.00 (G-New World)
Cabernet Sauvignon, '98, Napa Vly., Generations $80.00 (5)
Cabernet Sauvignon, '99, Napa Vly. Estate $23.00 (4)
Cabernet Sauvignon, '99, Napa Vly. Rsv. $40.00 (7)
Chardonnay, '00, Monterey Co. Estates $15.00 (8)
Chardonnay, '00, Napa Vly. Rsv. $20.00 (7)
Merlot, '99, Napa Vly. Rsv. $24.50 (6)
Pinot Noir, '98, Napa Vly. Rsv. $21.00 (S-New World)
Sauvignon Blanc, '00, Napa Vly. Rsv. $11.00 (B-Riverside)
Zinfandel, '99, Napa Vly. Rsv. $22.00 (5)

RED ROCK

P.O. Box 2325, Merced 95340

Chardonnay, '00, California (S-Pac. Rim)
Zinfandel, '98, California $10.00 (2)

REDWOOD CREEK WINERY

Address Not Available
www.redwoodcreekwine.com

Cabernet Sauvignon, '98, California $8.00 (3)
Chardonnay, '00, California $8.00 (3)
Sauvignon Blanc, '00, California $8.00 (S-W. Coast)
Sauvignon Blanc, '01, California $8.00 (B-State Fair)

RENAISSANCE

P.O. Box 1000, Renaissance 95962
www.renaissancewinery.com

Cabernet Sauvignon, '95, Premier Cuvee (2)
Cabernet Sauvignon, '97, Sierra Foothills $24.00 (2)
Cabernet Sauvignon, '98, Sierra Foothills Rsv. $39.00 (B-Orange)
Merlot, '97, Sierra Foothills $23.00 (B-Orange)
Pinot Noir, '00, Sierra Foothills $28.00 (2)
Red Rhone, '00, Sierra Foothills Mediterranean Red $19.00 (2)
Syrah, '00, Sierra Foothills $21.00 (3)
Viognier, '01, Sierra Foothills (S-Pac. Rim)
White Dessert, '97, Sauv. Blanc, Sierra Foothills $24.00 (S-Orange)
White Dessert, '99, Semillon, Sierra Foothills $25.00 (G-Orange)

White Varietals, '00, Rousanne, Sierra Foothills $37.00 (G-Orange)

RENWOOD WINES

12225 Steiner Rd., Plymouth 95669
www.renwood.com

Red Italian, '99, Nebbiolo, Amador Co. (G-State Fair)
Syrah, '00, California, Sierra Series (S-State Fair)
Syrah, '99, Amador Co. $25.00 (2)
Zinfandel, '00, California, Sierra Series $11.00 (3)
Zinfandel, '99, Amador Co., Grandmere $23.00 (S-Orange)
Zinfandel, '99, Amador Co., Grandpere $35.00 (4)
Zinfandel, '99, Amador Co., Old Vine $20.00 (5)
Zinfandel, '99, Shenandoah Vly., D'Agostini Vnyd. (Σ-State Fair)

REY SOL

Address Not Available

Red Italian, '00, Barbera, South Coast $15.00 (G-Orange)

RICHARDSON VINEYARDS

2711 Knob Hill Rd., Sonoma 95476

Cabernet Sauvignon, '98, Home Vnyd. $27.00 (B-Orange)
Pinot Noir, '99, Carneros Special Select (S-Pac. Rim)
Syrah, '00, Carneros Estate Grown $22.00 (S-Riverside)

RIDEAU VINEYARD

1562 Alamo Pintado Rd., Solvang 93463
www.rideauvineyard.com

Dry Riesling, '01, Santa Barbara $12.00 (B-W. Coast)
White Varietals, '01, Chenin Blanc, Santa Barbara $15.00 (2)

RIO SECO VINEYARD

Address Not Available

Bordeaux, '99, Cabernet Franc, Paso Robles $24.00 (2)
Cabernet Sauvignon, '99, Paso Robles (G-L.A.)
Zinfandel, '99, Paso Robles, Rio Seco Vnyd. $24.00 (B-Orange)

RIOS-LOVELL WINERY

Address Not Available

Cabernet Sauvignon, '00, Livermore Vly., Estate $18.00 (6)
Chardonnay, '01, Livermore Vly., Estate $14.00 (2)
Merlot, '00, Livermore Vly., Estate $17.50 (S-W. Coast)
Merlot, '00, Livermore Vly., Estate Rsv. $22.00 (3)
Petite Sirah, '00, Livermore Vly., Estate $18.00 (5)
Red Italian, '00, Barbera, Livermore Vly. Estate $17.50 (2)
Red Italian, '01, Barbera, Livermore Vly. Estate $19.00 (3)
Sangiovese, '01, Livermore Vly., Estate $18.00 (6)
Sauvignon Blanc, '01, Livermore Vly. $12.00 (B-San Fran)
Viognier, '01, Cienega Vly. $16.00 (S-Riverside)

RIVER GROVE WINERY

Address Not Available

Chardonnay, '00, Clarksburg Rsv. $10.00 (B-Riverside)
Merlot, '00, Clarksburg $14.00 (4)
Syrah, '00, Clarksburg Estate $12.00 (B-San Fran)

ROEDERER ESTATE

4501 Highway 128, Philo 95466
www.winery.com/roederer

Sparkling Wine, 'NV, Brut, Anderson Vly. $19.50 (G-Orange)

SPENCER ROLOSON

Address Not Available

Zinfandel, '99, Sonoma $24.00 (G-San Fran)

ROSENBLUM CELLARS

2900 Main Street, Alameda 94501
www.rosenblumcellars.com

Cabernet Sauvignon, '98, Mt Veeder, Rsv. (S-Pac. Rim)
Cabernet Sauvignon, '99, Mount Veeder, Yates Vnyd. $59.00 (3)
Chardonnay, '00, Edna Vly., Paragron Vnyd. $19.00 (3)
Chardonnay, '00, Russian River Vly., Loan Oak, Rsv. $25.00 (3)
Chardonnay, '01, Napa Vly. Selecy (G-State Fair)
Merlot, '00, Napa Vly., Mtn. Selection $27.00 (G-San Fran)
Merlot, '99, Russian River Vly. Lone Oak Vnyd. $21.00 (2)
Petite Sirah, '00, Dry Creek Vly. Rockpile Road Vnyd. $30.00 (3)
Petite Sirah, '00, Napa Vly. Picket Road $28.00 (3)
Red Rhone, '00, Mourvedre, Continente $14.00 (S-New World)
Red Rhone, '01, Cote Du Bone Roan, S.F. Bay (S-State Fair)
Syrah, '00, Santa Barbara Co., Rodney's Vnyd. $30.00 (S-San Fran)
Syrah, '00, Solano, England-Shaw Vyd. $37.00 (2)
Viognier, '01, Lodi, Ripkin Vnyd. $19.00 (4)
White Dessert, '00, Muscat Vin de Glacier Calif. $22.00 (B-San Fran)
White Varietals, '00, Marsanne, Dry Creek Vly. $28.00 (3)
White Varietals, '00, Muscat De Glacier, California $17.00 (3)
White Varietals, 'NV, Vintner's Cuveé, Calif. $8.00 (Σ-New World)
Zinfandel, '00, Alexander Vly., Harris Kratka Vyd. $28.00 (2)
Zinfandel, '00, Dry Creek Vly. Rockpile Road Vnyd. $25.00 (7)
Zinfandel, '00, Mendocino, Eaglepoint Vnyd. $24.00 (G-Orange)
Zinfandel, '00, Paso Robles Sauret Vnyd. $19.00 (4)
Zinfandel, '00, Russian River Vly., Alegria $34.00 (2)
Zinfandel, '00, Russian River Vly., Old Vines $23.00 (4)
Zinfandel, '00, San Francisco Bay, Carla's Vnyd. $23.00 (2)
Zinfandel, '00, San Francisco Bay, Continente Vnyd. $16.00 (2)
Zinfandel, '00, San Francisco Bay, Oakley Vnyd. $14.00 (S-Orange)
Zinfandel, '00, San Francisco Bay, Planchon Vnyd. $19.00 (4)
Zinfandel, '00, Sonoma, Samsel Vnyd., Maggie's Rsv. $40.00 (2)
Zinfandel, '99, Redwood Vly., Rhodes Vnyd. $27.00 (S-New World)
Zinfandel, 'NV, California Cuvee XXIV $9.50 (3)

ROSHAMBO WINERY

Address Not Available

Merlot, '99, Sonoma Co. (S-State Fair)
Syrah, '99, Dry Creek Vly., Frank Johnson Vnyd. (B-L.A.)
White Meritage, '00, Dry Creek Vly., Frank Johnson Vnyd. (B-L.A.)
Zinfandel, '00, Dry Creek Vly. (S-State Fair)
Zinfandel, '00, Dry Creek Vly., Taylor Vnyd. (B-State Fair)

ERIC ROSS

13404 DuPont Road, Sebastopol 95472
www.ericross.com

Pinot Noir, '00, Russian River Vly., Saralee's Vnyd. $30.00 (B-Orange)
Zinfandel, '99, Russian River Vly., Feeney Ranch $27.00 (2)
Zinfandel, '99, Russian River Vly., Occidental Vnyd. $30.00 (2)

ROUND HILL VINEYARDS

1680 Silverado Trail, St Helena 94574

Cabernet Sauvignon, '99, California $9.00 (3)
Chardonnay, '00, California $9.00 (3)

Merlot, '99, California (S-L.A.)
White Zinfandel, '01, California $4.50 (S-W. Coast)

JEFF RUNQUIST WINES

Address Not Available

Cabernet Sauvignon, '00, Paso Robles, Colina Poca $25.00 (4)
Petite Sirah, '00, Clarksburg, Salman Vnyd. $24.00 (6)
Pinot Noir, '00, Carneros, Sisters Vnyd. $28.00 (4)
Red Italian, '00, Barbera, Amador, Cooper Vnyd. $18.00 (7)
Sangiovese, '00, Amador Co., Pioneer Hill Vnyd. $20.00 (4)
Syrah, '00, Paso Robles $24.00 (3)
Syrah, '00, Paso Robles, Hilltop Vnyd. $24.00 (2)
Zinfandel, '00, Amador Co., Massoni Ranch $22.00 (7)
Zinfandel, '00, Amador Co., Nostro Vino Vnyd,. $24.00 (3)
Zinfandel, '00, Amador Co., Nostro Vino Vnyd. Primitivo $24.00 (6)

RUSACK VINEYARDS

1819 Ballard Canyon Rd., Solvang 93463

Pinot Noir, '00, Santa Maria Vly. $29.00 (2)
Syrah, '00, Santa Ynez Vly. (B-L.A.)

RUTHERFORD RANCH

1680 Silverado Trail, St Helena 94574
www.rutherfordranch.com

Cabernet Sauvignon, '99, Napa Vly. $14.00 (5)
Chardonnay, '00, Napa Vly. $14.00 (5)
Merlot, '99, Napa Vly. $14.00 (3)
Zinfandel, '99, Napa Vly. $14.00 (G-New World)

RUTHERFORD VINTNERS

1673 St. Helena Hwy. So., Rutherford 94573

Cabernet Sauvignon, '99, Stanislaus Co., Barrel Select $9.00 (5)
Chardonnay, '00, Stanislaus Co., Barrel Select $9.00 (6)
Merlot, '00, Stanislaus Co., Barrel Select $9.00 (3)
Syrah, '99, Stanislaus Co., Barrel Select $9.00 (3)
Viognier, '99, Lodi $9.00 (B-New World)
White Zinfandel, '00, Lodi, Barrel Select $8.00 (2)

RUTZ CELLARS

3637 Frei Rd., Sebastopol 95472

Chardonnay, '99, Russian River Vly., Dutton Ranch $38.00 (B-San
Pinot Noir, '99, Russian River Vly., Dutton Ranch $38.00 (B-San Fran)
Pinot Noir, '99, Russian River Vly., Maison Grand Cru $25.00 (S-San
Pinot Noir, '99, Russian River Vly., Martinelli Vnyd. $38.00 (S-San Fran)

S

SADDLEBACK CELLARS

P.O. Box 141, Oakville 94562

Cabernet Sauvignon, '99, Napa Vly. $48.00 (2)
Chardonnay, '00, Napa Vly., Barrel Ferm. $22.00 (S-Orange)
Merlot, '99, Napa Vly. $36.00 (B-Orange)
White Varietals, '01, Pinot Blanc, Napa Vly. $18.00 (S-Orange)

SALMON CREEK CELLARS

P.O. Box 317, Oakville 94562

Cabernet Sauvignon, '99, California $7.00 (3)
Chardonnay, '00, California $7.00 (6)
Chardonnay, '99, California $7.00 (B-New World)
Merlot, '00, California $7.00 (4)

Merlot, '99, California $7.00 (G-New World)
White Zinfandel, '00, California $7.00 (S-New World)
White Zinfandel, '01, California $7.00 (6)

SALVESTRIN WINE CO.

Address Not Available

Cabernet Sauvignon, '99, St. Helena (G-L.A.)
Sangiovese, '99, St. Helena (B-L.A.)

SAN SABA VINEYARD

1075 B South Main St., Salinas 93901
www.sansaba.com

Chardonnay, '01, Bocage, Monterey California $10.00 (2)
Chardonnay, '01, Monterey (G-L.A.)
Merlot, '97, Monterey $20.00 (S-Riverside)

SAN SIMEON CELLARS

679 Calf Canyon Hwy. 58, Creston 93432

Cabernet Sauvignon, '99, Paso Robles $20.00 (B-San Fran)
Chardonnay, '00, Monterey $15.00 (3)
Chardonnay, '99, Monterey $15.00 (S-L.A.)
Petite Sirah, '00, Paso Robles $20.00 (4)
Pinot Noir, '00, Monterey Co. $18.00 (2)
Syrah, '00, Monterey Co. $15.00 (6)

SANTA BARBARA WINERY

202 Anacapa St., Santa Barbara 93101
www.sbwinery.com

Cabernet Sauvignon, '00, Santa Ynez Vly. $18.00 (B-Orange)
Chardonnay, '00, Santa Barbara Co. $14.00 (B-New World)
Dry Riesling, '00, Santa Ynez Vly., Lafond Vnyd. $14.00 (B-Orange)
Pinot Noir, '00, Santa Barbara Co. (2)
Pinot Noir, '99, Santa Barbara Co. $18.00 (5)
Syrah, '99, Santa Ynez Vly. $22.00 (B-New World)
Zinfandel, '00, Santa Ynez Vly., Lafond Vnyd. LH $30.00 (4)
Zinfandel, '01, Beaujour, California $10.00 (2)

SAPPHIRE HILL VINEYARDS

Address Not Available
www.sapphirehill.com

Chardonnay, '00, Russian River Vly. $22.50 (S-W. Coast)
Chardonnay, '00, Russian River Vly. Rsv. $30.00 (3)
Pinot Noir, '00, Russian River Vly. Estate $36.00 (3)
Zinfandel, '00, Russian River Vly., Winberrie $30.00 (S-Orange)

V. SATTUI WINERY

1111 White Lane, St Helena 94574
www.vsattui.com

Cabernet Sauvignon, '00, Sattui Family, California $15.00 (2)
Cabernet Sauvignon, '99, Napa Vly. $21.00 (5)
Cabernet Sauvignon, '99, Napa Vly., Morisoli Vnyd. $32.00 (6)
Cabernet Sauvignon, '99, Napa Vly., Preston Vnyd. $32.00 (5)
Cabernet Sauvignon, '99, Napa Vly., Suzannes Vyd. $25.00 (8)
Chardonnay, '00, Carneros $17.75 (2)
Chardonnay, '00, Napa-Sonoma $13.00 (G-Riverside)
Chardonnay, '00, Napa Vly., Carsi Vyd. (S-Pac. Rim)
Dry Riesling, '00, California, Off Dry $15.00 (S-New World)
Dry Riesling, '01, California, Off Dry $15.00 (B-Pac. Rim)
Dry Riesling, '01, Dry Napa $15.00 (2)
Merlot, '99, Napa Vly. Lot 1 $24.00 (5)

Pinot Noir, '00, Carneros, Henry Ranch $35.00 (6)
Sparkling Wine, '97, Brut, Napa Vly. $20.00 (S-Orange)
Sparkling Wine, '98, Blanc de Blanc, Napa Vly. $21.00 (B-Orange)
White Varietals, '00, Muscat, California $15.75 (2)
White Varietals, '01, Muscat, California $16.00 (3)
White Varietals, 'NV, Angelica, California (B-State Fair)
White Zinfandel, '00, California $9.00 (5)
Zinfandel, '00, Contra Costa Co. Duarte Vnyd. $35.00 (4)
Zinfandel, '00, Napa Vly., Howell Mtn. $27.00 (3)
Zinfandel, '99, Napa Vly. Quaglia Vnyd. $22.00 (2)
Zinfandel, '99, Napa Vly. Suzanne's Vnyd. $20.00 (5)

AUCELITO CANYON

1600 Saucelito Creek Rd., Arroyo Grande 93420

Bordeaux, '00, Cabernet Franc, Arroyo Grande $21.00 (G-
Cabernet Sauvignon, '99, Arroyo Grande Vly. $25.00 (B-W. Coast)
Zinfandel, '00, Arroyo Grande Vly. $23.00 (6)

AUSAL WINERY

7370 Hwy. 128, Healdsburg 95448
www.sausalwinery.com

Cabernet Sauvignon, '99, Alexander Vly. $24.00 (2)
Red Italian, '96, Sogni D' Oro, Alexander Vly. (S-L.A.)
Sangiovese, '98, Alexander Vly. $15.00 (2)
Zinfandel, '99, Alexander Vly. $15.00 (2)
Zinfandel, '99, Alexander Vly. Private Rsv. $20.00 (4)
Zinfandel, '99, Century Vines, Estate $24.00 (2)

AWYER CELLARS

Address Not Available

Cabernet Sauvignon, '99, Napa Vly., Rutherford, Estate $46.00 (2)
Merlot, '99, Napa Vly., Rutherford, Estate $34.00 (2)
Red Meritage, '99, Bradford, Napa Vly., Rutherford $42.00 (2)

CHEID VINEYARDS

Address Not Available

Cabernet Sauvignon, '97, San Lucas Vnyd. $20.00 (B-New World)
Cabernet Sauvignon, '98, Monterey Co. $20.00 (B-New World)
Chardonnay, '00, Monterey Co. $18.00 (S-New World)
Dry Riesling, '01, Monterey Co., Riverview Vnyd. $12.00 (B-Orange)
Gewurztraminer, '01, Monterey, Viento Vnyd. $14.00 (B-Orange)
Pinot Noir, '99, Monterey, Riverview Vnyd. $25.00 (B-New World)
Sauvignon Blanc, '01, Monterey, San Lucas Vnyd. (G-State Fair)

CHRAMSBERG

1400 Schramsberg Rd., Calistoga 94515
www.schramsberg.com

Sparkling Wine, '95, Brut, J Schram, Napa $75.00 (G-New World)
Sparkling Wine, '96, Brut, J Schram, Napa Vly. $75.00 (4)
Sparkling Wine, '98, Blanc De Blanc, N. California Coast $30.00 (5)
Sparkling Wine, '98, Blanc De Noir, Napa Vly. $30.00 (3)
Sparkling Wine, 'NV, Mirabelle Brut, N. California Coast $16.00 (4)

CHUG

602 Bonneau Rd., Sonoma 95476
www.schugwinery.com

Chardonnay, '00, Carneros, Barrel Ferm. $19.50 (S-Orange)
Pinot Noir, '00, Carneros $19.50 (3)

SEBASTIANI VINEYARDS & WINERY

389 Fourth St. E., Sonoma 95476

Cabernet Sauvignon, '98, Sonoma, Four Generations $21.00 (5)
Cabernet Sauvignon, '98, Sonoma Vly. $30.00 (3)
Cabernet Sauvignon, '98, Madrone Ranch $24.00 (G-Orange)
Chardonnay, '99, Russian River Vly., Dutton Ranch $25.00 (2)
Chardonnay, '99, Sonoma Co. $16.00 (3)
Merlot, '98, Sonoma Co. $22.00 (3)
Merlot, '98, Sonoma Co. Four Generations $18.00 (S-Orange)
Merlot, '98, Sonoma Vly $22.00 (2)
Merlot, '98, Sonoma Vly., Madrone Ranch $30.00 (G-W. Coast)
Pinot Noir, '99, Russian River Vly. $22.00 (S-New World)
Zinfandel, '00, Sonoma Co. $15.00 (S-W. Coast)
Zinfandel, '99, Sonoma Vly., Domenici Vnyd. $24.00 (G-Orange)

SEGHESIO

14730 Grove Street, Healdsburg 95448
www.seghesio.com

Zinfandel, '00, Dry Creek Vly., Cortina $22.00 (Σ-Orange)

SELBY WINERY

3291 Westside Rd., Healdsburg 95448

Chardonnay, '00, Sonoma Co. $24.00 (B-New World)
Merlot, '99, Sonoma Co. $24.00 (S-New World)
Syrah, '99, Sonoma Co. $24.00 (B-New World)

SEQUOIA GROVE VINEYARDS

8338 St. Helena Hwy., Napa 94558

Cabernet Sauvignon, '98, Rutherford Rsv. $55.00 (S-New World)
Cabernet Sauvignon, '99, Napa Vly. $29.00 (4)
Cabernet Sauvignon, '99, Rutherford Rsv. $55.00 (3)
Chardonnay, '00, Napa Vly. Estate $29.00 (B-New World)
Chardonnay, '00, Napa Vly., Carneros $18.00 (2)

SEVEN LIONS WINERY

Address Not Available

Chardonnay, '00, Russian River, Buena Tierra $55.00 (B-W. Coast)
Pinot Noir, '00, Russian River, Hansen Vnyds. $55.00 (S-W. Coast)
Pinot Noir, '00, Russian River, Buena Tierra Vnyd. $75.00 (3)
Pinot Noir, '00, Russian River, Wes Cameron Vnyd. $65.00 (3)
Zinfandel, '00, Russian River, Joe & Emily's Vnyd. $60.00 (2)
Zinfandel, '00, Russian River, Poor Man's Flat Vnyd. $35.00 (2)
Zinfandel, '00, Sonoma Co., Three Amigo's Vnyds. $28.00 (3)

SEVEN PEAKS

5828 Orcutt Rd., San Luis Obispo 93401
www.7peaks.com

Cabernet Sauvignon, '00, Central Coast $14.00 (B-San Fran)
Cabernet Sauvignon, '99, Central Coast $14.00 (4)
Chardonnay, '00, Central Coast $10.00 (3)
Merlot, '99, Central Coast $14.00 (4)
Red Rhone, '99, Cab/Syrah, Paso Robles $20.00 (4)
Syrah, '00, Paso Robles $14.00 (2)
Syrah, '99, Shiraz, Paso Robles $14.00 (6)

CAROL SHELTON

P.O. Box 755, Windsor 95492
www.carolshelton.com

Zinfandel, '00, Cucamonga Vly., Lopez Vnyd. $24.00 (4)

Zinfandel, '00, Dry Creek Vly., Rocky Rsv. $32.00 (6)
Zinfandel, '00, Mendocino, Cox Vnyd., Wild Thing $28.00 (5)

SHENANDOAH VINEYARDS

12300 Steiner Rd., Plymouth 95669
www.sobonwine.com

Red Italian, '00, Barbera, Rsv., Shenandoah Vly. (Σ-L.A.)
Red Italian, '99, Barbera, Amador Co. $15.00 (S-Orange)
Zinfandel, '99, Primitivo, Organically Grown (S-L.A.)

SHYPOKE WINERY

Address Not Available

Red Italian, '99, Charbono, Napa Vly. $18.00 (2)
Sangiovese, '99, Napa Vly. (B-L.A.)

SIERRA VISTA

4560 Cabernet Way, Placerville 95667
www.sierravistawinery.com

Cabernet Sauvignon, '97, Five Star Rsv. $50.00 (B-San Diego)
Cabernet Sauvignon, '98, El Dorado Estate $16.50 (S-New World)
Cabernet Sauvignon, '99, El Dorado Estate $16.50 (S-Orange)
Red Rhone, '00, Fleur De Montagne, El Dorado $21.00 (5)
Sauvignon Blanc, '01, El Dorado Fume Blanc $12.00 (5)
Syrah, '99, El Dorado Red Rock Ridge $25.00 (2)
Zinfandel, '99, El Dorado Estate $12.50 (B-New World)
Zinfandel, '99, El Dorado, Herbert Vnyd. $16.00 (S-Orange)
Zinfandel, '99, El Dorado, Reeves Vnyd. $16.00 (B-San Fran)

SILKWOOD WINES

Address Not Available

Syrah, '00, Stanislaus Co. $22.00 (2)

SILVER RIDGE VINEYARDS

P.O. Box 317, Oakville 94562

Cabernet Sauvignon, '00, California $10.00 (G-State Fair)
Cabernet Sauvignon, '99, California Barrel Select $10.00 (5)
Chardonnay, '00, California Barrel Fermented $10.00 (2)
Merlot, '00, California Barrel Select $10.00 (4)
Syrah, '99, California Barrel Fermented $10.00 (2)
Viognier, '00, California (B-State Fair)

SILVER ROSE CELLARS

Address Not Available

Cabernet Sauvignon, '99, Napa Vly. $34.00 (4)
Chardonnay, '99, Napa Vly., D'argent $30.00 (2)
Merlot, '99, Napa Vly. $29.00 (2)
Merlot, '99, Napa Vly. Jupilles $38.00 (4)
Red Meritage, '99, Napa Vly., Dentelle $44.00 (6)

SILVER STONE

Address Not Available

Cabernet Sauvignon, '99, California $9.00 (2)
Chardonnay, '99, California $9.00 (2)
Chardonnay, '99, California, Barrel Ferm. (B-L.A.)

SIMI

16275 Healdsburg Ave., Healdsburg 95448
www.simiwinery.com

Cabernet Sauvignon, '99, Alexander Vly. $25.00 (S-San Fran)
Chardonnay, '00, Sonoma Co. $17.00 (2)
Chardonnay, '99, Gold Fields Vnyd. Rsv. $30.00 (S-San Fran)

Merlot, '99, Alexander Vly. (2)
Sauvignon Blanc, '00, Sonoma Co. $14.00 (2)
Syrah, '00, Alexander Vly. $20.00 (3)

SINGLE LEAF

7480 Fairplay Rd., Somerset 95684
Bordeaux, '00, Cabernet Franc, Fair Play $16.00 (2)
Cabernet Sauvignon, '99, Vines View Vnyd. $20.00 (G-Orange)
Zinfandel, '99, El Dorado $13.00 (3)
Zinfandel, '99, El Dorado Rsv. $16.00 (4)

SMITH & HOOK

37700 Foothill Rd., Soledad 93960
www.hahnestates.com
Cabernet Sauvignon, '99, Santa Lucia Highlands $18.00 (4)

SMITH WOOTEN

Address Not Available
Bordeaux, '99, Cabernet Franc, Napa Vly. $40.00 (S-New World)
Chardonnay, '99, Napa Vly. Estate $25.00 (B-New World)
Dry Riesling, '00, Napa Vly. Estate $17.00 (B-New World)

SMITH-MADRONE

4022 Spring Mountain Rd., St Helena 94574
www.smithmadrone.com
Cabernet Sauvignon, '99, Napa Vly. $37.00 (3)
Chardonnay, '99, Napa Vly. Estate $25.00 (5)
Dry Riesling, '01, Napa Vly. $17.00 (6)

SOBON ESTATE

14430 Shenandoah Rd., Plymouth 95669
www.sobonwine.com
Syrah, '00, Shenandoah Vly. Rsv. $24.00 (B-San Fran)
Zinfandel, '00, Lubenko Vnyd., Organic $18.00 (B-Orange)
Zinfandel, '00, Shenandoah Vly. Rsv. $24.00 (S-San Fran)

SOGNO WINERY

Address Not Available
Cabernet Sauvignon, '00, El Dorado (B-State Fair)
Red Italian, '00, Giocchino, El Dorado (B-State Fair)
Syrah, '00, El Dorado (B-State Fair)
White Varietals, '00, Muscat Canelli, El Dorado (B-State Fair)
White Zinfandel, '01, El Dorado (B-State Fair)
Zinfandel, '00, Primitivo, Sacramento Co. (B-State Fair)

SOLIS WINERY

3920 Hecker Pass Rd., Gilroy 95020
Sangiovese, '98, Santa Clara Vly. Estate (G-State Fair)

SONORA WINERY & PORT WORKS

17500 Rt. 5 Rd., Sonora 95370
www.sonorawinery.com
Sauvignon Blanc, '01, Amador Co. $13.00 (7)
White Meritage, '01, Sauvignon Blanc, Amador Co. (Σ-L.A.)
White Varietals, '01, Verdelho, California $13.00 (4)
Zinfandel, '00, Amador Co. $22.00 (2)
Zinfandel, '00, Amador Co. Linsteadt Vnyd. $22.00 (5)
Zinfandel, '00, Amador Co. TC Vnyd. $26.00 (2)
Zinfandel, '99, Amador Co. (B-Pac. Rim)
Zinfandel, '99, Amador Co. Linsteadt Vnyd. $18.00 (B-New World)
Zinfandel, '99, Amador Co. TC Vnyd. $24.00 (5)

ST. AMANT WINERY

1 Winemaster Way, Lodi 95240

Red Italian, '00, Barbera, Lodi $14.00 (2)
Syrah, '99, Amador Co. Rsv. $18.00 (B-Orange)
White Varietals, '01, Le Mystere, Amador Co. $18.00 (2)
Zinfandel, '00, Lodi, Mohr-Fry Vnyd. $15.00 (B-Orange)

ST. SUPÉRY

8440 St. Helena Hwy., Rutherford 94573
www.stsupery.com

Bordeaux, '99, Cabernet Franc, Napa Vly. Dollarhide $35.00 (9)
Cabernet Sauvignon, '99, Napa Vly. $24.00 (4)
Cabernet Sauvignon, '99, Napa Vly., Dollarhide Ranch $70.00 (6)
Chardonnay, '00, Napa Vly. $19.00 (3)
Chardonnay, '00, Napa Vly., Dollarhide Ranch $35.00 (3)
Chardonnay, '99, Napa Vly. $19.00 (5)
Chardonnay, '99, Napa Vly., Dollarhide Ranch $30.00 (3)
Merlot, '99, Napa Vly. $21.00 (6)
Red Meritage, '98, Napa Vly. $50.00 (7)
Red Meritage, '99, Napa Vly., Rutherford $60.00 (6)
Sauvignon Blanc, '01, Napa Vly. $15.00 (9)
Syrah, '00, Napa Vly. $25.00 (6)
White Meritage, '00, Napa Vly. $22.00 (7)
White Varietals, '00, Semillon, Napa Vly., Dollarhide $21.00 (6)
White Varietals, '01, Moscato, California $15.00 (9)

STARRY NIGHT WINERY

Address Not Available

Zinfandel, '00, Lodi $16.00 (2)
Zinfandel, '00, Russian River, Tom Feeney Ranch $24.00 (3)

STEELE WINES

4350 Thomas Dr., Kelseyville 95451

Bordeaux, '99, Cabernet Franc, Lake Co. $18.00 (B-San Fran)
Cabernet Sauvignon, '00, Shooting Star $15.00 (B-San Fran)
Chardonnay, '00, Steele Cuvée California $16.00 (B-San Fran)
Chardonnay, '99, Carneros Sangiacomo $26.00 (B-San Fran)
Chardonnay, '99, Bien Nacido Vnyd. $26.00 (B-San Fran)
Pinot Noir, '00, Carneros $18.00 (B-San Fran)
Pinot Noir, '99, Carneros, Sangiacomo Vnyd. $35.00 (B-San Fran)
Pinot Noir, '99, Carneros, Durell Vnyd. $38.00 (G-San Fran)
Pinot Noir, '99, Bien Nacido Vnyd. $36.00 (S-San Fran)
Red Italian, '00, Barbera, Shooting Star $14.00 (G-San Fran)
Syrah, '00, Lake Co., Shooting Star $11.00 (S-San Fran)
Syrah, '99, Lake Co. $16.00 (B-San Fran)
White Dessert, '97, Chardonnay, Carneros $50.00 (B-San Fran)
White Dessert, '97, Chardonnay, Mendocino $38.00 (B-San Fran)
Zinfandel, '98, Mendocino Co., Du Pratt Vnyd. $18.00 (B-San Fran)
Zinfandel, '99, Mendocino Co., Pacini Vnyd. $16.00 (B-San Fran)

STELTZNER VINEYARDS

5998 Silverado Trail, Napa 94558

Cabernet Sauvignon, '98, Stags Leap District $28.00 (B-Riverside)
Cabernet Sauvignon, '99, Napa Vly., Stags Leap District $32.00 (6)
Merlot, '99, Napa Vly., Stags Leap District (2)
Red Rhone, '99, Pinotage, Napa Vly. Stags Leap $26.00 (5)
Sangiovese, '99, Napa Vly., Stags Leap District $22.00 (4)

ROBERT STEMMLER

27000 Ramal Road, Sonoma 95476
www.robertstemmlerwinery.com

Cabernet Sauvignon, '98, Sonoma Co. $28.00 (3)
Chardonnay, '99, Sonoma Co. $20.00 (4)
Merlot, '99, Sonoma Co. $28.00 (3)
Pinot Noir, '00, Carneros, Sonoma Co. $38.00 (3)
Pinot Noir, '00, Sonoma Co. $28.00 (5)
Pinot Noir, '98, Sonoma Co. $25.00 (3)

STEPHEN'S

Address Not Available

Pinot Noir, '99, York Mtn. $24.00 (3)

STERLING VINEYARDS

1111 Dunaweal Ln., Calistoga 94515
www.sterlingvineyards.com

Cabernet Sauvignon, '99, Central Coast $13.00 (G-New World)
Cabernet Sauvignon, '99, Napa Vly. $24.00 (4)
Cabernet Sauvignon, '99, Napa Vly., Diamond Mtn. $40.00 (6)
Chardonnay, '00, Carneros, Winery Lake $25.00 (3)
Chardonnay, '00, Central Coast $13.00 (S-New World)
Chardonnay, '00, Napa Vly. $17.00 (2)
Chardonnay, '00, North Coast $17.00 (5)
Merlot, '99, Napa Vly. $22.00 (5)
Merlot, '99, Napa Vly., Three Palms $58.00 (4)
Pinot Noir, '00, Carneros, Winery Lake $25.00 (4)
Sauvignon Blanc, '01, North Coast $12.00 (3)

STEVENOT

2690 San Domingo Rd., Murphys 95247
www.stevenotwinery.com

Cabernet Sauvignon, '99, Calaveras Co. $16.00 (2)
Merlot, '99, Sierra Foothills $16.00 (B-San Fran)
Syrah, '00, Calaveras Co., Canterbury Vnyds. $18.00 (4)
Zinfandel, '00, Lodi Old Vine (B-State Fair)
Zinfandel, '00, Sierra Foothills, Costello Vnyd. $30.00 (3)

STONE CELLARS

9140 Owens Mt. Ave., Chatsworth 91311

Cabernet Sauvignon, '00, California (2)
Cabernet Sauvignon, '99, California $8.00 (B-Riverside)
Chardonnay, '00, California $8.00 (7)
Merlot, '99, California $8.00 (3)
Red Rhone, '00, Syrah/Cab, California $8.00 (7)
Sauvignon Blanc, '00, California $8.00 (B-New World)
Sauvignon Blanc, '01, California $8.00 (4)

STONE CREEK

9380 Sonoma Hwy, Kenwood 95452

Cabernet Sauvignon, '99, California $8.00 (B-New World)
Cabernet Sauvignon, '99, North Coast, Chairman's Rsv. $17.00 (2)
Chardonnay, '00, California, Special Selection $8.00 (B-W. Coast)
Chardonnay, '01, California, Special Selection $8.00 (B-State Fair)
Merlot, '00, California, Special Selection $8.00 (B-San Fran)
Merlot, '99, North Coast, Chairman's Rsv. $17.00 (3)
Zinfandel, '99, Lodi, Chairman's Rsv. $17.00 (B-W. Coast)

STONEGATE

1183 Dunaweal Lane, Calistoga 94515
www.stonegatewinery.com

Cabernet Sauvignon, '99, Napa Vly. $40.00 (6)
Chardonnay, '00, Napa Vly. Estate $22.00 (3)
Merlot, '99, Napa Vly. $28.00 (6)
Sauvignon Blanc, '01, Napa Vly. (B-L.A.)

STONEHEDGE

P.O. Box 5182, Huntington Park 90255
www.stonehedgewinery.com

Cabernet Sauvignon, '00, California $10.00 (2)
Cabernet Sauvignon, '00, Napa Vly. $25.00 (3)
Chardonnay, '00, Monterey Co. Rsv. $15.00 (4)
Merlot, '00, California $10.00 (B-Orange)
Merlot, '00, Napa Vly. $30.00 (2)
Merlot, '00, Russian River Vly., Diamond Ridge $20.00 (B-W. Coast)
Pinot Noir, '00, California $10.00 (3)
Sauvignon Blanc, '00, California $10.00 (G-New World)
Syrah, '00, California $10.00 (3)
Zinfandel, '00, California $10.00 (2)
Zinfandel, '99, Napa Vly. $20.00 (3)

STONY RIDGE WINERY

4948 Tesla Road, Livermore 94550

Bordeaux, '99, Cabernet Franc, Cienega Vly. Rsv. $20.00 (2)
Dry Riesling, '00, Monterey Co. Rsv. $10.50 (2)
Merlot, '99, Livermore Vly. Rsv. (B-State Fair)
Red Italian, '99, Nebbiolo, California (B-State Fair)
White Varietals, 'NV, Malvasia Bianca, California (Σ-State Fair)

STORRS

303 Potrero St. #35, Santa Cruz 95060
www.storrswine.com

Chardonnay, '00, Santa Cruz, Christie Vnyd. $24.00 (S-W. Coast)
Gewurztraminer, '01, Monterey, Viento Vnyd. $14.00 (B-Orange)
Red Italian, '00, Grenache, Central Coast $20.00 (S-W. Coast)
Red Rhone, '00, Carignane, Santa Clara Vly. (S-State Fair)
Zinfandel, '99, Santa Clara Co., Rusty Ridge $25.00 (3)

STRATFORD WINERY

1472 Railroad Ave., Saint Helena 94574

Syrah, '00, California $18.00 (G-Orange)

RODNEY STRONG

11455 Old Redwood Hwy., Windsor 95492
www.rodneystrong.com

Cabernet Sauvignon, '97, Alden Vnyds. $30.00 (G-New World)
Cabernet Sauvignon, '97, Northern Sonoma Rsv. $40.00 (9)
Cabernet Sauvignon, '98, Alexander Vly., Alden Vnyds. $30.00 (3)
Cabernet Sauvignon, '98, Alexander's Crown Vnyd. $28.00 (4)
Cabernet Sauvignon, '99, Sonoma Co. $18.00 (8)
Chardonnay, '00, Sonoma Co. $14.00 (3)
Chardonnay, '00, Sonoma Co., Chalk Hill Estate $18.00 (5)
Chardonnay, '98, Chalk Hill Vnyd. Rsv. $30.00 (5)
Merlot, '97, Alexander Vly., Northern Sonoma $26.00 (5)
Merlot, '99, Sonoma Co. $16.00 (5)
Pinot Noir, '00, Russian River Vly., Estate Vnyd. $18.00 (3)
Pinot Noir, '98, Northern Sonoma Rsv. $30.00 (G-Riverside)

Pinot Noir, '99, Russian River Vly. Rsv. $30.00 (4)
Sauvignon Blanc, '01, Charlotte's Home Vnyds. $12.00 (5)
Zinfandel, '99, Northern Sonoma, Knotty Vines $18.00 (6)

STRYKER SONOMA WINERY & VINEYARDS

Address Not Available

Chardonnay, '00, Russian River Vly. $22.00 (2)
Chardonnay, '00, L'Ancien Verger Vnyd. $24.00 (B-New World)
Sangiovese, '99, Alexander Vly. $22.00 (2)
Zinfandel, '99, Dry Creek Vly., Sommer Vnyd. $22.00 (2)
Zinfandel, '99, Old Vine, Alexander Vly. $25.00 (2)

STUART CELLARS

Address Not Available

Bordeaux, '00, Cabernet Franc, South Coast $25.00 (4)
Cabernet Sauvignon, '00, Temecula Rsv. $36.00 (S-New World)
Chardonnay, '00, Temecula (B-State Fair)
Merlot, '00, Limited Estate, South Coast $27.00 (3)
Viognier, '99, California Limited Bottling $21.00 (B-Riverside)
Zinfandel, '00, Temecula Rsv. $20.00 (B-New World)

STUHLMULLER VINEYARD & WINERY

Address Not Available

Cabernet Sauvignon, '98, Alexander Vly. $35.00 (S-Riverside)
Cabernet Sauvignon, '99, Alexander Vly. $35.00 (B-State Fair)
Chardonnay, '00, Alexander Vly. (G-State Fair)
Chardonnay, '99, Alexander Vly. $23.00 (4)

SUMMERS WINERY

Address Not Available

Merlot, '99, Knights Vly. $22.00 (2)
Red Meritage, '99, North Coast Chevalier Noir $32.00 (2)

SUNCÉ WINERY

1839 Olivet Rd., Santa Rosa 95401
www.suncewinery.com

Cabernet Sauvignon, '99, Dunnigan Hills $30.00 (B-New World)
Pinot Noir, '00, Sonoma Coast, Karah's Vnyd. (B-L.A.)
Pinot Noir, '01, Russian River Vly., Piner Ranch Vnyd. (B-State Fair)
Red Meritage, '00, California, Steyker's Vnyd. $35.00 (Σ-San Fran)
Red Meritage, '99, Dunnigan Hills $35.00 (B-San Fran)

SUNSET CELLARS

Address Not Available
www.sunsetcellars.com

Red Italian, '00, Barbera, Napa, Twin Creeks Vnyd. $18.00 (2)
Zinfandel, '99, Dry Creek Vly. $23.00 (2)
Zinfandel, '99, Napa Vly. $18.00 (B-Riverside)

SUNSTONE VINEYARDS & WINERY

125 N. Refugio Road, Santa Ynez 93460
www.sunstonewinery.com

Chardonnay, '00, Santa Barbara Co. $18.00 (B-Riverside)
Merlot, '00, Santa Barbara Co. (B-State Fair)
Merlot, '99, Santa Ynez Vly. Rsv. $30.00 (2)
Red Meritage, '99, Eros, Santa Ynez Vly. $36.00 (B-Orange)
Sauvignon Blanc, '00, Santa Ynez Vly. $15.00 (B-Riverside)
Syrah, '99, Santa Ynez Vly. Estate $40.00 (2)
Viognier, '00, Santa Ynez Vly. (B-State Fair)
White Varietals, '99, Eros Santa Ynez Vly. $36.00 (S-San Fran)

SUTTER HOME

277 St. Helena Hwy. So., St Helena 94574
www.sutterhome.com

Chardonnay, '00, California $6.00 (6)
Gewurztraminer, '00, California $8.00 (B-New World)
Gewurztraminer, '01, California $8.00 (7)
Pinot Noir, '98, California $8.00 (B-San Diego)
Sauvignon Blanc, '00, California $6.00 (B-Riverside)
Syrah, '98, California Shiraz $8.00 (S-W. Coast)
Syrah, '99, California Shiraz $8.00 (B-New World)
White Varietals, '00, Chenin Blanc, Signature, California $6.00 (5)
White Varietals, '00, Moscato California $8.00 (3)
White Varietals, '01, Chenin Blanc, Signature, California (B-State Fair)
White Varietals, '99, Moscato California $8.00 (B-New World)
White Zinfandel, '00, California $5.00 (4)
Zinfandel, '98, California $6.00 (B-Riverside)

SWANSON

1271 Manley Lane, Rutherford 94573
www.swansonvineyards.com

Merlot, '99, Napa Vly. $30.00 (2)
Pinot Gris, '01, Napa Vly. Pinot Grigio $20.00 (2)
Red Rhone, '99, Alexis, Napa Vly. $50.00 (4)

SYLVESTER

5115 Buena Vista Dr., Paso Robles 93446

Cabernet Sauvignon, '99, Paso Robles, Kiara Rsv. $15.00 (2)
Chardonnay, '00, Paso Robles, Kiara Rsv. $15.00 (2)
Merlot, '00, Paso Robles, Kiara Rsv. $14.00 (2)
Merlot, '99, Paso Robles, Kiara Rsv. $14.00 (2)
Sangiovese, '99, Paso Robles, Kiara Rsv. (B-L.A.)
Syrah, '97, Paso Robles, Kiara Rsv. $14.00 (S-San Fran)

T

TAFT STREET

2030 Barlow Lane, Sebastopol 95472

Cabernet Sauvignon, '99, Dry Creek Vly., Mauritson Farms (S-L.A.)
Merlot, '99, Central Coast $12.00 (2)
Merlot, '99, Sonoma Co. $17.00 (2)
Sauvignon Blanc, '01, Russian River Vly., Poplar Vnyd. (2)

TALUS

P.O. Box 1290, Woodbridge 95258

Chardonnay, '00, California $9.00 (3)
Pinot Gris, '01, California Pinot Grigio $9.00 (3)
Syrah, '99, California $9.00 (3)
Zinfandel, '99, California $9.00 (4)

IVAN TAMÁS

5565 Tesla Road, Livermore 94550
www.ivantamás.com

Cabernet Sauvignon, '99, California $10.00 (S-New World)
Pinot Gris, '00, Monterey Co. Pinot Grigio $10.00 (2)
Pinot Gris, '01, Monterey Co. Pinot Grigio $10.00 (B-W. Coast)
Zinfandel, '99, Livermore Vly., San Francisco Bay (B-L.A.)

TARA BELLA WINERY

Address Not Available
www.tarabellawines.com

Cabernet Sauvignon, '98, Sonoma Co. $42.00 (B-San Diego)
Cabernet Sauvignon, '99, Napa Vly. $55.00 (2)
Cabernet Sauvignon, '99, Sonoma Co. $42.00 (2)

THORNTON

32575 Rancho Calif. Road, Temecula 92589
www.thorntonwine.com

Cabernet Sauvignon, '00, South Coast $14.00 (2)
Chardonnay, '00, South Coast Dos Vinedos Cuvee $10.00 (3)
Red Meritage, '99, Cabernet/Merlot, South Coast $14.00 (4)
Red Rhone, '99, Cote Red, South Coast $14.00 (7)
Sangiovese, '99, South Coast, Temecula Vly. Vnyds. $12.00 (6)
Sauvignon Blanc, '01, Temecula Vly., Luttgens Family Vnyd. (Σ-L.A.)
Sparkling Wine, '96, Brut, Rsv., California $21.00 (2)
Sparkling Wine, 'NV, Brut (B-L.A.)
Sparkling Wine, 'NV, Cuvee De Frontignan, California $12.00 (5)
Sparkling Wine, 'NV, Cuvee Rouge, California $12.00 (7)
Viognier, '00, South Coast $13.00 (4)
White Varietals, '00, Moscato, South Coast $10.00 (3)
White Varietals, '00, Pinot Blanc, So. Coast, Miramonte $10.00 (3)

TOAD HOLLOW

4024 Westside Rd., Healdsburg 95448
www.toadhollow.com

Chardonnay, '00, France Le Faux Frog $7.50 (B-Riverside)
Chardonnay, '00, North Coast, Francines Selection $14.00 (2)
Merlot, '00, Russian River, McDowell Vnyd. Rsv. $22.00 (S-San Fran)
Pinot Noir, '00, RRV, Goldies Vines Rsv. $22.00 (B-New World)
Pinot Noir, '99, Russian River Vly., Goldies Vines $22.00 (2)
Sparkling Wine, 'NV, Brut, France Amplexus $15.00 (B-Riverside)
Syrah, '00, France Le Faux Frog $7.50 (B-Riverside)

TOLOSA

Address Not Available

Chardonnay, '00, Edna Vly., Edna Ranch $24.00 (2)
Pinot Noir, '00, Edna Vly., Edna Ranch $30.00 (5)
Syrah, '00, Edna Vly., Edna Ranch (S-State Fair)

TOPOLOS AT RUSSIAN RIVER VINEYARDS

5700 Gravenstein Hwy., No., Forestville 95436
www.topolos.com

Syrah, '00, Sonoma Co., Ladi's Vnyd. $25.00 (4)
White Dessert, '00, Gewurztraminer, RRV $23.00 (Σ-San Diego)
Zinfandel, '00, Sonoma Co., Twin Oaks (S-L.A.)
Zinfandel, '99, Lodi, Eco-zin, Organic $12.00 (B-Orange)
Zinfandel, '99, Sonoma Co. Old Vine $20.00 (5)
Zinfandel, '99, Sonoma Vly., Rossi Ranch $27.50 (2)

TOTT'S CHAMPAGNE CELLARS

600 Yosemite Blvd., Modesto 95353

Sparkling Wine, 'NV, Brut, California $7.00 (5)
Sparkling Wine, 'NV, Extra Dry, Rsv. Cuvee, California $7.00 (6)

TREFETHEN

1160 Oak Knoll Ave., Napa 94558
www.trefethen.com

Chardonnay, '00, Napa Vly. Estate $22.00 (3)

Dry Riesling, '01, Napa Vly. Estate $15.00 (6)
Merlot, '99, Napa Vly. Estate $26.00 (5)

RELLIS VINEYARDS

P.O. Box 685, Novato 94945

Cabernet Sauvignon, '99, Sonoma Co. $16.00 (4)
Chardonnay, '00, Russian River Vly. $14.00 (2)
Chardonnay, '99, Russian River Vly. $14.00 (S-State Fair)
Merlot, '99, Sonoma Co. $17.00 (6)
Sauvignon Blanc, '00, Dry Creek Vly. $11.00 (2)

RENTADUE

19170 Geyserville Ave., Geyserville 95441
www.trentadue.com

Merlot, '99, Alexander Vly., Estate $18.00 (6)
Petite Sirah, '00, Alexander Vly., Estate $20.00 (7)
Petite Sirah, '99, Alexander Vly., Estate $18.00 (G-New World)
Red Italian, '99, La Storia, Sonoma Co. $32.00 (3)
Red Meritage, '99, La Storia, Alexander Vly. $45.00 (6)
Sangiovese, '99, Alexander Vly., Estate $14.00 (B-Orange)
Zinfandel, '00, Alexander Vly. Geyserville Ranch $20.00 (8)
Zinfandel, '00, La Storia, Dry Creek Vly. $30.00 (9)

I. TRINCHERO WINERY

P.O. Box 248, Saint Helena 94574
www.tfewines.com

Cabernet Sauvignon, '98, Family Selection $17.00 (2)
Cabernet Sauvignon, '98, Napa, Chicken Ranch Vnyd. $30.00 (4)
Cabernet Sauvignon, '98, Napa Vly., Mario's Rsv. $45.00 (4)
Cabernet Sauvignon, '99, Family Selection (B-Pac. Rim)
Cabernet Sauvignon, '99, Napa Vly. Lewelling Vnyd. $60.00 (6)
Chardonnay, '00, Family Selection, California $14.00 (5)
Chardonnay, '99, Napa Vly., Mario's Rsv. $30.00 (5)
Merlot, '99, Family Selection, California $14.00 (4)
Merlot, '99, Napa Vly., Chicken Ranch $25.00 (4)
Sauvignon Blanc, '00, Napa Vly. Mary's Vnyd. $20.00 (3)

INITY OAKS

P.O. Box 248, Saint Helena 94574

Cabernet Sauvignon, '99, California $10.00 (4)
Chardonnay, '00, California (G-Pac. Rim)
Chardonnay, '99, California $10.00 (4)
Merlot, '99, California $10.00 (4)
Zinfandel, '99, California $10.00 (3)

OUT GULCH VINEYARDS

18426 Chelmsford Dr., Cupertino 95014
www.troutgulchvineyards.com

Chardonnay, '00, Santa Cruz Mtns. $18.00 (B-San Fran)
Pinot Noir, '00, Santa Cruz Mtns. $22.00 (2)

LIP HILL WINERY

Address Not Available
www.tuliphillwinery.com

Chardonnay, '00, California $18.00 (B-W. Coast)
Chardonnay, '00, San Joaquin, Mt. Oso Vnyd. (S-L.A.)
Merlot, '00, San Joaquin, Mt. Oso Vnyd. $24.00 (S-San Fran)
Red Rhone, '00, Shiraz/Cab, San Joaquin $38.00 (2)
Syrah, '00, San Joaquin, Mt. Oso Vnyd. $32.00 (4)

TULOCAY

1426 Coombsville, Napa 94558

Cabernet Sauvignon, '99, Napa Vly., Cliff Vnyd. $30.00 (S-Orange)
Merlot, '99, El Dorado, Sierra Oaks Vnyd. $20.00 (B-Orange)
Zinfandel, '99, Amador Co. $18.00 (B-Orange)
Zinfandel, '99, Napa Vly., Chiles Vly. $18.00 (B-Orange)

TURNBULL WINE CELLARS

8210 St. Helena Hwy., Oakville 94562
www.turnbullwines.com

Cabernet Sauvignon, '99, Napa Vly., Oakville (B-L.A.)
Sangiovese, '99, Napa Vly., Oakville $22.00 (B-San Fran)
Sauvignon Blanc, '00, Napa Vly., Oakville $15.00 (2)

TURNING LEAF

3387 Dry Creek Rd., Healdsburg 95448
www.turningleaf.com

Cabernet Sauvignon, '00, California (2)
Cabernet Sauvignon, '99, Central Coast Rsv., Oak Aged $10.00
Chardonnay, '00, California $8.00 (S-New World)
Chardonnay, '00, Coastal Rsv., North Coast $10.00 (5)
Dry Riesling, '01, Monterey Co. Rsv. (S-L.A.)
Merlot, '00, California Rsv. $10.00 (2)
Merlot, '00, Coastal Rsv., Sonoma Co. $10.00 (2)
Pinot Noir, '00, California $8.00 (2)
Pinot Noir, '00, Coastal Rsv., North Coast $10.00 (4)
Sauvignon Blanc, '00, California $8.00 (B-New World)
Sauvignon Blanc, '01, California $8.00 (2)
Sauvignon Blanc, '01, California Rsv. $8.00 (2)
Zinfandel, '98, Coastal Rsv., North Coast $10.00 (3)
Zinfandel, '99, California $8.00 (G-New World)

V

VALLEY OF THE MOON

777 Madrone Rd., Glen Ellen 95442

Cabernet Sauvignon, '98, Sonoma Co. $20.00 (B-W. Coast)
Chardonnay, '00, Sonoma Co. $16.00 (4)
Pinot Noir, '00, Sonoma Co. $20.00 (S-San Fran)
Red Meritage, '98, Cuvee De La Luna, Sonoma Co. $25.00 (2)
Sangiovese, '99, Sonoma Co. $15.00 (3)
Syrah, '99, Sonoma Co. $17.00 (6)
White Varietals, '00, Pinot Blanc, Sonoma Co. $15.00 (S-Riverside)
White Varietals, '01, Pinot Blanc, Sonoma Co. $15.00 (S-State Fair)
Zinfandel, '99, Sonoma Co. $15.00 (2)

VAN ASPEREN

1680 Silverado Trail, Saint Helena 94574
www.vanasperen.com

Cabernet Sauvignon, '97, Napa Vly. Rsv. $34.00 (B-New World)
Cabernet Sauvignon, '98, Napa Vly. $22.00 (4)
Cabernet Sauvignon, '98, Napa Vly. Signature Rsv. $36.00 (3)
Cabernet Sauvignon, '98, Napa Vly., Robinwood (S-L.A.)
Chardonnay, '00, Napa Vly., Corbett Vnyd. $35.00 (G-Orange)
Sauvignon Blanc, '00, Napa Vly. $12.00 (2)
Zinfandel, '98, Napa Vly. $15.00 (B-New World)
Zinfandel, '99, Napa Vly. $18.00 (2)

VAN ROEKEL VINEYARDS

34225 Rancho California, Temecula 92591

Chardonnay, '00, Temecula Estate $10.00 (3)
Chardonnay, '01, Temecula $9.00 (3)
Chardonnay, '01, Temecula, A Boire (S-State Fair)
Gewurztraminer, '01, Temecula $11.00 (5)
Red Rhone, '98, K. Syrah Sirah, Temecula $15.00 (S-San Diego)
White Varietals, '01, Chenin Blanc, Temecula $11.00 (B-Riverside)

VAN RUITEN-TAYLOR WINERY

Address Not Available
www.vrtwinery.com

Chardonnay, '00, Lodi Rsv. $10.00 (2)
Red Rhone, '00, Shiraz/Cab, Lodi Rsv. $12.00 (8)
Zinfandel, '00, Lodi Rsv., Old Vine $15.00 (6)

VENDANGE

P.O. Box 1290, Woodbridge 95258

Merlot, 'NV, California $5.00 (4)
Syrah, 'NV, California $5.00 (B-W. Coast)

VENTANA VINEYARDS

2999 Monterey-Salinas Hwy., Monterey 93940
www.ventanawines.com

Chardonnay, '00, Monterey Arroyo Seco Goldstripe $14.00 (3)
Chardonnay, '99, Monterey Rsv. $18.00 (2)
Dry Riesling, '01, Monterey, Arroyo Seco, Estate $10.00 (3)
Gewurztraminer, '00, Monterey, Arroyo Seco, Estate $10.00 (2)
Gewurztraminer, '01, Monterey, Arroyo Seco, Estate $10.00 (4)
Merlot, '00, Monterey, Arroyo Seco, Estate $18.00 (2)
Red Rhone, '01, Dry Rosado, Monterey Arroyo Seco (B-L.A.)
Sauvignon Blanc, '00, Monterey, Arroyo Seco, Estate $12.00 (3)
White Varietals, '00, Chenin Blanc, Monterey $10.00 (4)
White Varietals, '00, Pinot Blanc, Monterey, Arroyo Seco $14.00 (3)
White Varietals, '99, Muscat D'orange, Monterey Co. $12.00 (2)
White Varietals, '99, Pinot Blanc, Monterey, Arroyo Seco $14.00 (4)

VIANSA

25200 Arnold Dr., Sonoma 95476
www.viansa.com

Chardonnay, '00, Carneros, Cento per Cento $38.00 (B-San Fran)
Merlot, '00, Sonoma Vly. $28.00 (S-San Fran)
Merlot, '99, Sonoma Vly., Lorenzo $38.00 (S-San Fran)
Pinot Gris, '00, Sonoma, Vittoria Pinot Grigio $20.00 (B-San Diego)
Sangiovese, '99, Napa-Sonoma, Thalia $38.00 (2)

VILLA MT. EDEN

8711 Silverado Trail, St Helena 94574
www.stimson-lane.com

Cabernet Sauvignon, '99, Napa Vly., Grand Rsv. $22.00 (5)
Chardonnay, '00, Bien Nacido Vnyd. Rsv. $14.00 (B-New World)
Chardonnay, '99, Santa Maria, Bien Nacido Vnyd. $32.00 (2)
Pinot Noir, '00, California Coastal $10.00 (3)
Pinot Noir, '00, Russian River Vly. Rsv. $22.00 (2)
Syrah, '98, California Grand Rsv. $20.00 (B-Riverside)
Zinfandel, '00, Napa Vly., Mead Ranch Rsv. $22.00 (3)
Zinfandel, '00, Sierra Foothills, Fox Creek Vnyd. $23.00 (3)
Zinfandel, '00, Sonoma Vly., Monte Rosso Vnyd. Rsv. $23.00 (4)
Zinfandel, '99, California, Old Vines $10.00 (5)

VILLA TOSCANO WINERY

Address Not Available
www.villatoscano.com

Sangiovese, '00, Sierra Foothills $24.00 (B-Orange)
White Meritage, '00, Shenandoah Vly. (B-State Fair)
Zinfandel, '00, Shenandoah Vly. $18.00 (B-San Fran)

VINO NOCETO

Address Not Available

Sangiovese, '99, Noceto, Riserva (B-L.A.)
Sangiovese, '99, Shenandoah Vly. (2)
Sangiovese, '99, Shenandoah Vly. Rsv. $22.00 (5)
Sangiovese, '99, Shenandoah Vly., Hillside $25.00 (G-San Diego)

VISTA DEL REY VINEYARDS

7340 Drake Rd., Paso Robles 93446

Zinfandel, '99, Paso Robles, Puno Hierro Estet $20.00 (3)

VOSS VINEYARDS

P.O. Box 128, Vineburg 95487
www.vossvineyards.com

Merlot, '99, Napa Vly. $22.00 (S-San Fran)
Sauvignon Blanc, '01, Napa Vly. $18.00 (2)
Syrah, '99, Napa Vly. $24.00 (2)
White Dessert, '00, Sauv. Blanc/Semillon, Napa $25.00 (B-San Fran)

W

WATTLE CREEK

P.O. Box 1272, Healdsburg 95448

Cabernet Sauvignon, '98, Alexander Vly. $45.00 (6)
Cabernet Sauvignon, '99, Alexander Vly. $45.00 (4)
Chardonnay, '00, Alexander Vly. $25.00 (5)
Chardonnay, '99, Alexander Vly. $25.00 (6)
Sauvignon Blanc, '00, Alexander Vly. $18.00 (5)
Sauvignon Blanc, '01, Mendocino Co. $18.00 (6)
Syrah, '98, Alexander Vly. Shiraz $35.00 (3)
Syrah, '99, Alexander Vly. Shiraz $35.00 (7)
Viognier, '00, Alexander Vly. $24.75 (4)

WEIBEL

1 Winemaster Way, Lodi 95240
www.weibel.com

Chardonnay, '99, Monterey (B-L.A.)
Sparkling Wine, 'NV, Almondine Flavored, California $7.00 (2)
Sparkling Wine, 'NV, Brut, Grand Cuvee, California (B-L.A.)
White Varietals, 'NV, Green Hungarian, California $6.00 (4)

WELLINGTON VINEYARDS

P.O. Box 568, Glen Ellen 95442

Cabernet Sauvignon, '00, Sonoma Vly. $25.00 (B-Orange)
White Varietals, '01, Roussanne, Russian River $20.00 (G-Orange)

WENTE VINEYARDS

5565 Tesla Road, Livermore 94550
www.wentevineyards.com

Chardonnay, '00, Livermore Vly., Vineyard Selection $11.00 (2)
Chardonnay, '00, Riva Ranch, Arroyo Seco $16.00 (4)
Merlot, '99, Livermore Vly. Crane Ridge Rsv. $19.00 (2)
Red Meritage, 'NV, Livermore & Baja, Mex. (B-Pac. Rim)

Syrah, '00, Livermore Vly., Vineyard Selection $11.00 (3)

WHITE CRANE WINERY

Address Not Available

Bordeaux, '00, Cabernet Franc, Cienega Vly., Rsv. $27.50 (G-

Merlot, '00, Napa Vly. Rsv. (B-State Fair)

WHITE OAK VINEYARDS

7505 Hwy. 128, Healdsburg 95448
www.whiteoakwinery.com

Cabernet Sauvignon, '00, Napa Vly. $18.00 (S-State Fair)
Chardonnay, '00, Russian River Vly. $17.00 (5)
Chardonnay, '99, Russian River Vly. Rsv. $40.00 (S-L.A.)
Merlot, '00, Alexander Vly. Estate $28.00 (5)
Merlot, '00, Napa Vly. $24.00 (4)
Sauvignon Blanc, '01, Napa Vly. $18.00 (4)
Sauvignon Blanc, '01, North Coast, 20th Edition $13.00 (7)
White Varietals, '01, Sauvignon Musqué $24.00 (B-San Fran)
Zinfandel, '00, Alexander Vly. Estate $33.00 (6)

WHITEHALL LANE

1563 St. Helena Hwy., St Helena 94574
www.whitehalllane.com

Cabernet Sauvignon, '99, Napa Vly. $40.00 (S-W. Coast)
Merlot, '99, Napa Vly. $26.00 (3)

WHITFORD CELLARS

4047 E. Third Avenue, Napa 94558

Chardonnay, '00, Napa Vly., Haynes Vnyd. (B-State Fair)
Chardonnay, '99, Napa Vly., Haynes Vnyd. (G-L.A.)

WILD HORSE

P.O. Box 638, Templeton 93465
www.wildhorsewinery.com

Cabernet Sauvignon, '99, Paso Robles (B-L.A.)
Merlot, '00, Paso Robles $18.00 (2)
Pinot Noir, '00, Central Coast $21.00 (3)
Red Italian, '99, Negrette, Calleri Vnyd. $18.00 (2)
White Varietals, '01, Arneis, San Benito $16.00 (2)
White Varietals, '01, Malvasia Bianca, Monterey $13.00 (3)
Zinfandel, '99, The Slacker, Paso Robles (2)

WILDHURST

P.O. Box 1223, Kelseyville 95451
www.wildhurst.com

Merlot, '99, Clear Lake, Plunkett Creek (S-State Fair)
Sauvignon Blanc, '01, Clear Lake (Σ-State Fair)
White Varietals, '01, Muscat Canelli, Clear Lake (B-State Fair)

WILSON CREEK WINERY & VINEYARD

Address Not Available

Cabernet Sauvignon, '00, Temecula, Rsv. $35.00 (4)
Chardonnay, '00, Temecula $18.00 (B-Riverside)
Dry Riesling, '01, Temecula $16.00 (2)
Merlot, '00, Temecula Rsv. $29.00 (2)
Red Rhone, '00, Mourvedre, Temecula $23.00 (2)
White Varietals, 'NV, Green Hungarian, Calif. $10.00 (B-New World)
Zinfandel, '00, South Coast, Double Dog Red (B-L.A.)

WILSON WINERY

Address Not Available

Cabernet Sauvignon, '97, Sydney Vnyd. Rsv. $40.00 (G-Riverside)
Merlot, '99, Dry Creek Vly. Sydney Vnyd. $24.00 (3)
Zinfandel, '00, Dry Creek Vly. Carl's Vnyd. $25.00 (3)

WINDMILL ESTATES

Address Not Available

Cabernet Sauvignon, '00, California (B-L.A.)
Chardonnay, '00, California (S-L.A.)
Merlot, '00, Lodi (G-State Fair)
Syrah, '00, Lodi $10.00 (2)
Viognier, '01, California (S-State Fair)
Zinfandel, '00, Lodi Old Vine (G-L.A.)

WINDSOR VINEYARDS

9600 Bell Road, Windsor 95492
www.windsorvineyards.com

Cabernet Sauvignon, '97, Alexander Vly., Private Rsv. $23.50 (2)
Cabernet Sauvignon, '98, Alexander Vly., Simoneau $19.75 (7)
Cabernet Sauvignon, '98, North Coast, Private Rsv. $20.75 (3)
Cabernet Sauvignon, '98, Paso Robles $12.50 (6)
Cabernet Sauvignon, '98, Sonoma Co., Signature Series $27.25 (5)
Cabernet Sauvignon, '99, Mendocino Co., Rsv. $16.75 (5)
Cabernet Sauvignon, '99, North Coast, Vintner's Rsv. $20.75 (2)
Cabernet Sauvignon, '99, Paso Robles $12.50 (5)
Chardonnay, '00, Alexander Vly. Murphy Ranch $15.75 (6)
Chardonnay, '00, North Coast $12.00 (5)
Chardonnay, '00, Russian River Vly. Preston Ranch $15.75 (4)
Chardonnay, '00, Russian River Vly., Signature Series $18.75 (6)
Chardonnay, '00, Russian River Vly., Vintner's Rsv. $21.75 (3)
Chardonnay, '00, Sonoma Co., Barrel Fermented $17.75 (4)
Chardonnay, '99, Murphy Ranch $15.50 (B-New World)
Chardonnay, '99, Alexander Vly. Simoneau Ranch $16.50 (2)
Chardonnay, '99, Russian River, Barrel Ferm. $17.50 (B-New World)
Dry Riesling, '00, Monterey Co. $8.25 (3)
Dry Riesling, '01, Monterey Co. $8.25 (2)
Gewurztraminer, '00, Alexander Vly. $9.50 (2)
Merlot, '00, Mendocino Co. Private Rsv. $15.75 (3)
Merlot, '98, Sonoma Co., Signature Series $25.25 (6)
Merlot, '99, 40th Anniversary, Dry Creek Vly. $40.00 (2)
Merlot, '99, Sonoma Co., Signature Series $25.25 (5)
Petite Sirah, '98, Mendocino Co. $12.50 (4)
Pinot Noir, '00, North Coast Private Rsv. $16.75 (3)
Pinot Noir, '00, Sonoma Co., Signature Series $18.75 (3)
Pinot Noir, '99, Sonoma Co. Private Rsv. $16.75 (5)
Red Meritage, '97, Sonoma Co., Signature Series $23.75 (5)
Red Meritage, '98, Sonoma Co. Private Rsv. $18.00 (5)
Red Rhone, '98, Carignane, Mendocino Co. $11.50 (6)
Red Rhone, '99, Carignane, Alexander Vly., Oat Vly. $16.75 (7)
Red Rhone, '99, Carignane, Mendocino Co. $11.50 (6)
Sauvignon Blanc, '00, Fume Blanc, North Coast $11.75 (3)
Sparkling Wine, '98, Brut, Sonoma Co. Rsv. $20.00 (2)
Sparkling Wine, '99, Blanc de Noir, Sonoma Co. Rsv. $22.00 (8)
Sparkling Wine, 'NV, California Private Rsv. $11.75 (B-Riverside)
Syrah, '99, Dry Creek Vly. Private Rsv. $15.75 (6)
White Dessert, '00, Muscat, Alexander V. Murphy Ranch $15.25 (4)

White Dessert, '01, Muscat, Alexander V. Murphy Ranch $15.25 (5)
White Varietals, '00, Chenin Blanc, California $8.25 (2)
White Varietals, '00, French Colombard, North Coast $7.25 (2)
White Varietals, '00, Semillon, Mendocino Co. Rsv. $15.75 (2)
White Varietals, '01, Chenin Blanc, California $8.25 (2)
White Varietals, '01, French Colombard, California $7.25 (6)
Zinfandel, '99, Mendocino Co., Signature Series $17.75 (4)
Zinfandel, '99, North Coast $12.00 (6)

VOODBRIDGE WINERY

P.O. Box 1260, Woodbridge 95258
www.robertmondavi.com

Chardonnay, '00, California $9.00 (2)
Chardonnay, '99, Twin Oaks, California (B-State Fair)
Pinot Gris, '00, California Pinot Grigio $8.00 (S-New World)
Syrah, '99, California $9.00 (2)
White Varietals, '98, Muscat California $12.00 (B-San Fran)
White Zinfandel, '00, California $6.00 (B-New World)
White Zinfandel, '01, California $6.00 (B-State Fair)
Zinfandel, '00, California $6.00 (S-New World)
Zinfandel, '99, Lodi, Old Vine $14.00 (S-Orange)

VOODEN VALLEY WINES

4756 Suisun Valley Rd., Suisun 94585

Cabernet Sauvignon, '99, Suisun Vly. (B-L.A.)
Chardonnay, '01, Suisun Vly. (S-State Fair)
Merlot, '99, Suisun Vly. (B-L.A.)
Pinot Noir, '00, Suisun Vly. (S-L.A.)

VOODENHEAD VINTNERS

Address Not Available

Pinot Noir, '00, Humboldt Co., Elk Prairie Vnyd. $42.00 (3)

Y

)AKIM BRIDGE

Address Not Available

Merlot, '99, Dry Creek Vly. $28.00 (B-San Fran)
Zinfandel, '00, Dry Creek Vly. (B-State Fair)
Zinfandel, '99, Dry Creek Vly. (S-State Fair)

)RK MOUNTAIN

7505 York Mountain Rd. West, Templeton 93465
www.yorkmountainwinery.com

Chardonnay, '00, Edna Vly. $20.00 (B-San Fran)
Pinot Noir, '00, Edna Vly. $20.00 (S-San Fran)
Viognier, '01, Paso Robles, Fralich Vnyd. (Σ-State Fair)
White Varietals, '01, Roussane Paso Robles $20.00 (2)

)RKVILLE CELLARS

25701 Hwy. 128, Yorkville 95494
www.yorkville-cellars

Bordeaux, '99, Cabernet Franc, Rennie Vnyd., Organic $17.00 (2)
Bordeaux, '99, Malbec, Rennie Vnyd. $17.00 (4)
Bordeaux, '99, Petite Verdot, Rennie Vnyd. $17.00 (4)
Cabernet Sauvignon, '99, Yorkville, Rennie Vnyd. $19.00 (5)
Merlot, '98, Yorkville Highlands, Rennie Vnyd. $18.00 (3)
Red Meritage, '98, Richard The Lion-Heart $25.00 (4)
Red Meritage, '99, Richard The Lion-Heart $25.00 (B-State Fair)
Sauvignon Blanc, '00, Yorkville, Randle Hill Vnyd. $12.00 (2)

White Meritage, '00, Eleanor of Aquitaine $17.00 (6)
White Varietals, '00, Semillon, Randle Hill Vnyd. $13.00 (3)

Z

ZACA MESA

6905 Foxen Canyon Rd., Los Olivos 93441

Chardonnay, '00, Santa Barbara Co. (2)
Red Rhone, '00, Santa Barbara Co. Z Cuvee $16.00 (5)
Syrah, '00, Santa Ynez Vly. Estate $20.00 (B-San Fran)
Syrah, '99, Santa Barbara Co. Zaca Vnyd. $20.00 (2)
Viognier, '00, Santa Barbara Co. $16.50 (3)
Viognier, '01, Santa Ynez Vly. Estate $14.00 (S-Riverside)

ZAHTILA VINEYARDS

Address Not Available

Zinfandel, '00, Sonoma Co. Old Vines (S-State Fair)
Zinfandel, '99, Napa Vly. Estate $30.00 (2)

ZINGARO

Address Not Available
www.parducci.com

Zinfandel, '99, Mendocino Co. $13.00 (B-Orange)
Zinfandel, '99, Mendocino Co., Rsv. $18.00 (3)

Kendall-Jackson Wine Center, Sonoma County

INEXPENSIVE GOLDS

The following wineries have listings in this book for wines $13.00 or less that have won at least one Gold Medal. (Those with a * have won two or more)

Bordeaux

Ironstone
Pepperwood Grove*

Cabernet Sauvignon

Bel Arbor
Beringer*
Butterfield*
Coastal Ridge
Corbett Canyon
Cypress*
Estrella River
Forest Glen
Foxhollow
Gallo of Sonoma
Hidden Cellars
Hrm*
Mc Manis*
Mirassou*
Monterra*
Napa Ridge*
Parducci
Peirano Estate
Pepperwood Grove
Round Hill
Silver Ridge
Sterling
Turning Leaf*

Chardonnay

Arrow Creek
Barefoot
Bogle
Butterfield
Canyon Road
Castoro
Cecchetti Sebastiani
Coastal Ridge
Diablo Creek
Gallo of Sonoma
J. Lohr*
Mc Manis
Meridian
Mirassou
Mission View
Montpellier
Napa Ridge*
Parducci*
Rutherford*
Salmon Creek
V. Sattui
Seven Peaks
Stone Cellars
Thornton
Trinity Oaks
Turning Leaf
Van Roekel*

Dry Riesling

Beringer*
Fetzer*
Gainey
Geyser Peak*
Jekel*
Kendall-Jackson
J. Lohr*
Maddalena
Stony Ridge
Ventana*

Gewurztraminer

Adler Fels
Fetzer
Firestone
Geyser Peak
Husch*
Meridian
Sutter Home
Van Roekel*

Merlot

Callaway
Camelot
Cecchetti Sebastiani*
Coastal Ridge*
Cypress
Gallo of Sonoma
Meridian*
Monterra
Pepperwood Grove*
Salmon Creek
Turning Leaf

Petite Sirah

Bogle*
Cilurzo*
Concannon
Kempton Clark*
Parducci

Pinot Gris

Gallo of Sonoma
Maddalena

Pinot Noir

Barefoot*
Beringer*
Cecchetti Sebastiani
Fetzer
Indigo Hills*
Meridian
Michael Pozzan
Stonehedge
Turning Leaf

Red Meritage

Curtis
Kendall-Jackson

Red Rhone

Thomas Coyne
Curtis
Stone Cellars
Van Ruiten-Taylor*

Sangiovese

Chatom
Forestville
Gallo of Sonoma
Emilio Guglielmo

Sauvignon Blanc

Amador Foothill
Baileyana
Canyon Road*
Maurice Car'rie*
Chatom
Clos Du Bois
Dry Creek
Estrella River
Fetzer
Firestone
Geyser Peak*
Granite Springs
Hacienda
Kendall-Jackson
Lockwood
Montevina
Sierra Vista*
Sonora*
Stone
Stonehedge
Turning Leaf
White Oak*
Windsor
Yorkville

Sparkling Wine

Ballatore*
Korbel
Thornton*
Tott's
Weibel

Syrah

Camelot
Canyon Road
Cecchetti Sebastiani
Coastal Ridge
Delicato
Foppiano
Forest Glen*
Forestville
Foxhollow
Ironstone
Kendall-Jackson
Monterra
Montpellier
Peirano Estate
Pepperwood Grove*
Wente

White Dessert

Quady*

White Meritage

Kendall-Jackson*

White Varietals

Baron Herzog
Black Sheep
Bonny Doon
Maurice Car'rie
Chateau Lasgoity
Concannon
Curtis*
Eberle
Fanucchi*
Gnekow*
Husch
Ironstone
Kendall-Jackson*
Mirassou
Navarro*
Perry Creek
Quinta Da Sonora
Rosenblum
Sonora
Sutter Home

White Zinfandel

Bel Arbor
Beringer*
Corbett Canyon
Fetzer*
Hacienda
Montpellier*
Rutherford
Salmon Creek
V. Sattui

Zinfandel

Bargetto
Beringer
Souverain
De Loach
Frey
Ironstone
Kempton Clark
Peirano Estate
Pepperwood Grove
Perry Creek*
Rancho Zabaco
Ravenswood
Rosenblum
Santa Barbara*
Trinity Oaks
Turning Leaf
Villa Mt. Eden

NOTES

NOTES